God's Credentials

God's Credentials

Belief and Unbelief in a Troubled World

Philip Blair

BOOKS

Plas Gwyn, Trelawnyd, LL18 6DT

2007

K & M Books

Plas Gwyn, Trelawnyd, LL18 6DT

God's Credentials
First published in Great Britain in 2007
by K & M Books

Copyright © Philip Blair

British Library Cataloguing-in-Publication Data
A catalogue record for this book is available from the British Library

ISBN 0 9523041 7 1

Printed, typeset and distributed by

Tentmaker Publications
121 Haretshill Road
Stoke-on-Trent
ST4 7LU
www.tentmaker.org.uk

For Alexander

Contents

Preface

'God bless America.'

'I have never been more comfortable with the fact that I don't believe in God.'

Two responses to the same fearful event: the devastating destruction and loss of life caused by the terrorist attacks on the World Trade Centre and the Pentagon in the United States of America on 11 September 2001. The first response was that of the President, George W. Bush, concluding his address to the nation the day after the tragedy, words taken to heart and echoed by citizens throughout the country; the second was spoken by a member of the British public on the B.B.C. radio channel 'Five Live' a week later, when the catastrophe was still the main focus of news coverage. The specific topic for discussion on the channel on this occasion was, 'Is religion the root of all evil?'

The above two statements represent contrasting reactions to the troubled world in which we live: one of belief, the other of unbelief. What, we may well ask in the light of such views, should people of the twenty-first century seriously make of the idea of God?

The increasingly intractable problems facing the world are fostering a polarisation of attitudes towards religious belief. On the one hand, a fair proportion of society seems ready to accept the reality of a spiritual dimension of some kind; on the other hand, declarations of agnosticism or atheism are becoming more and more common. As for orthodox Christian belief, there is little doubt that this is dwindling. Leading ecclesiastics admit that the Church has its back to the wall. The former Archbishop of Canterbury, Dr George Carey, has declared: 'A tacit atheism prevails. Death is assumed to be the end of life.' Perhaps his words exaggerate the situation; opinion polls have shown that belief in God in some form is still widespread, especially in America. It is undeniable, however, that – in the West, at least – there is trend towards religious uncertainty and unbelief.

What is driving people today to agnosticism or atheism? The purpose of this book is to examine this question by going back to the earliest period in human history and tracing the way in which belief in God has since that time developed, varied, and in modern times diminished.

From the beginnings of human civilisation (when records in some form began) until relatively recently, belief in a supreme spiritual being was normative. That is my thesis in Part I of this book. Some two and a half centuries ago, this view began to be undermined by thinkers who argued that belief in the Deity had become at the least irrelevant and at most impossible. A hundred years later, when such ideas were becoming accepted more widely as a result, in particular, of scientific research, intellectuals were confidently predicting the swift demise of the Christian Church. Up to the present day they have not ceased to do so; indeed, many are now proclaiming the 'death of God' as indisputable fact. Part II examines the way such atheistic ideas have developed and assesses their validity. Part III then investigates in some detail the data underpinning Christian belief.

The question of God and religion is being debated today as never before. Our world seems to be at a crossroads, with many not knowing where to turn. While some counsel a return to 'religious belief and values', a return to God as they see him, others, with equal vehemence, advise humanity to abandon the very notion of the divine as a worn-out and dangerous superstition. Few are asking the pertinent question, essentially unrelated to the issue of religion: Does human history and does the nature of the universe we inhabit demand that we affirm or deny the existence of a Creator?

Facts adduced in the following pages, I submit, demonstrate that many assumptions underlying the arguments of atheistic philosophers, scientists, historians and (even) theologians are highly questionable.

Philip Blair
August, 2006

PART I: BELIEF

Chapter 1
In the Beginning

Writers on primitive or comparative religion these days usually take for granted the idea that monotheism, belief in a single Creator-God, was a relatively late development in the story of humankind, post-dating and springing from a belief in spirits (or 'daemons') and gods of nature.[1]

Early humanity, it is generally held, considered all nature to be in some sense alive. And since it was alive, what happened in it could only be described in terms of personal activity, in stories or 'myths' about visible phenomena – stones, mountains, plants, trees, animals, birds, the moon, the sun – and about imagined spirits, cosmic powers, or gods lying behind that phenomena. Such a way of looking at life is described in the classic study of primitive myths, beliefs and speculations in the ancient Near East, *Before Philosophy*. The authors write, 'The fundamental difference between the attitudes of modern and ancient man as regards the surrounding world is this: for modern, scientific man the phenomenal world is primarily an "It"; for ancient – and also for primitive – man it is a "Thou"… The whole man confronts a living "Thou" in nature; and the whole man – emotional and imaginative as well as intellectual – gives expression to the experience.' That expression took the form of accounts or explanations of natural 'happenings' or 'individual events' in the form of stories. 'In other words,' the authors conclude, 'the ancients told myths instead of presenting an analysis or conclusions.'[2]

Perhaps the most important myth invented by the ancients, according to this construction of early religious development, was that of creation. This was often seen as analogous to the act of birth, a primeval couple being postulated as the parents of all that exists. Thus for the ancient Egyptians and ancient Greeks the first pair were Earth and Sky (as in the case of other 'primitive' peoples). Alternatively, creation could be seen as the act of begetting by a single parent – whether a mother goddess, as in Greece, or a daemon, as in Babylonia, or even a male figure, as with the Egyptian god Atum. As mythmaking developed, these primeval creative agents gathered around them a crowd of lesser gods, their 'children' or 'grandchildren', often corresponding to natural phenomena. Atum, for example, sun-god and creator, begot Shu and Tefnut, Air and Moisture, and they in turn begot Geb (or Qeb) and Nut, Earth and Sky, from whom finally issued the great Egyptian god Osiris, possibly a personification of vegetation.[3]

Eventually, modern scholarship has it, there emanated from the increasingly complex cycle of myths the idea of a single, supreme deity, creator and lord of all life, spiritual and physical, gods and men. The Memphite Theology (or Drama), an Egyptian text thought to date from the fourth millennium BC, is probably the earliest known written statement of such belief. This identifies the supreme deity and creator as Ptah. As the text reads, 'Ptah, the Great One; he is the heart and tongue of the Ennead (ninefold pantheon) of gods ... who begot the gods.' Yet Ptah is seen by modern interpreters as a relatively late invention of man, almost a first attempt to rationalise an earlier mythology, with a pantheon of gods. To quote again from *Before Philosophy*, 'In the Memphite theology, the Egyptians, at one point, reduced the multiplicity of the divine to a truly monotheistic conception and spiritualised the concept of creation.'[4]

Such, very briefly, is the generally accepted view of the development of religion, culminating in monotheism. The idea of God, belief in a single, supreme, creative, spiritual being, was – as with belief in the lesser gods – no more than the construct of our early forbears as they sought to explain the strange world in which they lived. Even if a monotheistic faith arose earlier than was once thought, it was not an innate consciousness of reality; it was most certainly not a truth revealed to man through some manifestation of, or message from, the actual Deity.

Is this view correct? Is it true that monotheism grew out of polytheism, both being an invention of man's mind? Or is there evidence that humankind has always revered a Supreme Creative Spirit, has always believed in one God? Let us look more closely at the data.

Tribal religion

'The sun falls in the evening time, but He is always there.' So a tribesman of the Ashanti hinterland witnesses to the Sky-God, or Supreme Being, assuring an inquirer that members of his tribe are not sun-worshippers.[5]

The Ashanti hinterland comprises the northern territories of Ghana, West Africa, where there are a number of diversely named tribes, the majority of whom speak languages having a common base. The root of the word used by all these tribes for the Sky-God is *we* (sometimes *wu*). This word certainly means 'the sun'. To distinguish that heavenly body from the Supreme Spirit, however, the former usually has some other word prefixed or suffixed. It might superficially appear that the Supreme God for these people is in fact the sun. Yet the idea of the sun *as the sun* being a god does not occur to them. Hence the above statement made by the tribesman to the inquirer.

My father, the late Harold A. Blair, conducted research into the language, customs and religion of some of the Ashanti tribes in the 1920s and 30s, publishing his findings in government reports and other articles and books. Among the Konkomba (more properly Kpunkpamba), a general name covering several closely connected tribes in the Ashanti region, the Sky-God is called Nawuni (*na* meaning 'chief'). In his work *A Creed Before The Creeds*, my father recounts their 'myth' of creation and fall. This is his rendering of the story, as he heard it from some of these people in their own language:

In the old dark days, Nawuni created man and set him to live on a rocky plain, full of holes, chasms and abysses. The surface was so slippery and the chasms were so horrible that men dared not move at all. They prayed to Nawuni, who then created sand, gravel and clay, which he ordered his messengers to spread abroad over the earth. This they did, but with a high angelic carelessness, which accounts for the number of rocky hills still projecting above the surface.

Man, now able to walk where he would, became proud and ceased to care for Nawuni and his worship. So Nawuni thought out a scheme for enforcing the allegiance of men and angels. He called them to him, and showed them a wonderful and new thing which he had created, the belly, for before that men had had no bellies.

Men were foolishly delighted with these, especially when Nawuni explained the pleasure which they brought with them, the solid joy of eating and the wild exhilaration of drink. So men prayed Nawuni to give them bellies, which Nawuni gladly did. Thus men became dependent upon Nawuni for their daily bread.

The angels were wiser and refused to pray for these gifts; so they preserved their independence, and were given positions of rule and authority in the earth. They became the tingbana *(perhaps the 'skins of earth'), each with his or her own territory on earth of which the rights, fertility and power belonged to them.*

The story goes on to describe the coming of death, caused by the seduction of man's messenger, the dog, by an evil Djinnee. The dog was carrying man's prayer for Life to Nawuni, but was delayed by the Djinnee; meanwhile the malignant goat reached Nawuni with a false message that man chose Death. So Death was decreed as the lot of man.[6]

In this story, or 'myth', we have a number of strands, some of which – despite their fascinating character – I shall leave aside for the moment. What is interesting for our present purpose is the centrality of Nawuni, the Supreme God and Creator, throughout the tale. It is difficult to imagine this figure having been invented at a later time than his 'messengers' or 'angels', who become gods of the land. There is some plausibility to the speculation (it is no other) that the Egyptian god Ptah was a piece of rationalisation, reducing the multiplicity of the divine to a monotheistic conception, but in the Konkomba mythology the person of the Creator can scarcely have been tagged onto an earlier story about local gods. Most interesting is the fact that the creation of Nawuni's messengers or angels, who became the *tingbana* (singular, *tingbane*), or territorial gods, is not even mentioned. This therefore is not an account of how the *tingbana* came to be, unlike the account of Ptah begetting divine progeny; it is an account of how these messengers of God came to possess earthly authority.

Other West African tribes, besides those from the Ashanti hinterland, acknowledge a Supreme Being. The Bura, Margi and Kilba tribes of Northern Nigeria, for instance, call him 'Hel' or 'Hyel'; these tribes do not identify or associate him with the sun, but regard him as the Sky-God and Creator, with prayers being addressed to him directly. As his name suggests the Semitic 'El', it has been conjectured that there might at some early time have been some Semitic influence on this region of Nigeria, but etymological speculation of this kind is notoriously unreliable.[7] The Yoruba of Nigeria give the name Olodumare to the single Deity. Other African tribes who venerate a single, supreme Creator include the Ganda of Uganda, and the Zulus of southern Africa, who call him Ukqili.[8]

In other parts of the world, too, primitive tribes are known to have revered one great God. To several aboriginal Australian tribes he was known as Bunjil; he was, they believed, concerned about morality, justice and peace. The Andaman Islanders, who gave the name Puluga to the Creator, believed he was immortal, utterly opposed to evil but compassionate to those in distress. The first Christian missionaries to Greenland found, somewhat to their surprise, that the Eskimos were sure there was a Supreme Being who had made all things and was inherently good, worthy of love and honour.[9]

Of course, though these tribes and peoples acknowledge a Supreme Creator, they also have their religious cults, involving sacrifices and other rites and ceremonies, taboos and fetishes. These are associated not with the Creator but with lesser male and female deities, gods and spirits of rain, crops, human reproduction, tribal health and so on. These cults are served by priests and sacred families, sometimes by the chief himself. Ancestor-worship, veneration and appeasement or propitiation of the ancestral ghosts, also plays a major role in such tribal religion. H.A. Blair explains how with the Konkomba tribes, or at least among those who claim to be 'people of the land' (for they comprise several strata of aboriginals, immigrants, and invaders), there is no divorce between ancestor-worship and the honour given to the local guardian of the land, the *tingbane*. He writes, 'The spirits of the departed are taken into the spirit hierarchy of the tribe which is also guardian of the tribal territory. Worship is of the *do ut des* type ['I give so that you might give']: there is peace on earth, at least within their boundaries.'[10]

There seems no particular reason for thinking that the Supreme God venerated by these tribes was an imaginative invention by their distant tribal forefathers *after* their invention of territorial gods or other spirits. There seems little reason to believe that it was an 'invention' at all. Leaving aside the question of how or when *homo sapiens* originated, what real evidence is there that humankind has not from the first taken for granted the existence of the Supreme Deity, together possibly with a retinue of messengers, 'angels' or lesser 'gods'? As E.O. James has written, 'The universal occurrence of High Gods among low races suggests a probability in favour of the concept being part of the original substratum of religious consciousness.'[11]

Mesopotamia
It is commonly taught that human civilization arose in Mesopotamia some six thousand years ago, in the Tigris-Euphrates valley or 'plains of Sumeria' (now Iraq), where great cities – Ur, Erech and Kish – once flourished. It is to the Sumerians, as far as we know, that we owe the invention of writing, their pictographic script from which was derived the cuneiform script being the earliest known system of recording information. This development probably occurred around the middle of the fourth millennium BC. It was in this period, sometimes called the

Proto-literate period, that there was a great increase in the population, planned and large-scale irrigation began, and villages expanded into cities, with imposing new buildings and monuments. Most impressive were the new temples appearing on the plain, often sited atop huge artificial mounds of sun-dried bricks, the famous *ziggurats*. The new city-states needed political organisation, and this developed into a primitive form of democracy. It was at this time, too, it has been conjectured, that the Mesopotamian understanding of the universe 'found its characteristic form'.[12]

The early Mesopotamians, like the tribes in Africa and elsewhere to this day, acknowledged a Sky-God; they called him Anu, which was their everyday word for 'sky'. Anu was the highest of the gods, indeed, father of the gods, and prototype of all fathers. His was the seat of authority; as the 'pristine king and ruler' he was also the prototype of all rulers. The Mesopotamians themselves sum up Anu's attributes in 'The Myth of the Elevation of Inanna',[13] in which the great gods address Anu:

> *What thou hast ordered (comes) true!*
> > *The utterance of prince and lord is (but)*
> > *What thou hast ordered, (that with which) thou art in agreement.*
> *O Anu! Thy great command takes precedence,*
> > *Who could say no (to it)?*
> *O father of the gods, thy command,*
> > *The very foundation of the heaven and earth,*
> > *What god could spurn (it)?*

The terms in which Anu is described, in particular the fact that his command is 'the foundation of the heaven and earth', suggest that the universe itself is considered to have come into being through his word, his divine *fiat*. Anu is in fact Creator, whose word is absolute, and absolutely efficacious.

Later in the history of Mesopotamia we meet the Babylonian god Marduk, who is the hero of a creation myth. The assembly of the gods confers kingship upon Marduk, son of Ea. He is given absolute authority so that everything in the universe conforms to his will and what he orders immediately comes to pass. What is especially interesting in the story, however, is that his command is seen as being identical in essence with Anu, so that the gods exclaim, 'Thy word is Anu.'[14] Clearly, even to the later polytheistic Babylonians, a memory of Anu as Supreme God remained.

Interesting archaeological discoveries relate to the view that the earliest form of Mesopotamian religion was monotheistic. Henri Frankfort, already cited as co-author of the work *Before Philosophy*, was Field Director in Iraq for the Oriental Institute of the University of Chicago from 1929 to 1937. In his *Third Preliminary Report on the Excavations at Tell Asmar (Eshunna)*, in the chapter headed 'The Religion of Eshunna in the Third Millennium B.C.', he writes, 'In addition to their more tangible results, our excavations have established a novel fact, which the student of Babylonian religions will have henceforth to take into account. We have obtained, to the best of our knowledge for the first time, religious material complete in its social setting. We possess a coherent mass of evidence, derived in almost equal quantity from a temple and from the houses inhabited by those who worshipped in that temple. We are thus able to draw conclusions, which the finds studied by themselves would not have made possible. For instance, we discover that the representations on cylinder seals, which are usually connected with various gods, can all be fitted in to form a consistent picture in which a single god worshipped in this temple forms the central figure. It seems, therefore, that at this early period his various aspects were not considered separate deities in the Sumero-Akkadian pantheon.'[15] Dr Frankfort's statement suggests that in Mesopotamia polytheism developed from monotheism, not vice-versa.

The reign of the famous Hammurabi, the principal Amorite ruler of Babylon (once dated around 2300 BC, but nowadays as late as the eighteenth century), marks an important stage in the history of Mesopotamian civilization. After governing the small city-state of Babylon for thirty years, he united under one rule the hitherto independent Babylonian states of southern Mesopotamia. In this period religion was most clearly polytheistic, the gods being divided into high gods and others of secondary power. The king was, of course, supreme head of the state, as well as enjoying the privilege of being a demigod. The deification of kings was practised before the time of Hammurabi, though it was only fairly late in the dynasty of Ur that the practice grew of deifying the king while still alive, instead of waiting for him to take his seat among the gods after death. Evidence of Hammurabi's divine nature is seen in the use of names like 'Hammurabi-ilu' ('Hammurabi is god'), as well as in the coupling of his name with those of the gods in oaths.[16]

The outstanding feature of Babylonian religion in Hammurabi's time was the unique position in the pantheon of gods newly assigned to

Marduk. Percy Handcock explains this development, 'Marduk owed his exaltation to what we may without undue levity call local interest. The dynasty of which Hammurabi was so illustrious a monarch was the first dynasty of the city of Babylon itself; and Marduk the local god of Babylon naturally shared in the good fortune and prosperity of the people over whose welfare he presided. To Marduk belonged the real credit, honour and glory of his people's success, what wonder then that he should be accorded the post of honour in the hierarchy of heaven!'[17] If loyal Babylonian subjects usually resorted to the shrine of Marduk, it was still thought prudent from time to time to seek the favour and assistance of other gods. The most prominent among other deities worshipped were: Anu, lord of heaven; Ishtar, mother of the gods and goddess of love and war; Ea, god of the deep; Sin, moon-god and patron of the people of Ur; Ninib, god of war; and finally Adad, lord of the weather.

Marduk, it must be emphasised, was originally responsible for just one city, Babylon; he was thus one of many 'gods of the land', corresponding to any one of the local spirits or gods (messengers or 'angels' of the Sky-God) who were guardians of the tribal territories of the Konkomba peoples of northern Ghana. Yet, under Hammurabi, Marduk's supremacy was so firmly established that approaching two millennia later we find Cyrus the Persian, who captured Babylon in 539 BC (replacing its last native rulers, Nabonidus and his son and co-regent Belshazzar), ascribing victory to the Babylonian god. 'Marduk', the cuneiform inscription has it, 'sought out a righteous prince, a man after his own heart whom he might take by the hand, and he called his name Cyrus.'[18]

The creation myth involving Marduk, to which we have already referred, played a major role in later Babylonian culture. From the third millennium BC down to Hellenistic times, a New Year Festival lasting several days was celebrated. It became customary during the festivities to recite the story of creation, in which Marduk had defeated the powers of chaos on the First New Year's Day, when the world was created. At the same time, a mock battle was fought in which the king impersonated the victorious god. This event was, in fact, part of the highly organised state religion, which included a powerful priesthood and temples that were commercial centres as well as seats of learning. Serving in the temple was a profitable business and the privilege could be bought, sold or mortgaged. Once obtained, however, such privileges were – if not sold – inalienable, being transmitted from father to son.

Assyria (the region earlier known as Accad), with its capital at Nineveh, was originally a small kingdom in Mesopotamia situated around the Tigris River to the north of Babylon. During the second millennium BC and into the first, however, it increased in power, eventually overwhelming Babylon and becoming an empire that stretched from the eastern Mediterranean to modern Iran. In 626 BC, following the death of the last great Assyrian ruler, Ashurbanipal, Babylon again asserted her independence under the Chaldean dynasty headed by Nabopolassar.

Assyrian religion was Babylonian in origin and character. Gods from the Babylonian pantheon, notably Anu, Bel, Ea, Marduk, Adad, Sin and Ishtar, were venerated and temples erected in their honour. However, the local god Ashur, who gave his name to the first known capital city and eventually to the country itself, was elevated to first place in the pantheon. Ashur was the divine impersonation of Assyria, as Marduk was of Babylonia, though for the former the identification was more pronounced, for when Assyria declined and the empire crumbled the god himself virtually 'died'. Marduk, by contrast, maintained his influence during the period of Babylon's eclipse; foreign conquerors, like the Persian Cyrus, as we have seen, were swift to do him honour.

On becoming king of Babylonia, Cyrus sent foreign prisoners back from Babylonia to their own lands; he also, more interestingly, aided the restoration of their temples and returned their gods. This edict would have included the Jews.[19]

Egypt
The Memphite Theology, to which we have already referred, is a text thought to date from the very beginning of Egyptian history, that is, the fourth millennium BC. The actual 'document' is a battered stone, now housed in the British Museum, which bears the name of a pharaoh who ruled in about 700 BC. However, the pharaoh in question claimed to have been copying an inscription of his ancestors, and the language and physical arrangement of the text bear this out. The text clearly originated from the time when the first Egyptian dynasties made their new capital at Memphis, the city of the god Ptah.

As we have seen, the monotheistic character of the Memphite Theology is considered by most modern scholars to have been an attempt at rationalisation of an earlier, polytheistic form of religion. J.A. Wilson puts it thus, 'Memphis as the centre of a theological state was an upstart;

it had had no national importance before. To make matters worse, Heliopolis, a traditional religious capital of Egypt, the home of the sun-god Re and of the creator-god Re-Atum, was only twenty-five miles from Memphis. It was necessary to justify a new location of the centre of the world. The text in question is part of a theological argument of the primacy of the god Ptah and thus of his home, Memphis.'[20]

The question at issue is whether the statement in the Memphite Theology of Ptah's pre-eminence was a result of inter-city rivalry – rather as the elevation of Marduk to the head of the Babylonian pantheon of gods was a result of local pride – or whether it reflects a deeper, older awareness of a supreme Deity. The terms in which Ptah's creative power are described could be held to suggest the latter. Other texts dealing with creation, such as those from Babylon (later in date) or the Egyptian Book of the Dead (also probably later), are relatively crude. In the Book of the Dead, for example, the creator-god Re-Atum simply appears from some primeval matter, as if self-generated. The text reads (with explanatory glosses by John Wilson), 'I am Atum when I was alone in Nun (the primordial waters); I am Re in his (first) appearances, when he began to rule that which he had made. What does that mean? This "Re when he began to rule that which he had made" means that Re began to appear as a king, as one who existed before (the air-god) Shu had (even) lifted (heaven from earth), when he (Re) was on the primeval hillock which was in Hermopolis.' The text goes on to emphasise that the god was self-created and that he then brought into being 'the gods who are in his following'.[21]

As we have already seen, in the Memphite Theology Ptah is assumed to be antecedent to the creator-god Atum. He in fact 'created' Atum, and he did so in a remarkable manner. The text reads (again, with glosses by John Wilson), 'There came into being in the heart, and there came into being on the tongue (something) in the form of Atum.' Indeed, Ptah's creative power, through his 'heart' and 'tongue', is extended further, 'Great and mighty is Ptah, who has committed (power to all gods), as well as their spirits, through this (activity of the) heart and this (activity of the) tongue ... It has come to pass that the heart and tongue control every member (of the body) by teaching that he (Ptah) is throughout every body (in the form of the heart) and throughout every mouth (in the form of the tongue), of all gods, of all men, of (all) animals, of all creeping things, and of what (ever) lives, by (Ptah's) thinking (as the heart) and commanding (as the tongue) anything that he wishes.'[22] Wilson describes this as a 'creation by thought conception and speech delivery', adding that the idea comes close to the Logos doctrine of the New Testament, 'In the beginning was the Word, and the Word was with God, and the Word was God.'[23]

Interestingly, the Memphite Theology gives us another biblical parallel, this time with the Old Testament – indeed, with the very beginning of the Old Testament, the book of Genesis. After the text has summarised the range of Ptah's creative power as heart and tongue, it concludes, 'And so Ptah rested after he had made everything.' Wilson comments that the translation 'rested' might better be rendered 'was satisfied', but even so the parallel with the book of Genesis, where we read that God 'rested on the seventh day from all his work which he had done', is remarkable.[24]

Wilson and others assume that in the Memphite Theology the more fanciful religious concepts of Egypt (like the creation stories of Atum and his Ennead of gods) are for the first time subsumed into a higher philosophy. Yet let us not forget that the text we are dealing with comes, as we have already pointed out, 'from the very beginning of Egyptian history'; it is, in fact, the oldest Egyptian document we have. Let us remember, too, that in the first period of Egyptian history, the Old Kingdom, 'the word "god" is used in the singular', which, as Wilson concedes, is sometimes 'the creator or supreme god'.[25] This being so, might not the 'higher philosophy' of the Memphite Theology be the oldest concept of all? Might not an original notion of a Supreme Creative Spirit lie behind the 'developed' understanding of the god Ptah that we find in this text?

If this is so, it would accord with the findings of archaeology in general, both in Egypt and in Mesopotamia, with regard to the progress in these lands of human civilization. For there is no evidence of a movement from the crude to the more developed, no evidence in these regions of earlier generations of primitive, aboriginal man. As Dr H.R. Hall has written, 'When civilization appears it is already full grown.'[26] J.A. Wilson writes thus, 'The emergence of Egypt into the light of history seems to be a very sudden phenomenon, symbolised in the abrupt appearance of stone architecture of the highest technical perfection.' He talks of 'the sudden surge of vigour and the zest for action and accomplishment which characterised the Old Kingdom of Egypt', which also saw 'some of Egypt's highest intellectual achievements.' He concludes, 'The reasons for this sudden spurt of power are not clear ... they [the Egyptians] sprang upward with a suddenness which is miraculous to us.'[27] In the opinion of many, the Egyptians of the earliest fully visible period 'reached heights which were never surpassed later – in technical ability (as in the Great Pyramid and in sculpture), in science (as in a remarkable surgical papyrus and in the institution of a calendar), and in philosophy (as in the Memphite Theology).'[28]

As for Mesopotamia, whose history is if anything older than that of Egypt, L.W. King writes, 'Although the earliest Sumerian settlements in Southern Babylonia are to be set back in a comparatively remote past, the race by which they were founded appears at that time to have already attained to a high level of culture.'[29] Or as the famous archaeologist Sir Leonard Woolley wrote about Sumeria in the era of 3500 BC, 'It is astonishing to find that at this early period the Sumerians were acquainted with and commonly employed not only the column, but the arch, the vault, and the dome, architectural forms which were not to find their way into the western world for thousands of years. That the general level of civilization accorded with the high development of architecture is shown by the richness of the graves.'[30]

It was not until relatively late in the history of Egypt, in the days of the empire, from the sixteenth century BC, that we find minor, local gods coming into prominence, after the supreme god and the pantheon of gods associated with him had become remote from common man. As Wilson writes, 'In the latter part of the Empire an Egyptian expressed a close personal relation to a specifically named god, who was his protector and controller.'[31] It was in the Empire period, too, that there developed the fourfold cycle of the cult of Osiris, the god most commonly linked in popular understanding with ancient Egypt.

The Old Kingdom of Egypt collapsed as a result of a breakdown of centralised rule, accompanied by (or perhaps resulting in) an influx into the Egyptian Delta of Asiatic immigrants. In the Middle Kingdom that followed, Osiris came more strongly to the fore; he was god of the dead, with entry into eternal life largely in his gift. In the earlier period, the supreme god, the sun-god, had been the judge of men; then there was, in Wilson's phrase 'a democratisation of the next world and Osirianisation', eternal judgement taking place before a tribunal of gods; finally, the fate of the departed was held to depend on a trial before Osiris alone.[32] The developed Osiris myth – his murder when reigning as king on earth at the hands of his wicked brother Set; the mourning of Isis, his sister/wife; the finding, then burial, of his dismembered body; a kind of resurrection, 'Osiris of the mysteries, who springs from the returning waters'[33] – need not detain us. It was well after the Middle Kingdom, in the days of the Empire, that Osiris became chief of the gods.

As already mentioned, a feature of Egypt in the later period of its history – as in the later Roman Empire – was the multiplicity of 'gods'. At around the time of Moses (see below), there were over forty petty states in Egypt, each with its own chief god, worshipped in his temple at the principal city. Each such god had other gods associated with him – a wife goddess, or sons – and each in his own territory was regarded as 'god almighty', creator and preserver of the world. Besides these, each town and village possessed its own god. All gods were given 'names', to distinguish one from another. The Thebian Recension of the 'Book of the Dead' gives the names of over 450, and altogether we now know the names of over 2200. As in Mesopotamia, with the proliferation and increased splendour of temples, there was an increase in their staffing and wealth. Temple activities eventually became the dominant factor in Egyptian political, social and economic life, overwhelming everything and everyone, both people and pharaoh.

A consistent picture, I submit, has emerged from 'the history of God' we have so far traced, amongst 'primitive' peoples in Africa and elsewhere, and in the ancient kingdoms of Mesopotamia and of Egypt. It is of belief in a Supreme Deity that steadily become eroded, not of a slow development of belief from the daemons or spirits of trees and other natural objects, through local territorial gods to a pantheon of high gods, then on finally to one Great Creative Spirit. We could illustrate the same pattern from other parts of the world, notably China. It is little appreciated that some fifteen hundred or more years before the blossoming of Taoism and Confucianism in the fifth century BC, the ancient people of China served a single supreme God, had no myths or idols, and kept a strict moral code. Their name for God was ShangTi, meaning Heavenly Emperor, or literally 'Emperor Above'.[34] Yet this fact need not surprise us. Evidence suggests that the Chinese originally migrated from a site in Mesopotamia, their culture – in the arts, in the sciences and in government – showing marked similarity to that of the later Babylonians and Assyrians.[35]

At much the same time a famous family migrated from Mesopotamia to the land of Canaan. To that seminal event we shall now turn.

Chapter 2
Out of Ur

Abraham migrated to the land of Canaan from Ur, in southern Babylonia, Mesopotamia, probably sometime in the twentieth or nineteenth centuries BC, though possibly as early as the twenty-first century. His father Terah took the family as far as Haran, but then decided to settle there. From Haran, some time later, Abraham set out for Canaan with his wife Sarai, his nephew Lot, his family retainers and all his possessions. He did so, the Bible tells us, in obedience to the command of 'the Lord'.[1]

The patriarchs: a critical question

As soon as we start talking about the Hebrew patriarchs, whom we read about in the first book of the Bible, Genesis, we come up against the question of authorship, and historical truth. Karen Armstrong, for instance, asserts in her book *A History of God*, published in 1993, that the biblical account of these early wanderers and their immediate descendants was written down a thousand or more years after their lifetime, in about the eighth century BC, though earlier narrative sources were utilised. She refers to the critical method employed by nineteenth-century German biblical scholars, an analysis based on internal criteria, that of textual style and content. This, she writes, 'discerned four different sources in the first five books of the Bible: Genesis, Exodus, Leviticus, Numbers and Deuteronomy. These were finally collated into the final text of what we know as the Pentateuch during the fifth century BC. This form criticism has come in for a good deal of harsh treatment but nobody has yet come up with a more satisfactory theory.'[2]

The theory of multiple authorship of the Pentateuch to which Karen Armstrong refers is known amongst scholars as the Graf-Wellhausen hypothesis. The theory was finalised in the 1870s by Julius Wellhausen, who built on earlier scholarly work by K.H. Graf. The four sources Wellhausen isolated were: 'J', because the writer used the word 'Jehovah' for God (usually rendered 'the Lord' in English),[3] this source assigned by Wellhausen to the ninth century; 'E', because the writer used the word 'Elohim' for God, assigned to the eighth century; 'D', essentially the book of Deuteronomy, from the later seventh century (during the reign of king

Josiah); 'P', the Priestly source, from the fifth century. According to this reconstruction, the religion of the Hebrews evolved first into a national henotheism (the worship of one god from among many gods) and only much later, in the time of the literary prophets and the sixth century exile in Babylonia, into an ethical monotheism.

Generation after generation of students studying theology at universities and colleges all over Europe, in USA and elsewhere have been nourished on the above theory, the present writer being one of them. Alternative theories are seldom entertained, certainly not taught, apart from minor modifications by subsequent scholars of the same basic idea; any idea that Moses might have had a hand in writing the Pentateuch is dismissed out of hand. The student, therefore, almost inevitably finds himself going along with the German theory *faute de mieux*.

But is there really no alternative? This is not the place to argue the case comprehensively, but there is at least one satisfactory explanation for the data as we have it in Genesis, if not in the whole Pentateuch, and this dispenses entirely with the Graf-Wellhausen hypothesis.

Let us first make some general points about the latter theory. Firstly, it was propounded at a time when most scholars assumed that the contents of Genesis – known to us, like virtually all the rest of the Old Testament, in Hebrew – would if genuine have been handed down by word of mouth, written sources at such an early date being impracticable if not impossible. Archaeological discoveries that seriously suggested otherwise had not yet broken upon the world. As late as 1893, H. Schultz was writing, 'Of the legendary character of the pre-Mosaic narratives, the time of which they treat is sufficient proof. It was a time prior to all knowledge of writing.'[4] Secondly, even when, in the twentieth century, archaeological excavation was painting a somewhat different picture of the ancient world, biblical scholars initially paid little attention. As Edwin Yamauchi has written, 'One of the striking characteristics of the scholars who have approached the Bible primarily through literary analysis is the non-use or at least the grudging use they have made of archaeological evidence.'[5] Thirdly, Julian Wellhausen, though a brilliant and penetrating thinker, was a child of his time. He was strongly influenced by evolutionary concepts characteristic of the philosophy of Hegel. In other words, he did not come to the Old Testament with a fully open mind; there was an underlying desire to fit it into preconceived ideas about how historical processes worked.[6]

The theory which best fits the data we have in the book of Genesis is one first put forward by P.J. Wiseman in 1936. He realised that the oft-repeated phrase 'these are the generations of' (better translated 'these are the origins of' or 'the history of') could only represent a colophon in the text, a device giving the writer's name and often the date of writing, *referring to the preceding verses as a unit.* This would correspond exactly to Babylonian practice when using their cuneiform script, each unit of text constituting a clay tablet. He further identified Babylonian words in the early Genesis narratives, as well as literary mechanisms current among Babylonian scribes, like attempts at dating, section titles, the linking of passages in series and the use of catch-lines. Unlike the Graf-Wellhausen school, he proposed that ancient Mesopotamian or Mesopotamian-style sources lay behind most of Genesis. These sources were then combined with the Joseph narratives – which duly exemplify Egyptian words and names – to complete the book. He summed up his conclusions thus, 'The Book of Genesis was originally written on tablets in the ancient script of the time [i.e. in cuneiform, or possibly partly in the earlier pictographic script], by the Patriarchs who were intimately concerned with the events related, and whose names are clearly stated. Moreover, Moses, the compiler and editor of the Book, as we now have it, plainly directs attention to the source of his information.'[7]

Wiseman was aware that his conclusions were momentous and would not gain acceptance without careful perusal of all the evidence, yet he continued, 'When this evidence has been scrutinised, it will be found that it is attested by facts so numerous and verified by undesigned coincidences so overwhelming, that almost every critical difficulty regarding Genesis disappears.'[7] The present writer – trained both as a theologian and as a linguist – can testify that the evidence marshalled by P.J. Wiseman is immeasurably more convincing than that adduced in favour of the Graf-Wellhausen hypothesis, or any of its later modifications.

So much for the book of Genesis. What of the rest of the Pentateuch?

The general approach which assigns the compilation of the first five books of the Bible to dates between the ninth and fifth centuries BC, with its division into the four main sources noted above, has come in for strong criticism – as Karen Armstrong concedes. Some have pointed out that there are other explanations for the use of two divine names besides the idea that they denote two different sources, or that in any case there are no good grounds for using them as a criterion for documentary analysis.[8] Others have concentrated upon the supposed 'D' (Deuteronomic) and

'P' (Priestly) sources, finding difficulty in squaring the late dates postulated for their compilation in the Graf-Wellhausen scheme with internal data from the biblical books in question.[9] At all events, the latter scheme has been disposed of satisfactorily by P.J. Wiseman in his explanation of how Genesis was first written and later compiled.

The Hebrew patriarchs can clearly be taken seriously. To make such a statement is not superfluous because biblical scholars from the nineteenth century onwards have frequently cast doubt upon their very existence – witness the remark of M. Schultz, quoted above. The scholars H. Winckler and A Jeremias, specialists in Babylonia, suggested they were reflections of astral deities. Others, S.R. Driver, for example, have considered the patriarchs Abraham, Isaac, Jacob and his sons to be idealised creations, personifications of later tribes. They were perhaps invented at the time of the conquest of Canaan, or later, it has been suggested, to justify or legitimise the existence of the nation of Israel in the form of twelve tribes (descendants of the 'twelve' sons of Jacob) and, more especially, to reinforce its claim to the land. But not only can we be confident that the patriarchs were real people, who wrote (or had scribes write for them) records of their family history which they then preserved, we need also have no hesitation in believing that they worshipped one God. As we have seen, far from it being the (later) Hebrews who introduced true monotheism to the Near East and perhaps to the world (as some, like Karen Armstrong, seem to believe), the Babylonians, as well as the Egyptians, knew and honoured a Supreme Deity centuries before Abraham. It seems that their monotheistic belief slowly degenerated into polytheism, but there is no reason to think that the purer monotheistic faith did not survive in some circles to the time of Abraham. He was just one of those who maintained it.

After a brief sojourn in Egypt, because there was a famine in Canaan, Abraham, with Sarai, with his retinue and all his possessions, settled 'by the oaks of Mamre', at Hebron. His brother Lot, meanwhile, chose to dwell among the cities of the valley, finally settling at Sodom. At this point in Genesis (Chapter 14) we come across an extended passage which for long puzzled scholars, who duly dismissed it as unhistorical.[10] It concerns the invasion of four kings of the East – Amraphel, Arioch, Chedorlaomer and Tidal – against the kings of Sodom and Gomorrah. Yet the later archaeological discoveries of Nelson Glueck, W.F. Albright and others showed how the earlier scepticism about this account was too hasty. Although he had some forty years before been a sceptic himself, in 1961 Albright asserted that his studies 'have established the absolute antiquity of the contents of the chapter and have shown that it is strewn with indications of a very archaic verse tradition'.[11]

The above is just one example, albeit a significant one, of how archaeological research has corroborated the biblical accounts. On this whole matter, D.J. Wiseman, formerly Professor of Assyriology at London University, wrote in 1971, 'When due allowance has been paid to the increasing number of supposed errors which have been subsequently eliminated by the discoveries of archaeological evidence, to the many aspects of history indirectly affirmed or in some instances directly confirmed by extra-biblical sources, I would maintain that the historical facts of the Bible, rightly understood, find agreement in the facts culled from archaeology, equally rightly understood, that is, the majority of errors can be ascribed to errors of interpretation by modern scholars and not to substantiated "errors" of fact presented by the biblical historians.'[12]

According to the biblical account, the patriarchs met God in a number of ways, some of which we would today call anthropomorphic – that is, the describing of an experience in 'crudely' human terms. For example, in Chapter 18 of Genesis, we find God appearing to Abraham by the oaks of Mamre in the form of three men. On this occasion, we are told, the Lord promised Abraham that his elderly wife, Sarah (her name now changed from Sarai), would give birth to a son; it was also revealed to Abraham that God intended to investigate the sin of Sodom and Gomorrah. Or again, we are told in Genesis 28 that Abraham's grandson, Jacob, encountered God at Luz, which Jacob then renamed Bethel, when he had a dream of a stairway, or 'ladder', stretching from earth to heaven. (Perhaps Jacob had been thinking about *ziggurats* before going to sleep; he was at the time on a journey to Babylonia to find a wife.) God appeared above the stairway and promised that the land on which he lay would be given to him and to his descendants, who would spread abroad to the west, east, north and south. Jacob was also assured that he would be kept safe wherever he went and that he would one day come back to the land where he was.

These appearances of God, or 'theophanies' (to use the theological term), are considered legendary by most writers of popular religion.[13] Yet if, as P.J. Wiseman has established beyond reasonable doubt, the patriarchs themselves were the ultimate authors of these accounts, we must treat them with greater respect. At face value they refer to genuine experiences, as the many incidental touches of detail indicate. Whatever exactly happened, the accounts as we have them are the best way such experiences could have been described. Nor can they be other than 'anthropomorphic'; man can only describe the divine in his own terms. Of course, you can easily beg the question entirely by saying that the patriarchs did not exist, therefore the accounts have to be fictional inventions. But that is to make an *a priori* judgement. The alternative is to allow that the patriarchs existed and that they were (or could have been) the recipients of divine revelation, or at least had numinous experiences which may have been subjective but which they described as best they could. One can, of course, go further and say that the Divine is indeed a reality and that the patriarchs genuinely encountered this reality, though perhaps finding it difficult to make human thought-forms or language do justice to the nature of those encounters.

A lofty conception

The book of Genesis opens not with an account of anything personally to do with the patriarchs but with an account of creation. In this case the original author is not named, though we still have a colophon at the end of the narrative ('These are the generations [origins] of the heaven and the earth.'), which probably indicates that initially the account was inscribed on a separate clay tablet. The peoples of Mesopotamia likewise had their accounts of creation, as we have already seen, the most complete version of the Creation Epic surviving on a series of six, originally seven, clay Babylonian tablets. Today this Epic is normally referred to by its opening words *Enuma elish*, 'When on high'. The saga begins with a time when nothing exists except the watery deep or 'chaos'. Newly created gods represent order and they defeat rebellious elements, led by Tiamat (a monster personifying that same primordial 'watery deep'), only to be freshly opposed by them in strengthened form under another god, Kingu. Marduk, appointed champion of the gods, takes up the challenge, kills Tiamat and splits her open like an oyster to form the earth and the heavens. The stars and moon are then formed, this apparently taking place before the creation of animal and plant life. Finally, Marduk creates man from the blood of the slain Kingu, mixed with clay or dust from the earth.

The Genesis account of creation, with its lofty conception of God, bears little resemblance to the crude mythology of *Enuma elish*. As D.J. Wiseman has written of the latter, 'Any similarities with the Genesis record have to be rescued from the overlaying extraneous matter which forms the bulk of the poem; such can best be explained as due to both versions going back to common primary facts.'[14] If one has to postulate a relationship, it is easier to see the Babylonian story as a bizarre, half-remembered amplification of the dignified biblical account than the latter as a purified abbreviation of the former. As it happens, the Babylonian Epic may have been written as late as the eleventh century BC,[15] which would make it too late (on my dating of Genesis) to have influenced the writing of the biblical creation narrative.

The Gilgamesh Epic is another famous Babylonian saga. It is the story of a king of Uruk (biblical Erech, modern Warka) who searched for immortality. In the legendary accounts he is considered semi-divine but he can now be regarded as a real king who reigned about 2700 BC. The eleventh Gilgamesh tablet was published in 1872, creating a sensation because it contained parallels with the biblical account of the flood. The Gilgamesh flood story has been identified with a local flood at Tell Fara, where a flood deposit has been dated around 2700, when Gilgamesh himself was probably alive. On the other hand, as this flood episode is not an integral part of the Epic it may emanate from an older period. J.G. Frazer collected numerous flood stories from all over the world – the Near East, Greece, South Asia, the Pacific, the Americas – and this suggests there is a common memory of a much greater deluge.[16]

In 1965 another Babylonian text was published, the Atrahasis Epic. This includes both a creation and a flood account. As in the *Enuma elish* narrative, quarrelling gods are involved in creation, man being created to relieve the younger gods from having to work, and the flood being sent because men became too noisy for the chief god of earth to sleep. While parallels with the first chapters of Genesis exist – there is the creation, followed by rebellion and then a flood – the ethical and theological contrasts are significant. The Babylonians conceive of the event in polytheistic terms, the gods taking action because they have been inconvenienced; in the Bible, God acts in creation because everything he makes is 'very good', and he only sends the flood later because of man's wickedness. Once again, it is impossible to imagine borrowing by the biblical writers from this turgid Babylonian Epic.

We must pass swiftly over the remaining history of the Hebrew patriarchs, pausing only to note that in a poignant episode (so poignant for some that they hate reading it) we learn that the God of the Hebrews was not like the 'gods' of the surrounding nations because human sacrifice was abhorrent to him. The episode in question is that in which Abraham is, as the record has it, 'tested': God asks him to sacrifice his only son Isaac as a burnt offering, only to tell the obedient patriarch at the last moment to sacrifice a ram instead.[17] Isaac is of course the 'son of promise', the one through whom (according to the same record) God has already assured Abraham that the covenant, that of a multitudinous and blessed posterity, will be fulfilled. The author of the New Testament letter to the Hebrews realised the heavy irony involved in this 'test' because he tells us that Abraham believed God would raise Isaac to life again, after he had been slain as a sacrifice.[18] Yet Abraham and his successors would have had indelibly imprinted in their hearts and minds two crucial truths through this awful event: their God, the One True God, may have desired perfect obedience, but he did not desire the sacrifice of man's own flesh to please or appease him; he could not accept 'the fruit of my body for the sin of my soul';[19] when it came to such atoning sacrifice, God would provide.

Isaac's 'son of promise' was Jacob, who, following another encounter with God, took the name Israel. Jacob and all his sons except one eventually found their way to Egypt because of a famine in the land of Canaan, the way having been prepared by the arrival in Egypt ahead of them of Jacob's 'favourite' son Joseph, sold into slavery by his jealous brothers, yet ending up as Pharaoh's viceroy. On this note the book of Genesis ends, to be followed by the book of Exodus, which tells of the great increase in number of the children of Israel while they were in Egypt, of their oppression at the hands of a pharaoh 'who did not know Joseph', and of their deliverance under Moses.

Moses, 'Jehovah', and the prophets

The story of Moses is well-known: how, although himself a Hebrew, he was brought up as the son of Pharaoh's daughter (albeit cared for in early years by his own mother, acting as nurse); how he fled from Egypt after killing an Egyptian who was ill-treating one of his own people; and how, having lived for a while in Midian, he felt called to be Israel's deliverer. That call was very significant for the Hebrew understanding of the Deity.

The narrative in the third chapter of Exodus describes Moses' encounter with God after seeing a bush which was burning yet 'not consumed'. God then revealed to Moses that his true name was 'I am who I am', or simply 'I am'. The name consists of four Hebrew letters, corresponding to the English letters YHVH (or YHWH), rendered 'Jehovah', 'Yahweh', or more frequently 'the LORD', in English Bibles.[20] It is associated with the Hebrew verb *hayah*, meaning 'live'. The name came to be considered so holy by the people of Israel that they would not even utter it, fearing that they might in so doing be guilty of profanity, thus breaking the second of the ten commandments.

In the book of Exodus, Chapter six, verse two, we read these words addressed to Moses: 'I am the LORD. I appeared to Abraham, to Isaac, and to Jacob, as God Almighty, but by my name the LORD ['YHVH', 'Jehovah'] I did not make myself known to them.' The form 'God Almighty' translates the ancient title for God 'El Shaddai', probably better translated 'All Sufficient'. Moses would have come across this title frequently in his cuneiform sources and, partly because this title had become tainted by association with numerous local 'gods', all of whom were called 'god almighty' by their devotees, he substituted 'YHVH'. This accounts for the fact that the latter appears in our text of Genesis in connection with Abraham, Isaac and Jacob, in apparent contradiction of the above verse from Exodus.[21]

Many scholars in the past have suggested that it is only from the time of the exodus from Egypt under Moses and the conquest of Canaan under Joshua that the story of Israel begins – if indeed the exodus occurred, for some have doubted it. We have already seen, however, that there is no evidence, archaeological or documentary, to support such a truncated view of Hebrew history. Assuming, therefore, that the story of the patriarchs is genuine history, what we can undoubtedly say is that Moses began a new and very different stage in that history.

Moses is known as the Lawgiver, and in this role he was the prime instrument in the welding of his people into nationhood. One of Wellhausen's preconceived notions was that Law could not precede Prophecy. As the Hebrew prophets came well after Moses (not himself allowed to be a prophet), this was another reason why the Pentateuch, which in the book of Exodus includes accounts of the giving of the Law by Moses in Sinai, had in Wellhausen's view to be the work of a much later writer. Yet the 'Prophecy-before-Law' idea had to be abandoned when the Code of Hammurabi, dated in the eighteenth century BC, was unearthed at Susa, Mesopotamia, in 1901. The oldest law code now known is the twenty-first century Ur-Nammu Code. There are parallels between some of the 'case laws' found in these codes and laws in the Pentateuch, as for example legislation surrounding the problem of 'a goring ox'. But there are also significant differences, the Hebrew laws being generally more humane. For example, according to the Code of Hammurabi a Babylonian master could kill his own slave with impunity; in the Old

Testament, a Hebrew master who killed his slave would be tried for murder.

The exodus of the people of Israel from Egypt has been dated by scholars at around 1440 or, alternatively, 1270 BC. Archaeological evidence, though not conclusive, favours the latter. The question is bound up with the dating of the conquest of Canaan, which according to the biblical record occurred some forty years later, after the Israelites had wandered for that period of time in the wilderness of Sinai. Excavations have revealed signs of the violent destruction in the thirteenth century of Canaanite cities referred to in the Bible as having been taken by Joshua.[22] On the other hand, if the biblical Hebrews are to be identified with the Habiru of the fourteenth-century Amarna letters from Egypt, the earlier date might be preferable. The Habiru people, whose languages, like Hebrew, were West Semitic, is first mentioned in nineteenth century texts from Alishar, in what is now central Turkey. In the eighteenth-seventeenth centuries we find them in Haran (where Abraham stayed, as we have seen) and Mari, in the Euphrates valley. In the fifteenth century they appear in Egypt as 'Apiru', which W.F. Albright interprets tentatively as 'dusty one', that is, a donkey caravaneer. Finally, in the fourteenth century, they turn up in Palestine. Albright believes that the existence of the Habiru can help to explain the background of Abraham, while other scholars believe the movements of the biblical Hebrews may have been part of a broader movement of the Habiru.[23]

It is unnecessary to trace in detail the further history of the Hebrew people, or Israel. The important point to have established is that true monotheism began before Abraham, that he and the later patriarchs maintained it, and that it was only amplified through Moses, not invented by him – nor, indeed, by any later Hebrew prophet or writer.

An argument used by proponents of a late date for the emergence in Hebrew history of true monotheism is the fact that reference is made in the Old Testament to 'gods' or 'other gods' (also, more obscurely, to 'the sons of God') in a manner which implies they exist.[24] The following examples can be cited: in the 'Song of Moses' the question is asked, 'Who is like thee, O Lord, among the gods?'; the first commandment forbids the veneration of 'other gods before me'; the book of Deuteronomy describes 'Jehovah' as 'God of gods'; king Solomon declares that 'our God is greater than all gods'; finally, one of the psalmists seems to picture Israel's God as no more than the greatest deity in a pantheon of deities, after the manner of the myths of Mesopotamia and Egypt. As for the term 'the sons of God', referring apparently to heavenly beings, we find this early in the book of Genesis and also in the book of Job.[25] Should we understand, on the basis of such references, that the Hebrews accepted the existence (though perhaps also the powerlessness against themselves) of 'other gods'?

We should first remind ourselves just how often in the same Old Testament these 'gods' are charged with being effete, impotent – indeed, 'no gods' – in contrast to 'Jehovah', the mighty God of Israel.[26] Yet even after allowing for this, the feeling remains, from certain texts at least, that it is not so much the non-existence of 'the gods' that is at issue as the fact that they are given inappropriate obeisance. In other words, they exist, but do not deserve worship since they are not divine. I shall return to this point later.

If the prophets of Israel were not the inventors of monotheism they were certainly responsible for expanding their people's understanding of 'Jehovah', the one true God, frequently castigating the nation for its apostate behaviour. Isaiah, prophet during the second half of the eighth century to the southern kingdom of Judah (separated from northern 'Israel' after the death of Solomon), emphasised God's extreme holiness, looking for the coming of a leader imbued with his spirit – a messianic figure destined to rule over both Israel and the nations in power and justice.[27] Isaiah (or, in the view of some scholars, a 'Second Isaiah'[28]) talked also of a mysterious character, 'the righteous one, my servant', a kind of personification of Israel, whose task was to bear the sins and griefs of others through his own suffering and death.[29] One of Isaiah's contemporaries was Hosea, whose message was directed to the northern kingdom. As well as denouncing the people's faithlessness, he uttered words that shed light on the nature of the God he served, words quoted centuries later by Jesus. Speaking on God's behalf, Hosea declared, 'I desire steadfast love and not sacrifice, the knowledge of God, rather than burnt offerings.'[30]

At the end of the seventh century and into the sixth, the prophet Jeremiah called Judah to repent of its evil ways, especially the worship of 'other gods', warning that failure to do so would bring calamity – a warning fulfilled in 597 BC when Judah was overwhelmed by Nebuchadrezzar, king of Babylon, who ten years later destroyed Jerusalem and its temple, deporting all but the poor of the nation to Babylon.[31] Yet Jeremiah looked further ahead, to a re-gathering of all Israel (the northern kingdom having fallen to the Assyrians a century or so earlier, its people also taken captive) and eventually to the establishment of a new covenant between God and the nation. That covenant, in which the law would be written 'upon their hearts', would replace the covenant made with the nation under Moses, based on adherence to the law of Sinai.[32]

The message of Jesus, who lived and taught six centuries or more after Jeremiah, followed naturally on from that of the prophets of Israel. Before considering his contribution to man's understanding of God, however, we shall refer briefly to religious thinkers and movements active elsewhere in the world in the time of the later Hebrews.

Unlike 'Jehovah'

In Persia, at the beginning of the sixth century BC, a religious teacher called Zarathrusta, or Zoroaster in its Greek form, appeared on the scene – or his message first became prominent at that time, for it is possible he lived a lot earlier. He (or his followers) strove to purify the ancient faith of the country. Within fifty years Zoroastrianism was the state religion and by the second century AD a major world ideology. Zoroaster, who was ascribed divine powers by his followers though he had never claimed them, spoke of the age-long war between good, represented by Ahura Mazda, and evil, represented by Ahriman. The individual must support Ahura Mazda against Ahriman by doing what is right, confident that in the last days good will triumph, when Ahura Mazda finally prevails.

In India, during the first millennium BC, Hinduism and then Buddhism gradually replaced the older Vedic religion brought by Aryan invaders (from what is now Iran) nearly a thousand years earlier. The latter religion had seen a multiplicity of gods and many sacrifice rituals; it made no attempt, however, to answer questions like the origin and meaning of life. A desire for a deeper understanding of reality led to the appearance of new religious teachers, who, while not denying the existence of the old gods, sought to look beyond them. Between the eighth and fifth centuries BC many of these teachers wrote down their ideas, their writings being known collectively as the Vedanta (the end of the Vedas). In some of these tracts, called Upanishads, we encounter a form of pantheism – the view that the godhead is immanent in everything. The most important of these teachers was a man named Siddhartha Gautama, who about 538 BC left his wife, young son and fine home in north-east India to become a mendicant; he wanted to discover how *dukkha*, the pain or suffering he believed to be common to all existence, could be overcome. Following a mystical experience, he became the Buddha, or 'enlightened one'. In response to encouragement he received from two of the gods (as he claimed), he started travelling all over India preaching that the end of suffering, or *nirvana*, a state of existence transcending the sphere of the gods, was attainable through *dharma*, the right way of living.

In Greece, in the fifth century, Plato expounded a rather different and more rational view: beyond our physical world, he taught, exist eternal realities or archetypes. Aristotle further developed this philosophy, teaching that above a hierarchy of existences dwells the Unmoved Mover, or God. Unlike 'Jehovah' of the Hebrews, however, Aristotle's Deity was not Creator, nor was he even concerned about the universe, which was material and therefore flawed. The sole concern of this Supreme Being was the contemplation of himself, a spiritual exercise of pure thought.

The teaching of Jesus of Nazareth, born in the Roman province of Judea a few years before 1 AD (once thought to be the date of his birth), could hardly have been in greater contrast to that of the Indian and Greek thinkers.

Chapter 3
New Era

Jesus and a universal faith

It is frequently said that we know very little for certain about Jesus.[1] I shall dispute this at a later stage; my purpose now is to give his teaching in broad outline.

As far as the authenticity of the written records of Jesus' teaching is concerned, it will suffice at this stage to quote someone who sought to *discredit* Christian claims. In his book arguing that Christianity was founded on a mistake made by the first disciples, Rupert Furneaux writes, 'One thing seems certain, Jesus must have said most or many of the words attributed to him. Whatever else is doubtful, his basic teaching remains.'[2]

Jesus was a Jew, and like all Jews was an ardent monotheist.[3] He taught that this one God, though holy and demanding holiness from his devotees, was an infinitely loving Father to all who approached him in humility. This is clear from the teaching he gave in what is known as the Sermon on the Mount, recorded (or collected together) in Matthew's gospel, Chapters 5-7. The God he preached was concerned about individuals and their needs. God counts the very hairs of our heads, he said. Indeed, he cares no less for the birds of the air and the lilies of the field.

Of course, Jesus said more about God than that he was a loving Father – though it is this idea, together with the corollary that we must be similarly loving to our neighbours, that many people seem to think is the sole content of his 'original, simple message'. It is often forgotten that his ministry began with the call, reminiscent of the prophets of old, and echoing even more directly the message of his cousin and 'forerunner' John the Baptist, for people to 'repent, and believe the gospel'. This followed his electrifying announcement that 'the time is fulfilled, and the kingdom of God is at hand'.[4] Though not himself an austere man – for the criticism levelled at him by religious leaders for consorting with unsavoury elements in society must be taken seriously – the teaching of Jesus was starkly uncompromising: erring humanity has to turn from its evil ways and seek forgiveness from God. Above all, he hated insincerity; those religious teachers who took him to task for lax living frequently felt the rough edge of his tongue (with more than a touch of ironic humour). He had no time for their casuistic interpretation of the law, which, he told them, made a mockery of true holiness. It was on two such occasions that he turned to the prophet Hosea for a text (already cited above) with which to denounce their hypocrisy.[5] He once rebuked his disciples for a not dissimilar attitude, when they tried to stop people bringing children to him. In words that could be held to crystallise his purpose and mission, he told them, 'Let the children come to me, do not hinder them; for to such belongs the kingdom of God. Truly, I say to you, whoever does not receive the kingdom of God like a child shall not enter it.'[6]

But Jesus' teaching went further than this: there is no escaping the fact (though this is glossed over by non-Christian writers[7]) that Jesus considered himself to have a unique and exalted role in the process by which God's forgiveness would become accessible to man. His message was – unlike that of most religious reformers – extremely egocentric. People in general are prepared to admire Jesus as a teacher, conceding that he spoke sublime truth about life and (perhaps) about God. Yet they are apt to forget that inextricably bound up with such teaching is a consistent focusing of people's attention upon himself.

We can cite instances of Jesus' ego-centred teaching almost at random from the gospels. There are his words to two brothers out fishing together at the very beginning of his ministry, 'Follow me and I will make you become fishers of men.' A little later he was, on his own authority, declaring to a paralysed man, 'Your sins are forgiven you.' Not surprisingly, this incurred the wrath of some nearby clergy, who exploded, 'Why does this man speak thus? It is blasphemy! Who can forgive sins but God alone.' Soon after this he was taking it upon himself to change the Jewish rules about Sabbath observance; in other words, he was pronouncing on what did and what did not constitute sinful behaviour. A little later, when addressed as 'Son of the Most High God', he did not suggest the title was inappropriate. Nearer the end of his life he was telling the crowds that in following him they must be prepared to take up a cross, that if they wanted to 'save' their lives they must 'lose' them 'for my sake and the gospel's'. He then underlined this teaching by warning his hearers that if they spurned his words they would have to answer for it when they faced judgement before 'the Son of man' (a title he reserved for himself), who would one day come 'in the glory of his Father'. Finally, when challenged at his trial by the high priest to declare whether or not he was 'the Christ, the Son of the Blessed', he replied unequivocally, 'I am;

and you will see Son of man sitting at the right hand of Power, and coming with the clouds of heaven.'[8]

All the above examples of Jesus' teaching or deportment come from the brief gospel of John Mark, who, tradition tells us, was informed by Simon Peter, leader of the inner ring of disciples. We could multiply such examples of their master's self-glorifying stance from this gospel, as also from the other three gospels, not least that penned by 'the beloved disciple', almost certainly John Zebedee. It is this John who records that on one occasion Jesus declared, 'I and the Father are one', at which, we are told, 'the Jews took up stones again to stone him ... "for blasphemy; because you, being a man, make yourself God."'[9] To excise such sayings and actions of Jesus, implying his divine identity, from the passages in which they occur has no warrant in the text and does violence to the natural flow of the narrative, robbing the accounts of the compelling immediacy so impressive to the casual reader. There are no good grounds for saying that Jesus never said or did all this. Whether he was correct in his assumptions about himself, or about the world around him, is of course another matter.

Having told people to take up their cross and follow him, Jesus himself died on a cross. That might seem to be the end of the story, apart from the legacy of his teaching, but as the world knows his followers became convinced that though he had truly died he came back to life. Or rather, that he was resurrected, by the power of God (his own power, one could say, if he was himself divine), to a new and glorious form of bodily existence. This, anyway, is the traditional interpretation of the documents that comprise the New Testament, which, with the Jewish scriptures, or Old Testament, form the Christian Bible.

This chapter is not the place to discuss or defend the traditional view of the Christian faith. We are concerned at this point only to show that the idea of God, Creator and Lord of all life, Unique in Being and Power, was maintained by both Jesus and his first followers. The precise relationship of Jesus to that God – whether or not it was a relationship of such unbroken harmony that he could truthfully claim, as later his followers would assert, that he was by deed, right, and essence eternally united to Him – is an issue we must postpone.

The writers of the New Testament began to formulate the conception of a God who was truly one in his being yet having something like three manifestations or 'persons'. The argument was empirical: God 'the Father' they knew about as faithful Jews; God 'the Son' they had come to know in the person of Jesus; God 'the Counsellor' or 'Spirit', referred to several times by Jesus, they had discovered as a new power in their lives. The Christian doctrine of the Trinity, Three Persons in One Undivided Godhead, was not just an intellectual exercise, not the construct of academic eggheads speculating in a vacuum. It was, according to the evidence we have about early Christian thought processes, a theological necessity born of life-experience. As time went on, the trinitarian formula was explained more precisely, particularly in a creed promulgated by a council of Christian leaders held in Nicaea in north-west Asia Minor in 325 AD, primarily to combat the heresy of one Arius, who had been teaching that Jesus was not in essence divine. Finally, the so-called Athanasian Creed, a theological exposition in the form of a canticle, composed in the West towards the end of the fourth century, defined the doctrine of the Trinity more minutely.

The Council of Nicaea, the first ecumenical council held, was convened by the Roman Emperor, Constantine. This fact highlights for us the remarkable progress of Christianity from its first beginnings in Palestine three centuries earlier. To put it simply, when Constantine in 312 AD ascribed his victory in battle at the Milvian Bridge over his rival Maxentius to the intervention of the Christian's God, the true victors were the Christians. In other words, Christianity had finally conquered the Roman Empire – albeit without the Christians themselves having lifted an aggressive finger.[10] The historian Herbert Butterfield puts it thus, 'The spread of Christianity from that narrow and unpromising region where it had its birth, over the length and breadth of the civilized world, is one of the most moving stories that history has to offer us – one of the clearest cases ever known of the meek inheriting the earth. Islam was to be very different – it was to extend itself by military conquest. No one could accuse the followers of Christ of having made it their object, in the first three centuries, even to capture the Roman government.'[11]

What Christianity had 'conquered', of course, was not the empire but the pagan religion of that empire. Constantine retained the title Pontifex Maximus as head of the old Roman state religion, and indeed did not formally confess the Christian faith until on his deathbed, but following the Milvian Bridge victory he and his eastern colleague Licinius announced the crucial settlement of Milan. This settlement did not establish Christianity as the religion of the empire (as is often supposed) but it asserted the principle of toleration of all religious cults and, more specifically, declared that property confiscated from Christians in the recent persecutions would be restored. In other ways, too, Constantine showed that Christians enjoyed his special favour.

The Roman religious scene was one of 'gods many and lords many', the greatest of whom was the goddess Diana, whom people identified with the Greek Artemis, ancient mother goddess of Asia Minor. Until the time of Constantine, Christians were stigmatised by the Roman authorities as atheists because they did not recognise these 'gods' – except perhaps as demons. To these authorities, dismissal of the state gods, who normally included the emperor himself, was a form of treason. To the Roman populace in general, other factors put Christians out of favour: traditionalists viewed the rejection of the pantheon of gods and goddesses as uncultured and vulgar; tradesmen, whose business depended to a great extent on pagan religious practice, had no time for a god – the Christian God – who required no image, no sacrifice, no feasts; intellectuals, speculating with Aristotle about the Absolute, the Unknowable, the Unmoved Mover, found the idea of an incarnate suffering God unthinkable. Constantine's elevation of Christianity to the same level as the religion of the empire, or indeed to the level of other religions (such as Judaism) practised by its diverse peoples, was thus momentous in the extreme.

So it was that the Christian God, or the Christian view of God, became the heritage of the Western world. From that Western base, Christianity returned to the East in the latter half of the second millennium of our era through the work of Christian missions, after unsuccessful efforts to extend Christendom by the sword in the bloody and ignoble Crusades.

Not that the Crusades are the only example of the Christian Gospel being distorted. From the late nineteenth century, the movement called Christian Socialism has substituted the 'social gospel' for the traditional, spiritual understanding of the message of Jesus. Over the last fifty years or so, this movement has fostered (largely through the World Council of Churches) a form of the faith that concentrates on corporate ethical behaviour, effectively dispensing with God, discouraging evangelism and affirming that the chief duty of Christians is to work for change in the structures of society – through violent revolution, if necessary.

It is the mainstream churches that have been most deeply affected by Christian Socialism. Perhaps partly as a result of this, membership has tended to dwindle, except in the Catholic Church. The increase in Catholic membership, however, may have been less through the work of its missionaries than through the high birth rate of its existing members. Meanwhile, many evangelical Christian groups, especially the pentecostal churches, who have not ceased to proclaim a spiritual message, have seen their numbers rise.

One way and another, Christianity has become a universal faith: the God of Israel – albeit in trinitarian guise – is now confessed by almost a third of the world's population, from every nation on earth.

A spiritual form of Judaism

After the Jewish war with Rome, which began in 66 AD and reached a climax with the fall of Jerusalem to the Roman general Titus in 70, the religion of the Jewish people took on a new form. They had lost not only their capital city – 'Jerusalem, the joy of the whole earth' – but more significantly they had lost their Temple. The loss of the latter spelt the end of the priesthood because it meant the end of the system of animal sacrifices. One Jewish religious leader, however, an old man trapped inside the doomed city, saw what this signified for his nation. When Rabbi Johanan ben Zakkai was brought the news of the destruction of the Temple, and the messenger, one of his disciples, bewailed the loss of the place 'where they make propitiation for the sins of the Israel', he answered', 'My son let it not grieve thee; we have yet one propitiation equal to it, and what is that but the bestowal of kindnesses? – even as it is written, "I desired kindness and not sacrifice."'[12]

Johanan came to believe that the war with Rome had been a mistake: Jews must henceforth live by the spirit, not the sword. He took practical steps to bring this about, the first being remarkable. It is recorded that as the moment of supreme disaster for Jerusalem approached, he arranged with his disciples (through the connivance of Titus, rabbinical tradition has it) to be carried out of the walls of the city as one dead and ready for burial. Brought miraculously beyond the lines of danger, the rabbi arose from his coffin and made his way to the Emperor Vespasian. The emperor spared Johanan's life, granting his request to set up a school of rabbinical study in the little seaside town of Jabne (or Jamnia). In that unlikely spot Rabbi Johanan's new and more spiritual form of Judaism began to flourish.

The foundation for this new order of Judaism had already been laid in the form of an alternative organisation: the synagogue. It has to be remembered that not all Jews were living in Palestine at this time; over the centuries hundreds of thousands had been dispersed around the world, many of these in the later period forming quite large communities dotted around the Roman empire. The synagogue was a meeting place where Jews wherever they were living could come together for the reading and exposition of the law and for corporate prayer. The institution may have originated as a substitute for temple worship for the exiles in Babylon during the sixth century BC. By the first century of our era, however, as the New Testament bears witness, it had become an important institution in Palestine, not excluding Jerusalem. It was through the synagogue that the rabbis, respected teachers of the law, exercised their influence on the people. Most rabbis came from the party of the Pharisees and it was precisely this party that, because of its relative detachment from the temple order, was able to survive the catastrophic loss suffered at the hands of the Romans and reorganise the religious life of the people. The old Sanhedrin, or Council, made up of the chief priests and elders of the people, had perforce come to an end, so a new one was established. This, like the old one, comprised seventy-one members, but these were now doctors of the law, convening under the presidency of a leading rabbi. The new Council's chief function was the organisation of religious law.

Despite the necessary abandonment of the system of sacrifices, central to the religion of Israel prior to the year 70 AD, the God of Israel was still – and remains to this day – 'Jehovah', supreme and unique. This is clear from the definition by Raphael Loewe of what it means in our own times to be a believer in Judaism:

1. Acknowledgement of the uncompromisingly absolute, monotheistic sanction for Jewish ethical behaviour, including acknowledgement of its binding validity for oneself.
2. A sense of the meaningfulness of Jewish history.
3. An appreciation ... of the fact that Judaism enunciates its doctrines for the most part symbolically and by implication, using Jewish self-regulation (that is, *halakhah*, 'procedure, law') as its principal medium.[13]

For Loewe, Judaism is not merely a religion since it does not rest on dogma and enforces no ritual observances. It is also not a political movement, notwithstanding Zionism, since the latter has affected only a minority of Jews. It is, he summarises, 'a complex of faith and social ethics, of universal significance and possibly universal relevance [resting] upon the sanction of ... absolute monotheism'.[14]

Loewe's disclaimer of a political role for Judaism is difficult to credit since in the last fifty years or so it has become increasingly difficult to separate Judaism from the political aspirations of Israeli Jews. Zionism, the chief concern of which today is to maintain and strengthen the State of Israel *as a Jewish entity*, may in theory be espoused by only a minority of Jews but in practice it has coloured the whole Jewish scene. The majority of Jews undoubtedly support the broad aims of Zionism.

The religion of Israel as originally defined in the Hebrew scriptures (the Old Testament, to Christians) was theocratic. Possession of the land of Canaan was part of the contract God made with the sons of Jacob/Israel, who were commanded to *fight* for the territory, their 'promised land'. Religious Zionists today – many of whom are Orthodox rabbis from Israel and elsewhere – are sticking to this agenda. They believe that *Eretz Israel* (the biblical land of Israel) is theirs by divine right; this includes the West Bank, Gaza, the Golan Heights, as well as other areas. They view surrender of such territories, occupied by Israel following the Six Day War of June 1967, as a betrayal of the nation's covenant with God, their true King. In line with this, in July 1995 Zionist rabbis, including a former Chief Rabbi, issued a religious law announcing that it was unlawful for Israeli soldiers to evacuate Jewish settlers from the West Bank; the ruling put religiously minded soldiers in an impossible dilemma. The issue of the land, for many the holiest thing in Jewish religion, has accordingly been the chief stumbling block for every initiative designed to procure peace between Israel and the Palestinians.

There is also the issue of the Temple. Many Zionists would like to see a new one erected, with the sacrificial system reinstated; indeed, according to an Israeli journalist interviewed by the B.B.C. for the series *Crisis in the House of David* (1998), the rebuilding of the Temple is the ultimate goal of quite moderate Jews.

There are, of course, Jews who can be seen as modern adherents of the more spiritual form of Judaism promoted by Johanan ben Zakkai. The ultra-Orthodox sect known as the Netura Karta, for example, opposes a political expression of Judaism on the grounds that it is blasphemous to establish a Jewish state before the advent of Messiah. The sect even made a pact with the former Palestinian leader, Yasser Arafat, in whom ironically they saw an ally. There are also secular Jews who, on pragmatic grounds, argue that Zionism (in its more militant form, at least) has been misguided. But these are of limited influence in Israel today, where there has been an upsurge both in religious feeling and in the power of religious parties. The extreme Orthodox, indeed, argue that to be secular is to deny a true Jewish identity; if we go by Loewe's definition of Judaism, this would seem truly to be the case.

Islam and the theocratic ideal

Some five hundred years after the Jews had lost their holy city and Temple, a child was born in Mecca, traditional centre of Arabia for religion and trade, who was to proclaim a monotheistic faith that he believed had superseded both Judaism and Christianity. Muhammad bin Abdallah is revered as the Prophet and Founder of Islam. At the age of about forty, in around 610 AD, he began to preach the messages he had received, as he claimed, via the angel Gabriel (*Jibril*, in Arabic). Those messages concerned the oneness of God, the need for repentance, and the certainty of a Day of Judgement. Collected together, they form the Koran (*Qur'an*), the Muslim holy book. Muhammad encountered much opposition in his native city, especially from the merchant classes, which felt their lax morality, trade and polytheistic religion threatened by his stance. In 622, he was forced to make his exodus, or *hijra*, from Mecca to the city of Medina, where he established himself, achieving a position of power. During this time he fought three major battles with his Meccan enemies and in 630 was able to return in triumph to Mecca itself. He died just two years later.

Muhammad was influenced both by Jews and Christians living in Mecca while he was there. This is indicated by the fact that it was Gabriel, an angel who appears in both the Hebrew and specifically Christian scriptures (the Old and New Testaments), who brought God's message to Muhammad. But in any case the Koran is full of biblical stories, though these are sometimes slightly altered, or amplified, as with the account of Abraham making ready to sacrifice his son. Most significantly, Islam teaches the theocratic ideal, with sovereignty and law deriving from God via a special revelation to man, represented by Muhammad, just as in the religion of ancient Israel sovereignty and law was seen to derive from God through his revelation to Moses. Further, many specific applications of Islamic law (*shari'a*), such as those governing divorce or adultery, reflect Mosaic law, and Muslim ceremonial rites related to prayer, cleanliness and fasting reflect Judaic tradition.

The picture of Jesus given in the Koran (*Qur'an*) follows in rough outline the New Testament account, and this indicates the influence of Christianity, even if not of a wholly orthodox type: Jesus (*'Isa*), was born of Mary (*Maryam*), a virgin; he prophesied (as a new-born infant) that he would be blessed 'on the day of my death', praying for peace 'on the day when I shall be raised to life'; he performed miracles of healing and resurrection, as in the New Testament, though also creating a bird out of clay in a story that appears to come from an apocryphal gospel; the Jews did not kill or crucify Jesus, though they said they did and 'thought they did', but instead God 'lifted him up to His presence' – in a kind of resurrection; according to Islamic tradition (*hadith*), he is coming at the time of the end to destroy the 'Charlatan' (*Al-Dajjal*), a figure reminiscent of the antichrist of the New Testament; finally, Jesus is described not simply as God's apostle or messenger but also as 'His Word', and as 'a spirit from Him'.[15]

Despite the exalted view it has of Jesus, the Koran includes an explicit denial that God is 'Three', or, more specifically, that Jesus and his mother Mary should be worshipped. (The latter reference to people of the time apparently believing Mary divine, presumably as the third person of the Trinity, probably reflects contact between Muhammad and a distorted form of Christianity.) Islam, the message of Muhammad, is nothing if not monotheistic. In this, if not in other respects, it can be considered an heir to both Judaism and Christianity – the latter being as monotheistic as the former in terms of its own claims.

Perhaps the doctrine most commonly associated today in the West with Islam is that of Holy War, or *Jihad*, considered by some Muslims to be the sixth pillar of the faith. The word derives from an Arabic root meaning 'to strive', which can be interpreted simply in a spiritual sense, the striving of good Muslims against sin and sinful inclinations within themselves. However, historically it has a more literal sense. As we have seen, Islam is essentially theocratic; it encompasses the whole of life, including mankind's corporate life, which is politics. And politics involves wielding the sword. This is what is enjoined upon faithful believers in the Koran: 'Let those who would exchange the life of this world for the hereafter, fight for the cause of Allah; whether they die or conquer, We shall richly reward them ... Fight then against the friends of Satan ... perchance Allah will defeat the unbelievers ... Seek out your enemies relentlessly.' The faithful are thus commanded to take up arms for Islam, with its particular view of God. Underpinning this injunction to fight is of course the Koranic teaching that Islam is an exclusive faith: 'He that chooses a religion other than Islam, it will not be accepted from him and in the world to come he will be one of the lost.'[16]

Karma, nirvana and a missing dimension

Such exclusivism could not be laid at the door of another great world faith. Classical Hinduism is generally free from dogmatic assertions about the nature of God; indeed, it teaches that religion is not dependent on the existence or non-existence of God, or on whether there is one God or many. You can be a good Hindu as a monotheist, polytheist or even an atheist. As we have already seen, at the heart of Hinduism is the concept of *dharma*, or *sanatana* [eternal] *dharma*. *Dharma* has been defined as both 'law' and 'religion'. 'Law' can be divided between what we may call 'canon law', referring to clearly defined and explained legal treatises, as well as the religious assumptions on which those laws are based, and 'natural law', which in Hinduism is considered 'subtle' or difficult to know. Natural law occurring within the natural order (the laws of nature) does not in fact present a problem to the Hindu; natural law within the moral order, however, the Hindu only loosely defines.

There is one dogma, however, that is seldom if ever disputed by Hindus: the doctrine of the transmigration of souls or rebirth, more commonly known as reincarnation. The idea presupposes the law of *karma* or 'action', the law of cause and effect, from which we have the corollary that the condition into which every individual soul is reborn is the result of good or bad actions performed in former lives. All existence is ultimately subject to and conditioned by this law, which produces an endless causal past, the *dharma* of the universe. Within this *dharma*, which has neither beginning nor end, everything – the whole universe as well as the individual soul – is in bondage to the fetters of time and desire. Time itself, a revolving wheel that returns again and again to its starting point, can offer neither purpose nor salvation. From this wheel, therefore, the individual Hindu seeks escape, or *moksha*, a blessed state that is considered achievable, though whether through individual effort or by grace of a higher power no one can say.

The idea of *karma*, it should be pointed out, led to the Hindu caste system. During the 'classical' period of Hinduism, when Sanskrit was the sacred language and the Veda the holy and infallible book, the caste system, originated by the highest caste, the Brahmans, became increasingly central to the faith. Only the Brahmans, and the two other 'twice-born' castes, were allowed to benefit from the saving wisdom of the Veda; the lowest caste, as well as women and, of course, 'outcastes', were forbidden access to it. To satisfy the religious needs of the latter groups a devotional literature developed, written in various vernaculars and speaking of divine love for all, irrespective of caste. There was a strong monotheistic trend in this movement, concern for liberation from the bondage of time and matter giving way to adoration of the traditional gods, Vishnu and Siva, who were regarded as supreme Reality and absolute Lord. This religion of loving devotion or *bakhti*, somewhat analogous to pietistic movements within Christian Protestantism, became the real faith of the masses.

Until the latter part of the nineteenth century, acceptance of the caste system, and, to a lesser extent, recognition of the Veda as revealed truth, were considered by the orthodox to be the criterion of whether or not one was a Hindu. Today, not least as a result of the protest made against the caste system by Mahatma Gandhi, the situation is more fluid. Many would like to see the faith interpreted in more spiritual terms. Yet attempts at reform have in recent years faced a new challenge in the form of Hindu-sponsored violence in India, directed mainly against Muslims or Christians.[17]

The Buddha, with his *dharma* ('the Doctrine and the Path'; that is, his own teaching), was excluded from the Hindu fold not because of his philosophical views but because he did not accept the caste system and the Veda. The main thrust of his teaching was that instability is inherent in human existence, with no unchanging soul or God underlying this state of flux, but only moments ceaselessly passing. The law of *karma* (the force or consequence of a person's thoughts, words and deeds) dictates a kind of rebirth, but this occurs at every moment of this life as well as after 'death'; it is certainly not transmigration of the soul since no immutable soul exists to be reborn. Rebirth is simply the reordering into another complex or body of continuously changing, decaying elements. Pain or suffering, typical of human experience, is caused by trying to hold on to what is intrinsically fleeting, earthly life and possessions, so that *karma* takes its inevitable toll. To be free of suffering, which is to achieve *nirvana* (literally 'extinction' – of the flame of desire), one must renounce worldly attachments and seek enlightenment through self-reliance, strict moral behaviour, calm rationality, and above all meditation. The best way to achieve this stern self-discipline and so earn merit is the way of the Buddha himself, that of monastic self-denial.

Since the death of its founder, Buddhism has followed a separate path of development from Hinduism; yet some two and a half thousand years later it still has much in common with its parent religion. Most notably, it encompasses a wide variety of beliefs and practices, having little dogma. Its devotees variously emphasise good deeds, self-understanding through meditation, or the worship of the Buddha, yet all these strands go to make up the faith as we see it today. Robert Lester defines it thus: 'Buddhism is the pursuit of worldly prosperity, rebirth in heaven, and ultimately nirvana by making and sharing merit (good karma).'[18] There is no mention of God here; indeed, as we have seen, the Buddha rejected the idea that any eternal or unconditioned entity, like the soul or God, exists. The Buddha did not, we have also seen, dispense with the gods of early Hinduism (Brahmanism), but in his view their power was subordinated to the one who could conquer all desire. In other words, the idea of deity, whether one or many, is peripheral to Buddhist belief and practice. *Nirvana* itself may sometimes be described by Buddhists in terms which echo definitions of a Supreme Deity, but what is missing is the *personal* dimension intrinsic to the God of Jew, Muslim and Christian alike.

Buddhism made considerable headway in China in the early centuries of our era, though having to compete with both Confucianism and Taoism (Daoism). Confucius, the Chinese philosopher (*c.* 551- 479 BC), was not concerned with the supernatural; he appealed to reason, teaching that humans were perfectible through the self-knowledge brought by learning, which should lead in turn to love and respect of family, country and humanity as whole. Taoism, attributed to Lao Zi, said to have lived in China in the sixth century BC, stresses the importance of living in harmony with nature. The religion, in sharp contrast to Confucianism, is mystical in character, having probably been influenced by both the ancient Chinese mystics and Brahmanism. *Tao*, meaning both the Way and Being, is impalpable and inexpressible, but can be attained through compassion, humility and above all non-violence – all forms of violence being both wrong and self-defeating. Early Taoism rejected the idea of a personal God, or any gods. Later, however, the forces of nature, ancestral and other deities (including Confucius) were worshipped.

Several less prominent world religions may be mentioned briefly. Jainism was founded in India by Vardhamana Mahavira, a contemporary of the Buddha. Mahavira taught that non-violence and asceticism were ways to overcome suffering and death. Shintoism, native to Japan and dating from around the sixth century AD, is primarily a religion of nature and ancestor worship. Sikhism was founded in the Punjab, India, by Guru Nanak in the late fifteenth or early sixteenth century AD. It teaches the unity of the Godhead and the imperative of universal toleration. In the seventeenth century, further principles were enunciated and ceremonies instituted, including the abolition of all caste distinctions within the community.

Finally, in the modern era there has been a proliferation of relatively minor and very varied religious movements. At one end of the spectrum we have a sect like Mormonism, founded by Joseph Smith in New York State in 1820 as a legalistic faith based on Christianity but having its own extra holy book; somewhere in the middle is Transcendental Meditation, founded in 1958 by Maharashi Yogi, the followers of which (they included the Beatles in the 1960s) believe that collective meditation can solve the world's problems; at the opposite end of the spectrum must be the Aum Shinrikyo cult in Japan (one of an estimated 180,000), formed in 1987 by Shoko Asshara to prepare for 'Armageddon in 1997', with its strict hierarchy of 13 uniformed levels and cruel punishments for those who err. Other notable cults are Jehovah's Witnesses, Christian Science, New Thought, Unity, Children of God, the Unification Church, Hare Krishnas, Scientology, Rosicrucianism, Yoga, Rajneesh Ashram and the Divine Light Mission. To these can be added the New Age movement, which heralds the dawning of the astrological 'Age of Aquarius', and which is in essence a collection of cults, incorporating mystical, holistic, spiritualistic and vaguely occult beliefs.

God the self-evident

What have we learnt so far from this survey of man's 'religious quest', his teaching about or apprehension of the divine origin, meaning and ultimate purpose of life?

What seems clear from the evidence we have, particularly that which emanates from the earliest extant texts, is that there has never been a time when common people have not subscribed to the idea of a Supreme Deity – Creator, Maintainer, Ruler of All. This conclusion is supported by the findings of anthropologists, linguists and missionaries over the last two centuries about the religious perceptions of so-called primitive peoples all over the world. As that Ashanti tribesman said of God, 'He is always there.'

In contrast to the view that monotheism is a late development from polytheism, which had developed from even earlier 'primitive' animism or pantheism, everything points to an opposite process. What seems to have happened is a corruption of mankind's earliest, pure belief in God the Creator and the degeneration of this idea into a pantheon of gods, and finally into a multitude of local powers or spirits. Why, we may ask, did this happen?

The clue to the answer to this question is given in the creation narrative of the Konkomba tribes of the Ashanti region of Ghana, West Africa, recorded by Harold Blair. We pointed out above that in this tribal story the single, supreme Deity ('Nawuni') already has a retinue of messengers when he creates man and sets him on the earth. After man has become proud and neglected the worship of God, the story continues, these messengers are given positions of rule in the earth, having rights and power over particular territories. Harold Blair shows how this view of the world and the way it is ordered reflects the view Jesus held, which in turn drew upon ideas from the Old Testament. In an important passage, he explains the parallels.

Jesus said little, even indirectly, about idolatry: his preaching was to the people of Israel who were 'the Lord's portion', so that he had no occasion for discourses on idolatry in the ordinary sense. None the less the mission of the seventy showed that he accepted the belief of his time in angel guardians of the nations. It is easier to believe that he did so, because he clearly stated his belief in angel guardians of individuals (Matt. 18:10). He also showed in the story of the demoniac named Legion, a curious respect for the territorial rights of those demons; he did not banish them but let them banish themselves.

I have said that the Jewish belief in angel guardians of the nations was a monotheistic interpretation of the beliefs of those nations themselves in tribal and national gods; it was the insight of an inspired people into the claims of idolatry   (I Cor. 8). The gods of the nations were not imaginary in the sense of having no sort of existence in time; but their authority as gods was unreal. They existed but not for worship. Primitive religion today gropes towards this same realisation.[19]

Harold Blair's interpretation is illuminating. On only one point would I differ: instead of saying that primitive religion 'gropes towards' this realisation, this truth, I would prefer to say that primitive religion 'dimly recalls' it. What is important is the light this viewpoint sheds on the relationship of monotheism to polytheism and animism. It leaves us free – after a slight adjustment on the significance of the latter, that is, on what exactly we mean by the 'gods many' – to believe in both.

But perhaps we move too fast. Let us return to the issue with which we began, the question of whether or not mankind has from the first (whenever that 'first' was) had an innate sense of God the Creator,

Unique, All-knowing, All-powerful, All-loving. I submit that the evidence available – the evidence we have been considering, which is the only evidence possible – suggests that he has indeed had this sense. In other words, men and women in general have always considered the reality of God to be self-evident. Philosophers, scientists, teachers and gurus may sometimes have thought and taught otherwise, but that is something else.

To some of these latter thinkers, primarily those of the last three centuries, we now turn.

PART II: UNBELIEF

Chapter 4
Death of Divinity?

Age of reason

Francis Bacon, the English statesman and philosopher of the late sixteenth and early seventeenth centuries, outlined in his *Novum Organum* a new scientific method that was to rule the scientific scene. His approach to science, and that of René Descartes to philosophy, inaugurated what has been described as 'the age of reason'.

The new intellectual currents were flowing at a time when Europe was exhausted by a century of religious strife and warfare that had followed the spiritual and political revolution we call the Reformation. This had initially been set in motion by the protest against corruption within the Western (Catholic) Church made by Martin Luther in Germany, following earlier protests by John Wyclif in England and John Hus in Bohemia. The strength of Luther's protest, and that of contemporaries like Ulrich Zwingli in Zurich, Martin Bucer in Strasbourg, William Farel and John Calvin in Geneva, owed much to work already done by key Renaissance figures. The Dutch scholar Erasmus Desiderius, for instance, had edited the Greek text of the New Testament studied by Luther and which he was probably using when, early in 1513, he found peace and assurance through a verse in Paul's letter to the Romans, 'The just shall live by faith.'[1] It was said of Erasmus that he 'laid the egg which Luther hatched'. Yet the Renaissance movement, which began in Italy in the fifteenth century and soon spread to northern Europe, had looked back behind the period of intellectual and sometimes political domination by the Church, behind the era of the church Fathers, behind even the days of Jesus and the first disciples, to classical times. It was from the culture of ancient Greece that the scholars, philosophers, artists and scientific thinkers of the Renaissance primarily drew their inspiration. Plato and Aristotle can be considered the real fathers of what is sometimes called the Enlightenment.

The Thirty Years War, at first a conflict of Calvinist Protestants against Catholics but later a full-scale European war, was brought to an end in 1648 by the Peace of Westphalia; this defined the religious boundaries of modern Europe in the West. Meanwhile, the Eastern Church was quietly unaffected. After the fall of Constantinople to the Ottoman Turks in 1453, more and more of the Orthodox Church came under Turkish control. When, in 1589, the Patriarchate of Moscow was created it represented the only Orthodox Church both established and not under Muslim control. This situation in the East left little chance of creative intellectual activity. In the West, however, with peace finally established, the way was open for the development of new and sometimes daring thinking.

To Descartes, who was born in 1596 and died in 1650, belief in God was central, but such belief, he taught, should be the product of reason. Using the empirical method of his own mathematical theory, he sought to demonstrate God's existence in these terms. When he failed, finding chaos rather than design in nature, he turned to the fact of man's consciousness as evidence of irrefutable truth, and hence of the Divine, hitting upon the famous dictum, 'I think, therefore I am.' His views were developed by others, notably Baruch Spinoza (1632-1677), who was a Jew. After expounding philosophical views considered antagonistic to Judaism, Spinoza was excommunicated as a heretic by the rabbis of Amsterdam at the age of twenty-four. In 1663, however, he published his work on the philosophy of Descartes. While fervently upholding the existence of God, his searching examination of man's political institutions and religious literature persuaded many that the Cartesian system of philosophy was a dangerous one.

One of those who supplied a critique of the Cartesian method was Blaise Pascal. Born in 1623, he was a sickly but precocious child, his lifespan reaching only forty years. Like Descartes, he was a mathematician, as well as a physicist, though his fame today probably rests upon his theological insights. His standpoint was in sharp contrast to that of Descartes: God could not be found through rational thought but only as a result of personal experience – as in the revelation of God he had himself received. In his *Pensées*, published posthumously in 1669, Pascal outlined what this meant: faith is a gamble, for we can never prove God's existence, though neither can we disprove it. This is 'Pascal's wager', involving a finite risk but (possible) infinite gain. He went further than this, however, in asserting that when we accept the wager and exercise faith we will be blessed with signs of God's reality and presence, and be assured of salvation.

Isaac Newton, who lived from 1642 to 1727, believed he had demonstrated the existence of God through his contemplation and explication of the natural universe. His magisterial work *Philosophiae Naturalis Principia* ('The Principles of Natural Philosophy'), published in 1687, which introduced the concept of gravity as the crucial factor binding the universe together, described the relations between celestial and terrestrial bodies in mathematical terms. Central to this whole system was the Divine Mechanick, who had perfectly placed in their orbits the various heavenly bodies so that gravitational attraction would never pull them into collision.

John Locke, Whig philosopher and apologist for the 1688 revolution in England, was at much the same time expounding philosophical empiricism, the doctrine that all knowledge is derived from experience. His chief work in theoretical philosophy was his *Essay Concerning Human Understanding*, published in 1690, but in another work, *The Reasonableness of Christianity*, he argued that Christianity was the religion of reason and the only God was the God of Nature. The group of intellectuals called the Deists took Locke's arguments a stage further: they concluded that as natural religion was a reality, it was sufficient; revelation was at best superfluous, at worst superstitious. Meanwhile, theologians in England like Matthew Tindal and John Toland sought to interpret Christianity in strictly rationalistic terms, impatient of anything in the faith that smacked of mystery – which, Toland argued, led to 'tyranny and superstition'.[2]

The intellectual achievements of Newton and Locke were revered widely, on the continent almost as much as in England. Their conclusions paved the way for the almost universal adoption of the view that unrestricted scientific research and a latitudinarian and rationalistic approach to philosophy, political theory and theology would find the answer to man's every question and problem.

As a result of progress in the sphere of scientific investigation, some religious thinkers were becoming sceptical as well as rationalistic. Direct attacks were made on traditional Christian doctrines, especially in Calvinistic countries like Holland, where the State did not interfere with theological debate. A notable early sceptic was Cesare Vanini, a Neapolitan priest who recognised no God but nature. Then there was Richard Simon (1638-1712), another Catholic priest, who initiated a critical study of the biblical documents, though his primary aim was to confound the Protestants. Using methods of literary criticism similar to those used by nineteenth-century scholars, he concluded that the Pentateuch could not possibly have been written by Moses and that other historical books had over a long period been compiled from annals and chronicles by a guild of 'public scribes'. His views were expanded and popularised in the eighteenth century with considerable success by a Huguenot exile in Amsterdam called Pierre Bayle, who published a *Dictionary* which became a source book for Deists and sceptics who wished to attack the Bible. At around the same time, Herman Reimarus (1694-1768) wrote a critical study of Jesus, arguing that the founder of Christianity had never understood his mission in terms of atoning for men's sins but rather as the founding of a pious and godly nation, and that he died of despair when he realised his mission had failed.

In 1738, the Scottish philosopher David Hume published his *Treatise on Human Nature*. In this work he exposed the fallacies of an uncritical trust in logic and the human mind. In so doing, however, he undermined all traditional certainties – about God, man and the world. A.N. Wilson writes thus of Hume's legacy: 'Hume had delivered some mortal blows against the old arguments for the existence of God. Religion could choose to turn a blind eye to the calamity, or to rail against it, or to say that it did not, perhaps, matter. But if the process of human reason is the primary arbiter of truth, and if the strictures of empiricism rightly limit our criteria of what may be known to impressions created by 'sense impressions', then Hume's destruction of the religious position would seem to be absolute.'[3] Wilson makes his conclusion doubly conditional; the real question at issue – whether the 'religious position', that is, belief in God, is actually discredited if the human mind cannot validate it conclusively in argument – he sidesteps. He is right, meanwhile, to emphasise the impact Hume had upon the few who thought in such philosophical terms.

Hume claimed to be a Deist, though with how much conviction we cannot be sure. He was certainly no believer in institutional religion; he told the writer James Boswell that he had 'never entertained any belief in Religion since he began to read Locke and Clarke'.[4] In a famous incident in 1763, he was guest for dinner in the Paris home of Paul Heinrich, Baron d'Holbach, founder of what Rousseau called the *coterie Holbachique*, a group of mostly literary figures who regularly dined together. According to Denis Diderot, one of the group and d'Holbach's closest friend, Hume remarked to Baron d'Holbach that he 'did not believe in atheists, that he had never seen any', to which the Baron replied: 'Count how many we are here. We are eighteen. It is not too bad a showing to be able to point out to you fifteen atheists at once; the three others have not made up their minds.'[5]

The *coterie Holbachique*, or *les philosophes* as they are more often described, were said to be the fathers of the French revolution. Baron d'Holbach may have been exaggerating when he claimed that fifteen of those sitting round his table were atheists, but he himself almost certainly was. In 1770, when the group was reaching the height of its influence, he published (anonymously) *The System of Nature; or Laws of the Moral and Physical World*, with a foreword by Jacques-André Naigeon, another member of the group. The book quickly became a bible for atheistic materialism, Naigeon in his foreword pouring scorn on belief in God and religion, and d'Holbach arguing that there was no need to postulate a First Cause (God the Creator); better, if anything, to think of the universe as eternal, itself the nearest thing to a First Cause. Belief in 'God', he said, was dishonest, a denial of real experience; the Deity was simply a construct of men, who, after abandoning animistic belief, had created him in their own image.

Denis Diderot is probably the best known member of the group. In *A Letter to the Blind for the Use of Those who See*, published as early as 1749, he appeared to dispense with God. The book is cast in the form of an imagined dialogue between a man born blind (an actual Cambridge mathematician called Nicholas Saunderson, who had died in 1739) and a believer in God of Newtonian outlook. The conclusion to the debate was that an aberration of nature such as Saunderson exemplified, and all other such natural 'monsters', invalidated Newton's argument from design for the existence of God. Diderot's own view, like that of d'Holbach, was based on the assumption that matter, having its own creative character and obeying its own laws, is the foundation and source of life. At the most, God is (in) nature; at the least, nature exists, and there is no God. Diderot is usually cited as an uncompromising atheist, yet when challenged about the above book by François Voltaire, he retorted, 'I believe in God, although I live very well with the atheists ... But to believe or not to believe in God is not important at all.'[6]

New approaches
Hume destroyed easy confidence in a rationalistic approach to questions about life. In so doing he left behind him something of a void, leaving the way open for other independently minded thinkers to pioneer new approaches. Foremost amongst these was the German philosopher Immanuel Kant (1724-1804).

Kant said that Hume had awakened him from dogmatic slumber, a revival that moved him to ask the question, 'What is reason?' He was in fact responding to the problem, identified by Hume and other eighteenth century empiricists, of how we can be sure of truth or reality – how, in other words, we know anything. Cartesian philosophy had led to the formulation of two theories: firstly, that the human mind was capable of working things out according to their own inner and necessary logic, according, that is, to self-evident Reason; secondly, that the human mind was a 'clean slate', upon which reality projected itself through sense impressions. Kant came up with a different answer. He argued that we perceive reality in space and time through an innate understanding or concept of it, giving us a framework with which to organise our actual, day-to-day impressions or perceptions. He then went a step further in proposing that our sense of right and wrong, the moral or 'categorical' imperative, is also innate. This idea, that the human mind has built-in, pre-programmed capacities or tendencies, finds an interesting parallel today in Noam Chomsky's view that humans are born with a language learning facility, the mind being 'pre-wired' with grammar universals.[7]

Kant effectively elevated the human mind to a position of importance and centrality that it had not before attained, and the nature-loving freethinkers and poets we call the Romantics responded eagerly to this apparently humanistic development. His philosophical conclusions also indirectly encouraged confidence in the importance of scientific progress. If, as he seemed to have demonstrated, metaphysical questions about truth and reality were ultimately unanswerable, except in the subjective terms of the inner workings of the human mind, the only remaining way forward for the discovery of truth – if only the truth about phenomena – was through physical science. Of course, Kant's conclusions also constituted a reminder to scientists that their findings could never answer questions about *why* things were what they were, but this crucial proposition was largely brushed aside. (It is often wholly contradicted by today's scientists.) Meanwhile, for Kant himself the pre-eminence of the human mind, with its innate capacity for perceiving reality, led in a rather different direction: man's experience of the moral imperative made belief in God necessary – even if that God was located as much within the human mind as outside it.

The German theologian F.D.E. Schleiermacher (1753-1834) adopted an approach to the question of belief in many ways similar to that of Kant, arguing that people's feeling of absolute dependence – feeling being understood as an intuitive contact with truth or reality – constituted grounds for asserting the reality of God. Schleiermacher, whose influence on later theologians was profound, had in his early years been influenced by the Pietists (as indeed had Kant), a Christian group who emphasised the Lutheran principle of individual faith. This approach, with personal devotion to Jesus its central feature, was reflected in his theology.

Pietism had its origin in a book entitled *Pia Desideria* published by J. Spener (who died in 1705); it was later taken up by Count von Zinzendorf and in due course begot the Christian movement known as the Evangelical Revival. The leading figure of this movement was John Wesley, who in 1738 attended a meeting in London of the Moravians – Christians who had earlier fled from persecution in Habsburg lands and been offered refuge by Count Zinzendorf. As the speaker delivered his message, Wesley had the experience he famously described in the words: 'I felt my heart strangely warmed.'[8] Another key personality in the revival was Wesley's friend, the fiery preacher George Whitefield, who crossed the Atlantic and, joining local figures like Jonathan Edwards, helped promote a parallel revival in America, usually called 'The Great Awakening'. Evangelicals were dismissed by contemporary churchmen and others, including David Hume (in early life a devout Presbyterian), as overly enthusiastic. One English bishop personally confronted John Wesley on the issue: 'Enthusiasm is a horrid thing, Mr Wesley, a very horrid thing'.

'Enthusiasm' of this kind played little part in the life of G.W.F. Hegel. During a lifetime that ran almost concurrently with that of Schleiermacher, he poured contempt on his contemporary's views: dogs feel absolute dependence on their masters, he pointed out, so according to Schleiermacher they must be the best Christians. He rejected Schleiermacher's teaching that only phenomena can be known by pure reason. Everything, he affirmed, even the Absolute itself, is accessible to the human mind. The world is ordered according to a rational principle, the Absolute Idea, and nature and history are a dialectically evolving process that gradually gives birth to Spirit, a Spirit which has become self-conscious in man. Man at his highest – the philosopher, in fact – can fully apprehend truth as pure thought. For the ordinary person, however, this truth has to be translated into religious pictures and symbols.

At times, Hegel's language seems religious, with God a reality. He speaks, for instance, of the study of history as 'a theodicy, a justification of the ways of God'.[9] But it is in the relentless dialectic of history, the three phases of thesis, antithesis, synthesis, culminating (for him) in the German phase, that we find his identification of ultimate power. God himself, he implies, could be swept aside in the process – as the great god Zeus had disappeared with the demise of Greek civilisation. In other words, God for Hegel is not an objective reality but rather the creation of human imagining, a product of the collective mind. He distinguished between phenomena (or appearance), on the one hand, and truth (or reality), on the other; the latter, as we have seen, he virtually banished to the mind. This approach, which came to be described as Idealist, was shared by the majority of other nineteenth-century philosophers, who felt themselves to be following in the footsteps not only of Hegel – the great Idealist – but also of Kant.

One thinker of the period attacked Hegelianism vigorously, however, and by implication Marxism, with its economic determinism based on Hegel's thought. This was the Danish philosopher and theologian Søren Kierkegaard, who protested against the collectivism of the rationalists, and their depersonalisation of the individual. God was the Wholly Other, whom the individual must encounter in personal experience. The advances in the natural sciences should also be viewed with suspicion, he warned, 'sciencemongery' being especially dangerous when it invaded the realm of the spirit. As for the Church, it was apostate; genuine New Testament Christianity no longer existed on earth. Yet Kirkegaard's contribution to the debate was short-lived; in 1855 he died, in his early forties. Few took any real notice of what he had said; some church people in Denmark said he had gone mad.

Biblical criticism, Hegelian philosophy and God in the image of man
In 1795, the German scholar and philologist Friedrich August Wolf published *Prolegomena*, a study of Homer's classic saga, *The Odyssey*. In this work, he proposed that the famous narrative poem was not the product of a single person called Homer (who he said had never existed), but of several editors or redactors, who at a late date had woven together a number of strands of 'Homeric' tradition. The persons and places referred to in the book he dismissed as mythological. The critical method Wolf employed was described as 'higher' or literary criticism. This can be defined as a form of study seeking to determine questions of authorship, date, and composition of a literary text on the basis of vocabulary, style and consistency. 'Lower' or textual criticism is concerned with ascertaining the original text by comparing manuscripts and ancient versions.

Wolf's approach, especially his attempt to explain the content of an ancient text in terms of mythology, greatly influenced scholars engaged in biblical studies. We have referred to early attempts at such criticism – distinctly negative in nature – made by Richard Simon, Pierre Bayle and

Herman Reimarus. There were others, prior to Wolf, whose aim it was to subject the scriptures to critical scrutiny, though not always of a destructive kind. The most significant was J.G. Eichorn (1752-1827), a fairly conservative-minded Rationalist. Between 1780-1783, he published a three-volume introduction to the Old Testament, a work which earned him the title of 'father of Old Testament criticism'.[10] While commending the literary grandeur of the Hebrew scriptures, Eichorn was worried about the nationalistic tone which, in his opinion, characterized the Old Testament. He was interested in source-analysis, and pursued the path laid down earlier in the century by H.B. Witter and Jean Astruc, who saw in the different divine names used in the Pentateuch the key to an identification of its underlying sources. These earlier critical scholars, however, still inclined to the view that it was Moses, and not later schools of scribes, who had compiled the first five books of the Bible.

At the end of the eighteenth and into the nineteenth century, a number of scholars extended the scope and range of Old Testament source-criticism. At the turn of the century, a Scottish Roman Catholic theologian, A. Geddes, published his conclusion that the Pentateuch had been compiled during the time of Solomon from a mass of fragments. A German scholar, J.S. Vater, developed this view, publishing a commentary on the Pentateuch in 1805. While allowing that some of the 'forty' fragmentary sources dated from the time of Moses or before, he assigned the Pentateuch in its final form to the period of the Babylonian exile, in the sixth century BC. Another German scholar, W.M.L. De Wette, who published his views in 1807, argued that the earliest portions of the Pentateuch could only be dated from the time of David and that the different books were compiled by separate redactors drawing on independent fragmentary sources. In a work published in 1835, a further German theologian, Willhelm Vatke, concluded that much even of the *Grundschrift* (the 'Foundation Document'; the proposed underlying Pentateuchal source, incorporating 'Priestly' material) was of exilic date. As for the Torah, or Mosaic law, Vatke considered this to have been the product of the Hebrew state rather than the basis on which it was founded. Vatke was deeply influenced by the philosophy of Hegel, and he effectively rewrote the history of ancient Israel along the lines of the deterministic and evolutionary concepts characterizing that philosophy.

From the above, the picture emerges of an increasingly successful onslaught on the integrity of the Old Testament. There were, in fact, some whose critical studies led them in a different direction, persuading them that the traditional view of scripture was the more credible. E.W. Hengstenberg (1802-1869), for example, who was unhappy about the rationalist assumptions of the source-critics, in a string of publications argued cogently against the various documentary hypotheses.

The strong trend of critical studies throughout the nineteenth century, however, was to undermine confidence in the biblical narratives. As far as the Old Testament is concerned, this trend reached its apogee in the work of Julius Wellhausen (1844-1918). The work in which his conclusions were first placed before the general public was published in 1877.[11] He immediately acknowledged his debt to an earlier scholar, K.H. Graf, who himself owed much to the work of Willhelm Vatke.[12] Graf's main contribution had been to underline and extend Vatke's conclusions by arguing that, apart from one 'Priestly' section (Leviticus 18-26), the whole 'Foundation Document' was even later than Vatke had supposed; Graf assigned it to the time of Ezra, in the fifth century BC. Wellhausen applied the developmental approach of Vatke to the study of Hebrew religious institutions, combining it with the successive arrangement of ritual laws made by Graf, to 'prove' that almost all the 'Priestly' source (P) emanated from the fifth century. A final revision and editing of the entire corpus of the Pentateuch, he suggested, took place in about 200 BC.

The main outline of the Graf-Wellhausen hypothesis has been given in Chapter 2. I would like now, however, to emphasise once again the essential character of this theory, in the words of R.K. Harrison:

> Although Wellhausen had added little or nothing that was specifically new to the critical conclusions of Graf, his method brought to a climax the investigations of earlier liberal scholars and served to show the fundamental difference between the nineteenth-century *Zeitgeist* ['spirit of the age'] and the theological exegesis of an earlier age. Wellhausen had contrived to reduce the elements of law, covenant, religion, and history to one comprehensive and controlled scheme, consisting of three major periods of Hebrew historical development in which simple forms evolved into progressively differentiated aspects. His scheme bore all the marks of Hegelian evolutionism, and by its very simplicity and comprehensiveness it commended itself to an age which was endeavouring to resolve the many into the one by means of a single interpretative principle.[13]

We have so far been looking almost entirely at the application of 'higher' critical methods to the Hebrew scriptures, what Christians call the Old Testament. What, then, of the New Testament, the specifically Christian scriptures?

The scholar who corresponds in New Testament criticism to Wellhausen in that of the Old Testament is F.C. Baur of Tübingen (1792-1860), who together with his associates comprised what came to be called the Tübingen School of biblical criticism. Though some have disputed it,[14] Baur also seems to have been strongly influenced by Hegelian philosophy. The philosophic dialectic of history proposed by Hegel is reflected in Baur's reconstruction of the early progress of Christianity: Paul, representing Gentile Christianity, advocated freedom from the law (thesis); Peter and his party, representing Jewish Christianity, reacted against this teaching and so advocated adherence to the law (antithesis); second-century Christians achieved a resolution of this conflict (synthesis), which we can see in the New Testament book called Acts.

Possibly even more influential than Bauer among the Tübingen scholars, however, was David Friedrich Strauss, whose book *The Life of Jesus, critically examined* was published in 1836; it is referred to by Don Cupitt as 'perhaps the most important single theological book of the nineteenth century.'[15] Strauss' doubts about Christian orthodoxy stemmed directly from his study of Hegel. Faced with the notion of an evolving world Spirit, he felt unable to expound his faith in accordance with traditional Church teaching. So he reinterpreted the life of the founder of Christianity in entirely mythological, non-literal terms. The radical theology of Albert Schweitzer, who many years later spoke of Jesus having been mistaken about his divine identity and role, dying a broken and disillusioned man, owed much to what Strauss had written.

A.N. Wilson, in his account of Western man's loss of faith, *God's Funeral*, speaks of the significance of the Hegelian approach for the Tübingen School, going on to stress the significance of the School and its work for the decline of religious belief.

> The Christian religion, and Christ Himself, were the products of the communities of faith which produced the Gospels. From this idea of Hegel's and his belief that religion manifests itself in myth, sprang the modern critical Germanic school of biblical criticism, centred largely upon the Tübingen School of Divinity. And if any one phenomenon may be said to have been responsible for the destruction

of ordinary Christian faith in the nineteenth-century Protestant world
(and in the Catholic world, when they allowed themselves to become
aware of it), it was this critical approach to the scriptures.[16]

The question at issue for us today is whether, in view of the *a priori*
wish of the above scholars to interpret scripture in Hegelian terms, we
should take seriously either the Graf-Wellhausen or the Tübingen
reconstruction of why, when and how the scriptures were written. As we
have already seen, when briefly examining the Graf-Wellhausen approach
to the Pentateuch (especially Genesis) in Chapter 2, there are good critical
grounds for retaining a more conservative view as to the origin of these
Old Testament documents. Later in this book I shall argue that there are
just as weighty reasons for rejecting the approach of the Tübingen School
– even when much modified – to the New Testament, in favour of the
traditional Christian view.

German thinkers, Hegel and biblical scholars like Vater and De Wette,
much influenced the thought of the English philosopher, theologian and
poet, Samuel Taylor Coleridge (1772-1834). Coleridge was an inquirer,
and his views were seldom fully worked out. He was one of the first in
England openly to question the idea of the plenary inspiration of the
Bible and the notion that the truth of Christianity could be established
by reference to the fulfilment of biblical predictions or to miracles. The
divinity of scripture, he argued, lay in its power to evoke personal faith
in the reader. Besides the Germans, Coleridge drew upon the thought of
the founder of British Socialism, Robert Owen, an anti-clerical and
utopian agnostic whose philosophical Idealism strongly appealed to him.

Frederick Denison Maurice, who lived a generation later than
Coleridge, made no secret of his debt to the latter. The two of them
exerted great influence on future theologians in England and beyond,
the impact of Maurice rather surprising in view of the incoherence of
much of his thought and language.[17] Like Coleridge, Maurice took a broad
view of truth, both theological and philosophical, and was impatient with
those who condemned the new critical approach to the Bible. For
Maurice, the Church represented the universal family, a redeemed
humanity. The philosophy of the French thinkers Bayle, Montesquieu,
Voltaire and Diderot (who had built upon basic concepts from Locke
and Newton) had, he believed, rediscovered this truth, and the French
revolution of 1789 had blazoned it – a new humanitarianism – before
the world.

Maurice was the chief inspiration in England for the movement known as Christian Socialism, with its 'social gospel' programme of reform through participating in democratic political institutions. Elsewhere this movement drew more on the thought of Albrecht Ritschl (1822-1889), who was a disciple of Schleiermacher. Ritschl, perhaps the most influential theologian since the latter, followed up the tentative misgivings that his mentor had expressed at the end of his life about the doctrine of the Trinity. He concluded that the latter idea, which was an alien 'layer of metaphysical concepts, derived from the natural philosophy of the Greeks', had corrupted the original teaching of Jesus.[18] He saw Jesus as no more than a man, in line with the Hebrew prophets, who had delivered an exalted message about 'the kingdom of God', a kingdom to be understood in an ethical sense, as 'the organisation of humanity through action inspired by love'.[19]

Meanwhile, the trend in German philosophy was to deny the reality of God altogether. In 1819, Artur Schopenhauer (1789-1860) published a book entitled *The World as Will and Idea* in which he argued that there was no Absolute, no Reason, no God, nothing but an instinctive animal will to survive. Then, in 1841, the philosopher Ludwig Feuerbach (1804-72), a former pupil of Hegel, brought out *The Essence of Christianity*, the impact of which was considerable. In this work he argued that God was no more than the projection of human longings for perfection.

To Feuerbach goes the credit for having turned one of Hegel's assumptions on its head, leading Karl Marx to make his famous assertion that religion was 'the sigh of the oppressed creature ... the *opium* of the people, which made this suffering bearable'.[20] Hegel had, among other things, assumed that 'the Idea of the State' was subject, with society as its predicate. Feuerbach, however, wrote in *Introductory Theses to the Reform of Philosophy* (1843), 'Being is subject, thought predicate. Thought arises from being, not being from thought.'[21] In other words, 'society' is subject; 'the Idea of the State' is predicate. Feuerbach had in fact moved away from Hegel's Idealism to embrace Materialism – summed up in his well-known aphorism, 'Man is what he eats.' Marx (1818-1885) extended the logic of this conclusion from the realm of the abstract to the real world of politics, the state and society.[22] So, he concluded, the constitution does not create the people, the people create the constitution; similarly, religion does not make man, man makes religion. In other words, man makes God – in his own image.

Marx found support for his conclusions from an unexpected quarter. In December 1860, in a letter to Friedrich Engels, he was enthusing about a recently published scientific work. 'This is the book,' he wrote, 'that contains the basis in natural history for our view.'[23]

The author of this revolutionary new study was Charles Darwin.

Chapter 5
A Question of Substance

'Theologians and historians – even human intelligence itself – has capitulated to science,' writes the historian and philosopher Philip Sherrard. 'To understand the truth of this statement one has only to take into account the degree to which theologians accept the hypothesis of evolution … as axiomatic, and treat it as a kind of imperative condition to which everything, including theology itself, must accommodate itself.'[1]

Charles Lyell's *Principles of Geology*, published between 1830 and 1833, spoke of huge tracts of time being involved in the formation of the earth's surface. Then, in 1844, Robert Chambers published (anonymously) *The Vestiges of the Natural History of Creation*, placing before the public the idea – not in itself new – that a uniform natural law governed the appearance of the various species. It was fifteen years later, however, when Charles Darwin published *On the Origin of Species by Means of Natural Selection*, that the furore occurred, for in the data he presented he appeared to substantiate the idea of the evolution of all life from a common source.[2] Over a century later, in our own era, the biologist Richard Dawkins can write: 'Today the theory of evolution is about as much open to doubt as the theory that the earth goes round the sun, but the full implications of Darwin's revolution have yet to be widely realised.'[3]

Seeds of doubt

Richard Dawkins is one among many today who speak as if the truth of the Darwinian hypothesis had been conclusively established and was now unassailable. This is not the case. Many writers refer to unresolved problems inherent in the theory, not least unaccountable gaps in fossil evidence for the evolutionary chain of development. Signed-up evolutionists who concede such difficulties usually argue that answers will eventually be forthcoming, or that even the most improbable of mutational developments – the formation of the eye, for example, or the transition of creature life from the sphere of water to that of land, thence to the air, in winged flight – are feasible when account is taken of the vast periods of time involved.[4] In other words, anything is possible if you allow enough time.

Let me be more specific – as well as more personal.

I was brought up, at home and in school, to believe implicitly in evolution. Indeed, the idea was not presented as theory, but as indisputable, unchallenged fact – exactly as Dawkins presents it above. In the classroom would be those familiar posters depicting the 'geological column' (the strata of rocks in an evolutionary sequence), or the slow development of the horse family, or the 'ascent of man', showing a succession of primates with gradually straightening backs until *homo erectus* and then, finally, *homo sapiens* is reached. Not only had Darwin's ideas been scientifically proved, I was assured, they were inherently noble, testifying to the ongoing, upward march of humanity – of Life itself – to a glorious destiny. They were also fully compatible with Christian belief; or, rather, they complemented such belief, enabling the believer to understand his faith more perfectly. My father was an ardent admirer of Teilhard de Chardin, the famous Christian evolutionist and theologian.

Then, after I had left school, I came into contact with a certain medical practitioner – an eye specialist, as it happened – who drew my attention to the fact that the arguments and evidence for Darwin's reconstruction were not quite what I had assumed. The seeds of doubt having been sown, I started reading what I could find on the topic – books, articles, reviews, press reports – to discover that it was just as the good doctor had said: hard evidence for evolution was extremely difficult to come by, while much relevant data seemed to point in a quite different direction. This was years ago, but to this day I have maintained interest in the subject. As far as possible, I have taken note of published trends and developments, and, whilst living in different parts of the world, have engaged in minor geological field research. Of course, I cannot claim to be other than a layman in the subject. But then, of those millions of others ready to give their verdict on the matter, often with great passion, 99.9 per cent are also laymen – not excluding writers who have cited the 'fact' of evolution in support of their thesis.[5] On issues such as this, of far-reaching significance, the vast majority of us can only do our best impartially to weigh up the arguments and sift the evidence before coming to our necessary conclusion. We speak as we find. What we should not do is adopt a viewpoint simply because 'experts' hold it. History tells us that 'experts' are as likely – perhaps more likely – to be wrong than right.

Richard Dawkins is, of course, an expert on evolution. Leaving aside for a moment the question of whether he is right or wrong, it is interesting to learn what, for him, appears to constitute its chief significance. He writes, 'Darwin made it possible to be an intellectually fulfilled atheist.'[6] From which we might infer two things: firstly, that for Dawkins atheism is important, that is, it is something he wants or feels the need to embrace, because in it he finds fulfilment; secondly, if Darwin's theory alone makes such atheism possible, as he implies, then it is imperative for him that it is true. Which leads to a question: does Dawkin's conviction about the truth of evolution ultimately spring from evidence in its favour or from his need to believe in it? He is very ready to explain Christian belief in the latter terms.[7] Yet the atheist may have as much reason for wanting to be an atheist as the Christian has for wanting to be Christian. Not that it is unusual – or bad – to believe something because we want to believe it, as long as belief does not fly in the face of evidence. It is probably true to say that no one believes anything unless he or she really wants to.

Richard Dawkins is certainly wrong in his assumption that a Darwinian approach necessitates atheism.[8] He claims that Darwin's account of our origins answers the question of 'why we exist',[9] but the theory of evolution is not about the 'why' of life at all, it is about the 'how'. To say we exist *because* we evolved from one primeval, single-celled life-form is to be guilty of a *non-sequitur*. To go back further, and say we exist because in the beginning a 'Big Bang' brought the universe into existence is equally illogical. When we ask 'why' something is, we are not asking a question about the processes that were involved in its coming into being but about the reason for there being processes at all. Richard Dawkins says that science today has brought our knowledge about the past of our universe to the point where 'we are just that tiny fraction of a second away from the first moment.' He appears to think that this achievement, combined with Darwin's theory, explains everything, doing away with the need for a Deity. Yet as John Keegan has put it, 'In a search for origins, a fraction of a second is as large an interval as eternity.'[10] In any case, even if we could get back to that 'first moment', we would still not have answered the question of why there should have been one. Theism offers an answer, that behind everything is a Supreme Eternal Spirit. Dawkins waves this aside: 'The hypothesis of God offers no worthwhile explanation for anything, for it simply postulates what we are trying to explain. It postulates the difficult to explain, and leaves it at that.'[11] So it does, yet where there is no alternative to a hypothesis, as in this case, we do well to take it seriously.

Dawkins, as we have seen, argues that Darwinism provides an adequate alternative to the idea of God. It does so, he believes, because it represents a revolutionary view of the way life developed. He declares, 'The great beauty of Darwin's theory of evolution is that it explains how complex, difficult to understand things could have arisen step by plausible step, from simple, easy to understand beginnings.'[12] Yet as pointed out above, Darwin's theory cannot provide an explanation of the 'why' of life. Further, it remains – whatever extravagant claims are sometimes made for it – no more than a theory, one that has failed (unlike that of Copernicus) to persuade all. Doubts have persisted; doubters have persisted. As already intimated, I long ago joined the number of the unconvinced, having found the evidence adduced in favour of evolution – or rather the lack of it – to be leading me to another conclusion about life. Today, after having had access to a great deal more data, I remain extremely doubtful about Darwin's approach, even in modified form. It is time now to say something more about those doubts.

I will start where the doubts first started.

The fossil record and the nature of species

Evolutionists these days, as we have seen, readily concede that there are gaps between the various species in the fossil record.[13] The pattern displayed is one of sudden jumps, followed by long periods of stability – quite unlike the continuous, gradual process of change from one species to another proposed by orthodox Darwinism. Niles Eldredge, curator of the American Museum of Natural History and a leading fossil expert (and ardent evolutionist), speaks in sad terms of the lack of evidence for this process: 'Evolution cannot forever be going on somewhere else. Yet that is how the fossil record has struck many a forlorn palaeontologist looking to learn something about evolution.'[14]

In the 1970s, Eldredge, together with the palaeontologist Stephen Jay Gould, followed others (usually called saltationists) in acknowledging the existence of and seeking to explain these 'gaps', or 'missing links'. They spoke of 'punctuated equilibrium', which refers to the spasmodic nature of evolutionary change, in contrast to Darwin's gradualist approach. Asked once about the famous 'horse sequence', which shows a gradual increase in the size of the horse over time, Eldredge responded, 'There have been an awful lot of stories, some more imaginative than others, about what the nature of that history [of life] really is. The most famous example, still on exhibit downstairs, is the exhibit on horse evolution prepared perhaps 50 years ago. That has been presented as the literal truth in textbook after textbook. Now I think that that is lamentable, particularly when the people who propose those kinds of stories may themselves be aware of the speculative nature of some of that stuff.'[15]

In 1977 Gould published *Ontogeny and Phylogeny*,[16] an attempted identification of the mechanism by which short-term – and, by implication, rapid – evolutionary change might have taken place. He followed others in proposing that the timing of embryonic development (an organism's ontogeny) held the key. If, he argued, apparently small, outwardly insignificant changes occurred at an early stage in the development of an embryo, its adult form could be dramatically altered. The new form, appearing quite abruptly, might potentially constitute a new species.

In his book *Sudden Origins: Fossils, Genes and the Emergence of Species*, Jeffrey Schwartz takes Gould's argument a step further, taking account of more recent research into the genetics of development. He suggests that species may appear rapidly because of subtle changes occurring in the genes that control and organise the process of embryonic development (homeobox genes). He bases this idea largely, it appears, on the assumption that certain such genes operate in isolation during embryonic development. David Norman, director of Sedgwick Museum, Cambridge, takes issue with this assumption:

> In truth such genes operate in synergistic clusters with a range of other genes, in a very complex and necessarily integrated manner. Experimental developmental biologists and geneticists deal with small abstractions of these complexes in order to understand aspects of the processes involved, but are far from a synthetic view. The simplistic notion of mutating a homeobox gene and letting these altered genes spread (as recessive Mendelian alleles through populations) as Schwartz imagines is far more likely to introduce an element of chaos to the regulated pathway of development than a population of potentially new and "hopeful monsters" (a phrase coined by the geneticist Goldschmidt).[17]

The British palaeontologist Colin Patterson, and others of his school, approach the problem of 'gaps' in the fossil record from a rather different angle; indeed, they effectively sidestep the issue. These scientists, whose founding father was a German entomologist named Willi Hennig,[18] are usually called cladists; they are taxonomists of nature, labellers of natural categories or species among both present-day and fossil organisms. They believe that knowledge about what groups or categories exist must be acquired before any ideas about process can be tested. Until such knowledge is established in some detail, a common origin to living organisms can only be hypothesised. 'The concept of ancestry is not accessible by the tools we have', Patterson has said, commenting on one occasion that a fossil is no more than 'a mess on a rock'.[19] In other words, Darwin's theory of evolution – which involves time, change, process – simply cannot be read from the rocks.

Patterson's conclusion that it is impossible to find evidence for change or process in an examination of fossils is to some extent supported by the fact that so many of them, not least those once thought to represent long extinct forms, have been found to correspond to creatures living today. The case of the coelacanth is an obvious example. Thomas Huxley once said, in relation to the various species represented in fossilised form, 'The only difference between a fossil and a recent animal is that one has been dead longer than the other.'[20]

Darwin himself called the problem of explaining and defining species the 'mystery of mysteries'. Steve Jones, professor of genetics at University College London, author of a major 'update' of Darwin's 1859 work,[21] has confessed that the chapter he found most difficult to write was the one on the nature of species, what species are and what keeps them apart. '*On the Origin of Species*,' he says, 'is not really about the origin of species at all because Darwin never really gets straight what makes species happen, why they do not just blend into one another, how barriers to this arise. The short answer is we still haven't got it quite right on that.' The hope that molecular genetics would provide a solution to this problem, Jones largely dismisses: 'Molecular genetics is just anatomy plus a massive research grant. The fact that humans and chimps share 98.8 per cent of their DNA is fairly amazing, but it still does not explain the nature of differences between humans and chimps. You have to bear in mind that humans and mushrooms share 60 per cent of their DNA.'[22]

The sequencing and analysing of the human genome has shed little light on the nature of species. On completion of the project in February 2001, it was revealed that humans possess far fewer genes than was previously thought. 'There are about 30,000 to 40,000 protein-coding genes in the human genome – only about twice as many as in worm or fly,' reported the

International Human Genome Sequencing Consortium. 'There are only a few hundred genes ... that are not in the mouse genome,' commented Craig Venter of Celera Genomics, Inc. 'In fact, what has been said about the human genome, that it is the blueprint for humans, is not true. We don't think blueprint is the right metaphor.' The true directions for what makes a human being lie not in letters of code, it was stated, but in what the body does with that code – an unknown process. Man, in fact, 'remains a puzzle'.[23]

Mendel's laws of genetics can still be considered the clearest statement – if an indirect one – of what does and what does not constitute a distinct species.

Gregor Mendel was a nineteenth-century Austrian monk. A biologist of note, he experimented with garden peas and made the discovery that they do not vary in heredity in a haphazard fashion, but according to clear, orderly laws, which he duly formulated. He read a paper on the subject before the Natural History Society of Brunn, Austria, in 1855, but as his findings did not accord with evolutionary ideas (with which the scientific world was becoming preoccupied) his discovery was ignored – until 1900, when the same truth was rediscovered independently by Hugo de Vries and Carl Correns. Thereafter 'Mendelism' – the 'laws of Mendel', or the 'principles of genetics' to which his discovery led – became accepted as a part, and a very significant part, of the established corpus of modern science. This acceptance did not happen without a struggle, however, since Mendelism was quickly seen to be antipathetic to evolution. A notable evolutionist put it thus, 'Interesting and profoundly important as are the results of Mendelian investigation, it must be admitted that they have rendered but little assistance in making the evolution process more intelligent, but instead of removing difficulties have rather increased them.'[24]

The truths Mendel had isolated amounted to a contradiction of a basic assumption of Darwinism, namely, that individual species form a continuum rather than being inviolably distinct. Those truths can be summed up as follows: descent from generation to generation is orderly rather than disorderly; variation takes place within a natural species as a result of different combinations of materials already contained in that species, that is, within its genes; nothing new is ever added, apparently 'new' forms, or 'mutations', being the reappearance of old forms hidden (for long ages, perhaps) in 'recessive' genes of a species.

On the basis of those laws or principles, the biologist William Bateson, late President of the British Association for the Advancement of Science and specialist in Mendelian heredity, defined a species as a group of organisms with marked characteristics in common and freely interbreeding.[25] The definition allows for the variation known to exist in natural species, and yet acknowledges the existence of a wall of partition between species known as sterility, which has been cited as the true test of species.[26] Bateson said that until the rising of a new species permanently sterile towards its parent forms had been witnessed, evolution would not have been proved; he is also on record as having stated that had Darwin known of Mendel's work, he would never have written the *Origin of Species*.[27] Bateson remained a believer in evolution, but had no illusions about the theory's problems. 'When students of other sciences ask us what is currently believed about the origin of species,' he wrote, 'we have no clear answer to give. Faith has given place to agnosticism.'[28]

That there is a 'wall of partition' between species is confirmed by the lack of evidence from living forms that one species ever changes into another. Niles Eldredge has been taken to task by Alan Linton, emeritus professor of bacteriology at Bristol University, for neglecting this fact in his book proclaiming 'the triumph of evolution'. Linton writes,

> Where is the experimental evidence? None exists in the literature claiming that one species has been shown to evolve into another. Bacteria, the simplest form of independent life, are ideal for this kind of study, with generation times of 20 to 30 minutes, and populations achieved after 18 hours. But after 150 years of the science of bacteriology, there is no evidence that one species of bacteria has changed into another, in spite of the fact that populations have been exposed to potent chemical and physical mutagens and that, uniquely, bacteria possess extra-chromosomal, transmissible plasmids. Since there is no evidence for species changes between the simplest forms of molecular life, it is not surprising that there is no evidence for evolution from prokaryotic to eukaryotic cells, let alone throughout the whole array of higher multicellular organisms.[29]

Let me now return to the record of the rocks. The strata, we have seen, cannot tell us anything about the ancestry of species; perhaps, however, they can tell us something about their own origin. I will again begin with something personal.

A theory that fits

For eighteen months in the 1980s, employment took me to the Yemen, in southern Arabia. In no country on earth, perhaps, are geological strata so brilliantly displayed. This is because the mountainous terrain, rich in precipitous cliffs and stunning escarpments, have in many regions been rendered barren of soil and vegetation by the endlessly oscillating assaults from high wind, driving rain and scorching sun. I have stood atop the loftiest mountain in Arabia, some 13,000 feet above sea level, and contemplated the panorama of receding peaks and ranges. I have stopped my Land Rover and alighted on the roadside to examine, at an altitude only slightly lower, a stratum entirely composed of fossilised cockles, perfectly preserved, including in many cases the original dark colour. I have flown over these same mountains and looked down at the peaks, rifts, gorges, wadis, valleys and asked myself how they came into being. The answer was as clear as the vista was beautiful: water, water, water, overwhelming, surging, eddying, falling, cutting, receding, returning, falling again, cutting deeper, receding, drying. And sediment – the mix of earthly substances churned up by that water in vast quantities, then sifted and deposited, stratum upon stratum – drying, hardening, cracking, splitting, buckling, shifting, crumbling, collapsing, settling.

This, of course, is the layman speaking. But whether layman or specialist one can only speak as one finds, as I have said. The best evidence is first-hand, not what is culled from books or heard from others' lips.

Water, I say. Water, too, says the evolutionist, water to lay down strata of myriads upon myriads of sea creatures on ocean bottoms, watery silt from rivers or perhaps flash-floods to bury and fossilise land creatures, from dinosaurs to door-mice, in further strata – massive chunks of which, by up-thrusting pressure from clashing continental plates were, in an infinitely slow process, contorted and elevated to form mountain chains or lifted in vast horizontal slabs to make high inland plateaux. So, specialists tell us today, our world's crust – oceans, islands, continents, lowlands, highlands, snow-capped peaks – was (still is) largely fashioned by imperceptible yet relentlessly grinding movement over endless ages. So, however, to one observer of the world he lives in, it can never have been.

'How did the Earth move?' was the heading given to a letter published in *The Daily Telegraph*, 20 September 1992, the writer of which was Professor R. A. Lyttleton of Cambridge. The letter began, 'In his Advice to a Young Scientist the late Sir Peter Medawar wrote, "I cannot give any scientist of any age better advice than this: *the intensity of conviction that a hypothesis is true has no bearing on whether it is true or not.*" In failing to be guided by this dictum, the plate-tectonicists have concocted a worthless theory that has imposed on a vast army of proponents. The great sorrow of these plate drifters is that they cannot discover any engine capable of moving continents. Your science correspondent's article (September 13) is more than timely, as this absurd tectonic theory has been so widely promulgated as now even to be taught in schools as gospel.'

Professor Lyttleton refers to his own (and Herman Bondi's) preferred theory of how mountains were formed, a theory based on the existence of radioactive elements within the earth. Such elements may indeed exist, but they, like plate-tectonics, are superfluous to a satisfactory explanation of the formation of the world's stratified, fossil-bearing crust. I cite Professor Lyttleton's letter to demonstrate that the theory of plate-tectonics, though (as the professor points out) widely accepted, is not without grave weaknesses nor, in consequence of this, without its critics. There is another theory that fits the data I have gathered – sometimes through personal observation and investigation, though much more often through the published findings of others. It is not a new theory; it is one that was adhered to by the great majority (since it accorded with observed facts) until well into the nineteenth century, until, more specifically, the advent of Darwinism. It is the theory of a universal cataclysm or flood.

In front of me as I write these words is a chunk of mud-coloured rock I picked up from a pile of debris left after a mountainside in the Kyrenia range, Cyprus, had been demolished to make way for a new road. On one side of this piece of rock is the almost perfect impression of a fresh leaf, perhaps from a laurel tree. Other leaves can be seen half-exposed, as well as tubular effects indicating stalks or small twigs. In other words, this 'rock' was originally composed of countless bits and pieces of vegetation mixed up together in the sediment, all of which then petrified. I speak of 'sediment'. Let me now give the definition of this word, in a geological sense, given in the *Oxford Dictionary*: 'matter that is carried by water or wind and deposited on the surface of the land, and may in time become consolidated into rock.'

I am aware that a definition given in a general dictionary cannot be cited as an authoritative scientific statement. Nevertheless, on reading the above, a phrase leapt out at me, because it corresponds exactly to what I have always understood to be axiomatic to the prevailing view about the deposition and hardening of sedimentary strata. It is the phrase 'in time', which in the context of that dictionary sentence means 'over a period of time'. In other words, the sedimentary strata constituting virtually all the earth's crust was formed gradually. We have all been taught the approximate time-scale: it is to be measured in hundreds of millions, even billions of years.

My chunk of rock tells me a different story. It tells me that the process of petrifaction happened quickly, because had it been slow there would have been no beautiful leaf impression. The (laurel) leaf would have decomposed, just as fallen leaves shrivel and then disintegrate in my garden, or rot and become leaf mould if they are covered in. Of course, the vegetable material of the leaf *has* disappeared; it did, in fact, 'decompose' in the process of fossilisation. But it only did so after the sediment had become so hard that the perfect pattern and proportions of its fresh form were permanently preserved. Indeed, the fact that the bigger rock incorporating my chunk split open along the 'surface' of the leaf suggests that on decomposing it left behind it the tiniest fault-line. The actual stalks and twigs have also disappeared, in some instances leaving behind their fossilised forms but sometimes *leaving spaces or holes*. The latter fact is suggestive: it points to the sediment having hardened quickly – as if containing a cementing agent – so that spaces left behind by decomposing vegetation were not filled in.

Perhaps my story of a leaf does not convince; it will perhaps be argued that this area of sedimentary rock in Cyprus was exceptional, that something caused it to petrify more quickly than the norm. Let me turn to something else.

In the 'Dinosaur Museum' in Dorchester, Dorset, England, is a slab of rock, seven feet square and three inches thick, itself composed of several thin layers, on which footprints of two Megalosauri are preserved. It looks like a stretch of slightly undulating mud. Along this freshly deposited sediment strolled our dinosaurs, shortly before more sediment covered their tracks. The 'mud' has a crazed appearance suggesting some drying out, yet little time can have passed before it was covered because, if much time had elapsed, wind, rain, or other agents would have scarred its surface and obliterated the footprints. Hardening, preventing distortion due to pressure from above, must also have been swift. The shelf of rock must have split along the surface of the 'mud' during excavation (at Swanage in 1981), leading to the discovery of the footprints. This also suggests quick hardening, the two adjacent deposits not having coalesced. Another such example comes from Ardley, Oxfordshire, England, where quarrymen scraped away rock and clay to expose a trail of three-toed dinosaur footprints that extended for no less than 180 metres, the lengthening gaps between the prints at one point showing that the creature had broken into a sprint. Reporting the find, Tim Radford, who confessed to a gradualist approach to geology with continents shifting and landscapes sinking into and then rising out of the sea, commented: 'Some freak of time and geology preserved them.'[30] No. The answer to this and other such phenomena worldwide is simpler: a single, global cataclysm.

Dinosaur tracks preserved in stone are not, of course, unusual; ripple marks on the top of strata are positively common. Irregular, washboard markings, which form on the sandy bottoms of streams, lakes and oceans in storms or other disturbances and disappear as quickly as they have come, occur numerously at the separation of strata, whatever their composition. Some such marks are small, evidently caused in shallow water, others are immense, measuring over twenty feet between peaks, suggesting deep, violently agitated water. They bespeak a quick, though periodical, deposition of sediment, as from an ebb and flow, in a manner not paralleled by anything seen in existing waters. Speaking more generally, the line of contact between almost all strata is perfect, precise and smooth, irregularities indicating disturbance on the surface of each lower stratum being rare. The evidence points to a deposition of strata, one above the other, at such speed that the upper surface of each formation was soft and moist when the next even softer layer was superimposed on it.[31]

Other phenomena observable in the strata, usually glossed over or ignored in reports or books, suggest the same speedy formation. When a trunk of a tree, for instance, is found piercing a number of adjacent strata, it is difficult to resist the conclusion that those strata were deposited quickly, building up round the piece of timber lodged in a vertical or angled position. The case of a tree found in Craiglieth Quarry, England, can be cited. This tree trunk, over eighty feet in length and leaning at an angle of about forty degrees, intersected some twelve different strata of limestone. It had no branches or roots, and the bark had been converted into a thin coat of the finest coal. When it lay exposed in the quarry it had the appearance of charred wood, in contrast to the white rocks in which it lay. The same phenomenon has been found in beds of coal, fossil stems sometimes passing from the bottom into the strata above to a great height.[32]

Another pointer to swift deposition of sediment is the presence of very delicate and easily broken plants – such as horsetails, rushes and other plants of the Equiseta family – unbroken and intact in the hardest sandstone. A bed of stone three feet thick encloses such flora at High Whitby, in Yorkshire, England, where the accumulation of sediment must have been so rapid as to prevent decomposition of the cortical portions of the plants, the wearing away of their superficial structure, or the bending of their stem beneath a current of the water.[33] It was in a quarry near Whitby, too, that the near-complete fossil of an ichthyosaur, fifteen feet in length, was discovered early in 2000. This specimen of the extinct marine reptile was in such good condition that palaeontologists were able to work out what it had had for its last meal – an unknown form of squid. Needless to say, such an excellent appetite indicates that the creature was in good health when it suffered what must have been a sudden, violent form of death.[34]

Quarries all over England have yielded rich pickings for fossil hunters, the fossilised remains of many thousands of fish in rock blasted from these quarries telling the same story of a rapid deposition of sedimentary strata. Some individual examples show traces of colour on their skin, indicating burial before decomposition of their soft parts. Cuttle-fish found in rocks around Lyme Regis, England, must have been killed and entombed (overcome by encroaching sediment, we must imagine) with extraordinary rapidity since they retain the dark fluid with which their ink-bags are filled when alive. Scarcely any substance decomposes more speedily than the flesh of fish, as can be seen from the swift onset of decay – within a few hours – in fish left on beaches or river banks. Fossil fish in great numbers found in carboniferous strata, in magnesium limestone, in chalk and other rocky substances are frequently found in a condition of almost perfect preservation, no part of their structure being injured. The scattered fragments of marine creatures occasionally found in modern deposits are in stark contrast to this phenomenon, which requires that fossil fish were entombed almost immediately on their having been in some way overwhelmed. In some ways similar is the case of a fossil shark, yielded up by stratified shale in northern Ohio, USA. This great fish is compressed horizontally to the thickness of a quarter of an inch (though otherwise undistorted), with the tail not flattened but standing almost at right angles. The conditions point to burial alive, as if the shark had been swimming in murky water rapidly thickening into sediment.[35]

The famous 'drowned mammoths of Siberia' furnish further evidence of a watery catastrophe that not only killed these animals but also buried their bodies (together with those of other species, in one case a complete whale) under beds of loam or gravel, which then immediately froze, together with the carcasses. The catastrophe must, in fact, have been accompanied in that region by a great and sudden change of climate, from temperate to extreme cold. The strata beneath the surface of northern Siberia are composed chiefly of sand, which would be sandstone if it had consolidated. In some places this sand is mixed with layers of clay, and also of gravel. The year-round cold in the region means that the strata remain perpetually frozen to a great depth, except for a few feet of topsoil that thaws out briefly in the summer. The mummified remains (together with hoards of fresh bones of quadrupeds or marine creatures) have remained chilled and in perfect condition ever since first being frozen, so that bears, wolves and dogs have been known to feed upon the red meat of carcasses occasionally exposed – in the banks of seasonal rivers, for example. That these animals met a quick end by drowning can be inferred from the fact that some have been found with identifiable vegetation – their last meal – remaining in their stomachs and, in one case at least, in the mouth.[36]

The preservation of these mammoths, and sometimes of other large mammals, *in their flesh* has fascinated scientists and others, and led to unusual projects. In 1996 a Japanese team began hunting for sperm from frozen mammoths in Siberia, hoping to fertilize the sperm with an elephant ovum to create a female hybrid and then, through the latter, a near-mammoth. Not finding the sperm, they decided to try to clone a mammoth from frozen DNA samples. By July 2003 they had collected enough bone marrow, muscle and skin from mammoth remains to commence the experiment.[37]

The huge hoards of bones found in Siberia may represent the residue of animals drowned at a fairly early stage in the cataclysm, the carcasses decomposing and becoming dismembered as they washed around as flotsam, finally to be gathered together by the subsiding water and deposited in different areas. The latter effect would similarly account for mass deposits of bones from different species or sometimes of complete specimens found in strata all over the world, such as the 'mass graveyard of feathered dinosaurs with teeth' found recently in Utah, USA.[38] Evolutionary geologists, unable to believe in a universal deluge, have argued that the vast quantities of both the frozen remains and bones of mammoths and other species in Siberia could represent animals drowned in rivers of the region and later buried in some way. Such an explanation was offered, in December 1995, to account for the presence of the skull and tusk of a 'prehistoric elephant', twice the size of a modern African elephant, in a cliff (also containing 'molluscs and other fossils') in Norfolk, England. The animal had probably, it was recorded, 'died in a prehistoric river'.[39]

Catastrophes, small or large, are usually invoked to explain the demise of dinosaurs. Regional floods or sandstorms are suggested causes for the death and burial of some individual creatures,[40] while resort is made to a major cataclysm – the impact of a meteorite and/or a series of volcanic eruptions, leading to a belt of atmospheric dust blocking off light from the sun – to account for their extinction some '65 million years ago'.[41] Though evolutionists often claim that they do not have to posit catastrophic events – certainly not a general cataclysm – to account for data unearthed, they seem more than ready to do this when it suits them.

That the earth at some stage in the past suffered a great inundation is suggested by the phenomenon of 'dry rivers', which point to immense amounts of water having once drained off higher ground. These 'dry rivers' are wide, long valleys which now have comparatively small streams flowing in them, but which give the impression of having once contained vastly greater amounts of water. Horizontal terraces or 'banks' at different heights above the existing river show the level at which the water once flowed, representing expanses enormously wide and deep. Such terraces at varying heights up to 300 feet above sea level can be found in England along the River Thames or, in USA, hundreds of feet above the Spokane River.[42] In much of the Middle East, wide, usually dry wadis can strikingly evince this effect.

Uniformitarianism and the geological column

This talk of watery catastrophe contrasts radically with the perspective exemplified by the 'geological column', already referred to, displayed in today's textbooks, classrooms and natural history museums. The 'column', which places the various strata (and their fossils) in ascending chronological order, reflects the approach to prehistory usually called uniformitarianism, which can be encapsulated in a phrase coined by Sir Archibald Geikie, 'The present is the key to the past.'[43] By these words, Geikie means that the origin of sedimentary rocks should not be explained by invoking theories of catastrophe, but in terms of what is happening on the ocean floor today, extended over immense periods of time. The average rate of sedimentation, according to uniformitarians, is 0.2 millimeteres per year. It is postulated that each stratum was slowly formed beneath the seas and then lifted (by the movement of tectonic plates, presumably) to become dry land for a while, before being again submerged to allow the formation of a different stratum – and so on, again and again.

Richard Milton, in his book *The Facts of Life: Shattering the Myth of Darwinism*, writes thus of uniformitarian theory, 'Most non-geologists (and perhaps even some geologists) will be surprised to learn that observations of modern geological processes show that nowhere today are there rocks being formed anything like those in the geological column.'[44]

Milton describes the composition and formation of the main types of sedimentary rock exemplified in the geological column: sandstones, limestones, dolomites, siltstones, mudstones, shales, conglomerates and evaporites. He explains how lithification (transformation into solid stone) of sandstones, clays, siltstones and mudstones requires, chiefly, the presence of a cementing agent (very fine grains which bind bigger grains together). The process, he suggests, is similar to that of mixing sand, cement and water to form – in a matter of hours rather than millions of years – the rock-like substance familiar to every handyman. He goes on to speak of limestones and dolomites, explaining that the foramineferal ooze forming today on the Bahamas banks of the Atlantic (until recently cited by uniformitarians as a sedimentary limestone) is only superficially similar to the historical limestone we know as chalk, and that if, as is now widely believed, the aragonite and calcite crystals that compose chalk are non-organic, the chalk must have precipitated out of sea water. Such precipitation would require 'sudden and cataclysmic changes in the temperature and acid-alkaline balance of huge areas of chemically saturated water'. He concludes, 'Nothing of this kind can be observed anywhere today.' Of dolomite (the 'geological cousin' of limestone), he concludes, similarly, 'It is nowhere known to be forming today.'

Conglomerates are sands containing cemented gravels, pebbles and boulders. The process involved in the formation of a sedimentary conglomerate depends on the size of its largest constituents. Milton writes, 'The more fast flowing and the more turbulent, the heavier the object that can be transported. As water slows down, and becomes quieter, the particles suspended in it will begin to settle on the bottom, beginning with boulders, cobbles and pebbles, followed by sand and finally the finest particles of silt and mud. This is precisely the type of sequence that crops up in deposits all over the world, strongly suggesting that the sediments were laid down not gradually, but as a result of violent flood conditions which then abated.' The areas covered by deposits of conglomerates can be vast, like that of the Colorado plateau, which covers an area of 125,000 square miles. No such deposits are forming today, because the catastrophic flood conditions needed to produce them do not exist.

Deposits of what are called 'evaporites' are extensive, immensely thick beds of common salt, gypsum and anhydrite, found on most continents.

Nothing happening today can be compared to the process that must have been involved in their formation. An estimated ocean full of water – millions of billions of tons of sea water – would have to evaporate to create the 1,100 metres depth of salts in the Stassfurt deposits of northern Germany. Milton again suggests a 'catastrophic' origin for evaporite deposits, through precipitation from chemically saturated waters, a process similar to what he suggests for the formation of limestones.

Richard Milton concludes his survey of the formation of sedimentary strata with what he describes as 'the greatest anomaly of all'. He writes, 'Nowhere today are there known to be any *fossiliferous* rocks forming. There is no shortage of remains, no lack of quiet sedimentary marine environments. Indeed there are the bones and shells of millions of creatures on land and sea available. But nowhere are these becoming slowly buried in sediments and lithified. They are simply becoming eroded by wind, tide, weather and predators.'[45]

As explained above, the uniformitarian model of the world's past, represented by the 'geological column', places the various strata in ascending chronological order, with fossils assigned to each period to show how life gradually developed. Scientists now consider that the simplest living forms (microbes that could use sunlight to 'photosynthesise') began nearly 4,000 million years ago. This, it is proposed, was followed by an immensely long and mysterious period called 'Pre-Cambrian'. The 'Cambrian' period followed (from around 600 to 500 million years ago: the age of trilobite molluscs), then the 'Ordovician' (500 to 440 million: gastropod molluscs), the 'Silurian' (to 395 million: bivalve molluscs, terrestrial plants, jawless fish), the 'Devonian' (to 345 million: goniatite molluscs, jawed fish), the 'Carboniferous' (to 280 million: spiders, first reptiles), the 'Permian' (to 225 million: Eryops – a large mammal), the 'Triassic' (to 200 million: ammonites, and Megazastrodon – a shrew-like mammal), the 'Jurassic' (to 135 million: sea urchins, large dinosaurs), the 'Cretaceous' (to 65 million: marine gastropods, and Pteranodon – a gliding reptile), the 'Tertiary' (to 1.8 million: Eohippus – 'ancestor' of the horse); the 'Quartenary', replacing the older 'Pleistocene' (to the present day: butterflies, and Australopithecus – a man-like creature).[46]

It all looks very tidy, but in fact there is often a great mix of fossils in each stratum, as in the case mentioned above of the giant elephant skull and tusk found in a Norfolk cliff, which also contained 'molluscs and other fossils'. One early geologist, referring to 'aluminous or lias (limestone) strata', writes: 'Here we see crocodiles and other large saurians; fishes, great and small, nautilites, ammonites, belemnites, and myriads of other shells, associated with trees and fragments of wood, and all, with few exceptions, lying parallel to the plain of the strata. Such an assemblage, and so arranged, could have been formed only by ocean currents, collecting these substances together, and depositing them in their places.'[47]

Dating of strata and fossils often gives the impression of being circular: types of strata are dated by the fossils found in them (the 'youngest' type, normally); thereafter, fossils otherwise unknown may be dated by the particular type of strata in which they are found. Dating techniques based on radioactive decay, once thought to provide reliable corroboration of the dating of strata on less 'scientific' grounds (although in fact many sedimentary rocks contain no radioactive material), has run into problems.[48] In any case, whatever system of dating is used, many anomalies occur. These are sometimes explained by invoking an abnormal circumstance lying behind the presence of a fossil in the 'wrong' environment.

A major anomaly for the uniformitarian model of prehistory is the existence of inverted strata. A stratum having very simple fossils, supposed to have evolved early, is frequently found on top of a stratum containing very complex fossils, supposed to have evolved late. When this is the case, uniformitarian geologists talk of the strata having 'reversed' their position since being deposited. Geikie, for example, writes, 'We may even demonstrate that strata have turned completely upside down if we can show that fossils in what are the uppermost layers ought properly to lie beneath those in the beds below them.'[49] 'Ought properly', of course, refers to his assumption that the strata should show a gradual development of life from simple to complex. The statement begs the question at issue. It would of course not do for him to entertain the thought that the fact of inverted strata might mean sediments were laid down in a manner different from that proposed by evolutionary theory.

It should be pointed out, before going further, that in general the simpler forms of life are found in lower strata and more complex forms are found in upper. This accords with evolutionary theory, but it accords equally well with the hypothesis of a cataclysm, of a gigantic flood. If the action of water buried the fossils, we should expect heavy objects to be buried lower down in strata than light objects. We have already referred to this principle in relation to the formation of conglomerates. So it would be with fossils: we should expect, for example, marine forms (shells, corals and the like) to end up in lower strata than fish, and fish to end up in lower strata than land animals. The last mentioned, having a tendency to float, we would normally expect to be in the topmost strata. The cataclysm or flood theory of geology is wholly compatible with this general picture, but it has the advantage that it is capable of accounting for exceptions – like inversion of strata. This is because the waters of a cataclysm would not have been quiet but massively turbulent, especially initially. The water would have surged and rushed, abated for a while, then returned, the cycle probably repeating itself many times, allowing new currents to bring different sediment and detritus and pile them up layer upon layer (as with coal, fossilised vegetation, fifty seams of which have been known to alternate with sand, sandstone, clay or gypsum), or to deposit simple 'early' fossils on top of complex 'late' fossils.

Reversal of strata certainly poses a problem for uniformitarians. It stretches credulity to breaking point to imagine how, in the uniformitarian scheme of things, 'Cambrian' and 'Pre-Cambrian' strata *7,000 square miles in extent* in Montana, Alberta and former British Columbia have managed to end up on top of a 'Cretaceous' stratum, or how many similar upside-down areas identified all over the world came into being. The problem is not alleviated by proposing that the process took many millions of years. Evolutionary geologists obviously have to attempt an explanation of how such reversals occurred, however; this they do by speaking of 'faults' in the earth's surface – monster thrusts or massive folds of strata, whereby vast areas have risen up and slid or turned over so that they now lie horizontally, the top on the bottom and the bottom on the top. Yet the areas of inverted strata do not exhibit signs of previously deposited sediment having been disturbed. The layers containing simple or 'early' organisms lie quite naturally on the top of layers containing complex or 'late' forms.[50]

Of course, sizeable collapsing, buckling and up-thrusting of strata have occurred, as is evident from what I have seen personally many times in the barren mountains of the Yemen and Oman. Strata can be steeply angled – almost vertical – the fragmented ends forming peaks and the surface of the top stratum forming steep, smooth mountainsides. An example of the latter faced the house I used to live in just outside Muscat. Such phenomena are perfectly naturally explained if we allow that a vast inundation was responsible for the present state of the earth's surface. Subsiding water produces exactly these effects, as can be observed on the muddy banks of tidal rivers, where this happens in miniature. When the earth's strata were first laid down they would have been soft, like river mud, but (as we have

seen above) they would quickly have hardened. As the water drained off
the topmost layers, it would have cut rifts and gorges, finally creating wide
valleys – as we see in any mountainous or hilly terrain. Then, when the
water flowed along the low-lying courses it had created in the strata, it would
have cut into and under the 'banks' (or 'cliffs') along their edge until
sections of the land above broke off and collapsed. If by that time the strata
had largely hardened, the 'inland' end would be thrust heavenward as the
'cliff' end descended into the flowing stream or valley below.

I will now turn to the most emotive aspect of evolutionary theory.

The 'ascent of man'

'The more we find out about the origins of man the less we know.' These
words headed an article written in 1995 by Stuart Wavell, surveying the
latest findings on human evolution. Wavell summarised his conclusions:
'The scientists themselves are confused. A series of recent discoveries has
forced them to tear up the simplistic charts on which they blithely used
to draw linkages from *australopithecus africanus* to *homo habilis* to *homo
erectus* to *homo sapiens*. The classic family tree delineating man's ascent
from the apes, familiar to us from school, has given way to the concept
of genetic islands. The bridgework between them is anyone's guess.'[51]

'Genetic islands' is the key phrase, referring to the failure of scientists
(palaeoanthropologists) to find conclusive evidence of an intermediate
form or forms linking man with his proposed ape forebear, or linking
proposed intermediate forms with each other. Not that there is a shortage
of (often hotly disputed) candidates for the roles. Some relatively recent
additions to the list include *sahelanthropus tchadensis* from Chad, assigned
an age of 7 million years; twelve bones of an 'upright hominid' from
Kenya, assigned 6 million years; *australopithecus ramidus* from Ethiopia,
4.4 million years;[52] and *kenyanthropus platyops* ('the flat-faced man of
Kenya'), around 3.5 million years[53]. Prominent contenders from an
earlier period of palaeoanthropological research are: from Kenya,
australopithecus anamensis, 4.1 to 3.9 million years; from Ethiopia,
australopithecus afarensis ('Lucy'), 4 to 3.6 million years; from South Africa,
australopithecus africanus, 3.5 to 2.5 million years; from Tanzania, *homo
habilis*, 2 to 1.5 million years.

The above 'missing links' in the proposed chain of human evolution
are from Africa, once the unchallenged 'cradle of humanity' – as the
'Eve' hypothesis, based on (flawed) statistical analysis of DNA from people

around the world, long maintained.[54] Yet in August 1995 came news from China of 'epoch-making evidence' that apes, monkeys and the ancestors of humans came from East Asia, and in July 2006 it was argued that fossilised skulls from Dmanisi in Georgia, said to be over 1.7 million years old, had established a link between Tanzania's *homo habilis* and Kenya's *homo erectus*, represented famously by the 'Turkana Boy', assigned an age of 1.6 million years.[55]

Homo erectus, conceived as still slightly ape-like in feature, is said to have dispersed across Africa, Asia, Europe and America and to have flourished for over a million years. Two final English 'links' in the chain to *homo sapiens* are 'Anglia Man', said to have lived 700,000 years ago, and 'Boxgrove Man', 500,000 years ago, hailing from East Anglia and West Sussex respectively. The latter is described as of wild though essentially modern appearance, this being depicted for us on the basis of a shinbone and tooth – body parts, experts have decided, of distinct individuals.[56]

The very plethora of candidates for the role of man's earliest ancestor(s) raises difficulties for specialists in human origins, as Wavell explains: 'The problem is that mankind can only have evolved from one ancestor, and there is an embarrassing number of contenders, which is growing by the week. Their relationships to one another remain clouded in mystery and nobody has conclusively identified any of them as the early hominid that gave rise to *homo sapiens* ... There are at least five hypotheses, none of them provable, relating to 14 hominid species.'

Having traced in outline the evolutionary 'ascent of man', in so doing revealing problems encountered by the theory's own exponents, it scarcely seems necessary to comment further. To the layman the reconstructed picture is, at best, speculative; much argument rests upon minimal data. Worth recording here, however, is the fact that even unflinching evolutionists are prepared to acknowledge the paucity – even non-existence – of data relating to man's ancestry. Richard Lewontin, Harvard University geneticist and one-time president of the American Society for the Study of Evolution, has written, 'Despite the excited and optimistic claims that have been made by some palaeontologists, no fossil hominid species can be established as our direct ancestor.'[57] In conversation with Tom Bethell, researching the article on evolution already cited, he commented further, 'The only way you can know that some fossil is the direct ancestor [of the human species] is that it's so human that it is human. There is a contradiction here. If it is different enough from humans to be interesting, then you don't know whether it's an ancestor or not. And if it's similar enough to be human, then it's not interesting.'[58]

Despite this concession, Lewontin adheres to the view that man evolved, like every other every living creature, from simpler life forms; he has stated, 'Evolution is fact, not theory ... Birds evolve from nonbirds, humans evolve from nonhumans.' On being invited by Bethell to justify such claims, he responded, 'Those statements flow simply from the assertion that all organisms have parents. It is an empirical claim, I think, that all living organisms have living organisms as parents.' Bethell comments, 'What struck me about Lewontin's argument was how much it depended on his premise that all organisms have parents. In a sense, his argument includes the assertion that evolution is true. Lewontin maintains that his premise is "empirical", but this is only in the (admittedly important sense) that it has never to our knowledge been falsified.'[59]

I have now, in looking at the evidence (or rather, arguments) for human evolution, come full circle. I started this appraisal of Darwinism, orthodox or modified, by examining statements made by Richard Dawkins, whose belief in the truth of evolutionary theory seems, I suggested, to spring from his atheism, from a need to believe. In other words, his argument, like that of Lewontin, 'includes the assertion that evolution is true'; it is circular. Lewontin himself, in conversation with Bethell, ultimately concedes the point: 'Either you think that complex organisms arose by non-natural phenomena, or you think that they arose by natural phenomena. If they arose by natural phenomena, they had to evolve. And that's all there is to it. And that's the only claim I'm making.'[60]

I should point out (as already argued in slightly different terms) that neither Dawkins nor Lewontin has actually, by embracing Darwinism, obviated 'non-natural phenomena'. The premise underlying Lewontin's argument (and that of Dawkins, we must presume) is self-defeating: if all living organisms have living organisms as parents, what are we to make of the first living organism? Lewontin (or Dawkins) is free to assert that this original life-form did not, for some reason, need a living parent; Lewontin's premise, however, tells me that it did. Could that parent have been the 'living organism', the 'non-natural phenomenon', we call God?

What appears to underlie the widespread acceptance of Darwinism, and its vigorous promotion by people like Dawkins and Lewontin, is materialist philosophy – the atheistic view of life that seems largely to have taken over the scientific community. Phillip Johnson, in an article reviewing the evidence for 'Darwinism's mechanism of random mutation and natural selection as defined by Richard Dawkins', explains how this has come about:

> If there is no God, and if matter had to do its own creating, then something at least roughly like Darwinism has to be true. Dawkins himself makes this point by his doctrine of Universal Darwinism, which asserts that the Darwinian mechanism is the only one that can, in principle, explain life's complexity ... As long as materialism rules the dialogue, Darwinism-in-principle is effectively unfalsifiable. Only the details are open to debate.[61]

The last sentence in that quotation, incidentally, has considerable resonance with me. For in my reading around the subject, I have constantly found that its protagonists do indeed only talk about details; the broader picture, 'Darwinism-in-principle', is not discussed. Dawkins himself furnishes an example of this, stating on the first page of *The Selfish Gene*, 'This book is not intended as a general advocacy of Darwinism. Instead, it will explore the consequences of the evolution theory for a particular issue.' He and most other writers on evolution appear to believe that the argument (for or against evolution) is over; the battle to establish its truth has long since been won. Thus their reluctance to discuss broader aspects of the theory is probably not because of apprehended weaknesses in the argument. While conceding this, the seeker-after-truth finds it frustrating that the conclusion of the overall thesis is always being assumed. (I might point out that I used to suffer the same kind of frustration in the discipline of theology.)

Phillip Johnson, at all events, believes the evolutionary boot to be on the other foot. He concludes his article with these words, 'If materialism is true, Darwinism has to be true. But the empirical evidence when it is considered without a huge materialist bias, is against Darwinism in every speciality.' His conclusion is one with which I readily concur, as will be gathered from all the foregoing.

There is a last point to be considered before ending this discussion of evolution; it can be summed up in a single word.

Entropy

The term 'entropy' was invented by the German physicist Rudolf Clausius in order to define a property of the Second Law of thermodynamics. This law, formulated by William Thompson (Lord Kelvin), states that all physical processes are irreversible because a certain amount of energy is always dissipated as heat. In other words, all processes are inefficient – making perpetual motion impossible, amongst other things. Put differently, all natural processes exhibit a degree of randomness or tendency to chaos, and it is this property that Clausius, taking the Greek word *en* ('in') and *trope* ('turning round or back'), labelled *entropy*. Let it be emphasised, he was talking about every kind of process, small or large, even one bounding the universe; *all* processes, he decided, are ultimately thermodynamic and irreversible; all are therefore subject to entropy. What is more, the entropy – the randomness or tendency to chaos – inevitably involved in any process increases the longer that process continues. Alone among the laws of physics, therefore, the Second Law of thermodynamics includes the arrow of time; entropy and time advance together. Clausius' concluding statement, encompassing both the First and Second Law, makes the point with beautiful simplicity: 'The energy of the Universe is constant; *the entropy of the Universe tends towards a maximum.*'[62]

Entropy can be understood more loosely as the transition from order to disorder, and expressed in these terms we immediately become aware of a paradox, of a question needing to be asked – and answered. The question was posed some years ago in an article entitled 'Arrows to the heart of Time' by Eric Bailey: 'If the universe amounts to a progressive cosmic degradation, how do we explain the formation of life, which represents a formidable process of organisation, evolution and improvement?'[63] In other words, if entropy is an indisputable, universal fact, how can life today in all its complexity, represented in particular by us humans, have evolved from simple beginnings – even if over immense tracts of time? More simply, how can we square Darwin's theory with the Second Law of thermodynamics?

Being an evolutionist, Bailey can only answer his own question as follows: 'The second law of thermodynamics raises more questions than it answers: it works when applied to a steam engine, but not necessarily when applied to the universe.'[64] Which seems to me a very weak statement. (Have we not heard something like it before, in relation to Mendel's laws of genetics?) Bailey is effectively saying that Thompson and Clausius and many others got it wrong, that the Second Law can, after all, be negated by a natural process. Yet it has never to our knowledge been contradicted, as Sir Arthur Eddington has testified:

The law that entropy always increases – the Second Law of thermodynamics – holds, I think, the supreme position among the laws of nature. If someone points out to you that your pet theory of the universe is in disagreement with Maxwell's equations – then so much the worse for Maxwell's equations. If it is found to be contradicted by observation – well, these experimentalists do bungle things sometimes. But if your theory is found to be against the Second Law of thermodynamics I can give you no hope; there is nothing for it but to collapse in deepest humiliation.[65]

Eric Bailey does not entirely abandon the field having made his 'weak' statement. He refers to a group at the Free University of Brussels who, while studying the behaviour of chemicals mixed together, found that the molecules formed transient symmetrical patterns. He writes:

> The patterns were apparently spontaneous, and disappeared as the chemicals moved towards the complete mix – its state of equilibrium, and maximum entropy. The patterns suggest that the molecules "know" where to go to create the brief semblance of order. Could it be that the beginnings of life were self-organising in the primeval soup? If so, the arrow of time implied by thermodynamics remains intact.[66]

This explanation of how evolution and the Second Law of thermodynamics might be reconciled seems to rely on a new factor in the equation, which looks uncommonly like personal intelligence, in other words a designer. True, the intelligence, or designer, is located inside the molecules rather than outside them – they control themselves rather than being controlled externally. But outside or inside, once such intelligence has been introduced into the picture you no longer have the Darwinian mechanism of random mutation and natural selection. The reconciliation is a sleight of hand: evolution driven by intelligence can of course contradict the imperative of entropy because it is no longer a natural process; it is a non-natural process (or, if you like, a supernatural process), in principle the same as creation by divine fiat. Bailey is following in the pathway trodden by Richard Dawkins, who seeks, as Phillip Johnson puts it, 'to solve the problem [of random mutation having to supply new genetic information in astronomical quantities] by smuggling an intelligent designer into his illustrations'. Dawkins, for example, makes much of the analogy of the way in which a random letter generator can produce a coherent sentence as long as the computer has been suitably pre-programmed, enabling the letter generator to 'discover' the sentence. 'Of course it can,' writes Johnson, 'and a properly programmed computer with a sufficiently rapid random letter generator can also produce the complete works of Shakespeare in a matter of hours. It is nearly as fast as printing the whole thing out from memory, because that is exactly what it amounts to.'[67]

The most fundamental question of all, concerning the very beginnings of life, remains unanswered. In his book proclaiming 'the triumph of evolution', Niles Eldredge can only offer the following statement on the matter: 'All biochemical steps leading to the formation of the first organism ... have yet to be deciphered.'[68] Robert Matthews sums the matter up:

Any viable theory has got to get from simple, off-the-shelf chemicals to relatively complex organisms that can grow and recreate themselves. It's a tall order, but now Japanese scientists think they have solved one of the problems: where the so-called amino acids come from. Amino acids are the building blocks of proteins, chemicals crucial for all living things ... But while the amino acid problem may now be solved, another enigma remains: where on earth – or beyond it – did self-replicating molecules like DNA come from? Without their instructions, amino acids are merely so many Lego bricks lying forlornly in a box.[69]

I began this discussion of evolution with Richard Dawkins – probably the most famous contemporary Darwinist – and it seems appropriate to be ending with him. I will quote one more of his statements: 'We cannot prove that there is no God, but we can safely conclude that He is very, very improbable indeed.'[70] In the light of the above data and arguments, I would suggest a small alteration to this sentence, as follows:

We cannot prove that there is no Evolution, but we can safely conclude that It is very, very improbable indeed.

Chapter 6
Biggest Bang

Rudolf Clausius declared: 'The entropy of the Universe tends towards a maximum.'

This all-embracing law has an important corollary, as Professor Roy Peacock has pointed out, 'Rather like mountaineering, the approach to a maximum can only be from a point of lower entropy [i.e., less chaos = more organisation] Whichever way the peak is climbed, it is always from a lower altitude. If a maximum is being approached then a minimum must have existed. If there was no overall reduction [in entropy] en route, a condition of the Second Law, it is an unavoidable fact that the minimum was a beginning. For us to live in a universe in which the Second Law of thermodynamics holds, then, it must be a universe that has a starting point.'[1]

That there was such a 'starting point' to the universe is today taken for granted by most scientists, and it is interesting to trace how this viewpoint has come to prevail.

Starting point

Theories of how the universe began (or did not begin) have oscillated over the last hundred years. In 1915, Albert Einstein propounded his General Theory of Relativity, which showed that time and space could not exist without matter. In 1924, Edwin Hubble found stars in the Andromeda galaxy, indicating that the universe was billions of times bigger than had previously been believed; then, in 1929, he concluded from the 'Red Shift' of light emitting from galaxies that the universe was expanding, a fulfilment of one of Einstein's predictions. In 1948, Fred Hoyle, Herman Bondi and Thomas Gold advanced their 'steady state' (or 'continuous creation') theory of an infinitely old universe, that is, one that has no beginning or ending. In contrast to this theory, however, the view had been gaining ground that the simplest explanation of Hubble's expanding universe made up of millions of galaxies was to say that everything had emerged from a point, or singularity – a massive explosion or fireball. This 'Big Bang' – an ironic term coined by Hoyle to reflect his disbelief in it – was dated to about 15 billion years ago (now usually reduced to 13 billion years). In 1965, the American radio astronomers Arno Penzias and Robert Wilson decided that a weak hiss of radio noise coming from every direction in space (known now as 'cosmic background radiation') was an echo of the Big Bang, and this new data caused Herman Bondi to change his mind and accept the idea of a finite universe. In 1987-88, Alan Guth and Stephen Hawking independently proposed an infinite series of universes inside each other. Then, in 1990, Hoyle and others put forward the 'modified steady state theory', which involves an infinite number of localised big bangs. Finally, in 1992, Professor George Smoot announced that the Cobe (Cosmic Background Explorer) satellite launched in 1989 and monitored by his Nasa team had discovered evidence of the earliest solidifying of matter – the beginning of the universe – in the form of 'whispy ripples of matter'. The latter finding convinced a majority of scientists that the Big Bang was no longer theory, but fact.

A point often made by those who accept that the Big Bang happened is the extreme delicacy of the balance in the substances and forces it produced that are required both to hold the universe together and to allow for development conducive to life. John Barrow and Frank Tipler, for example, write that 'most perturbations of the fundamental constants of nature away from their actual numerical values lead to model worlds that are still-born, unable to generate observers and become cognisable. Usually, they allow neither nuclei, atoms nor stars to exist.' As an illustration, they cite a simple system consisting of deuterium (a proton, a neutron and an electron) and diproton (two protons), whose existence 'hinge precariously on the precise strength of the nuclear force.' They continue, 'If the strong interaction were a little stronger the diproton would be a stable bound state with catastrophic consequences – all the hydrogen in the Universe would have burnt to diproton during the early stages of the Big Bang and no hydrogen or long-lived stable stars would exist today.... If the nuclear force were a little weaker ... elements heavier than hydrogen would not form.'[2] The physicist Paul Davies speaks of 'an almost unbelievable delicacy in the balance between gravity and electromagnetism within a star.' More generally, he concludes,

> The Big Bang was not, evidently, any old bang, but an explosion of exquisitely arranged magnitude. In the traditional version of the Big Bang we are asked to accept not only that it happened, but that it happened in an exceedingly contrived fashion. The initial conditions had to be very special indeed ... It was a highly orchestrated explosion.[3]

To the average layman, of course, a question arises: what came before the Big Bang?

Many scientists simply dismiss the question. Professor John Wheeler, of the University of Texas, has said, 'It is a meaningless question. There was no 'before'. It is like asking what is north of the North Pole.'[4] (Bernard Levin's response to this bears repeating: 'It is a perfectly meaningful question, only Professor Wheeler doesn't know the answer. Nor do I, for that matter, but unlike him I can try to banish my own residuary doubts by speculating on the idea of the Creation, which, after all, does demand a Creator – a much more likely solution than Professor Wheeler's cop-out.')[5] Others are agnostic, like Wheeler, but more circumspect. British cosmologist Michael Rowan-Robinson, professor of astronomy at London University, has said, 'Time before the Big Bang is more or less unknowable, but I agree with Saint Augustine and with Stephen Hawking, that Time begins with the universe ... so there is no before.'[6] Others again are only too happy both to ask and answer the ultimate question. One such is Michio Kaku, professor of theoretical physics at the City University of New York, who writes,

> What happened before the Big Bang? ...A remarkable consensus has been developing recently around what is called 'quantum cosmology', in which scientists believe that a merger of quantum theory and Einstein's relativity may resolve these sticky theological questions.... In the beginning was Nothing. No space, no matter, no energy. But according to the quantum principle, even Nothing was unstable. Nothing began to decay; that is, it began to 'boil' with billions of tiny bubbles forming and expanding rapidly. Each bubble became an expanding universe. If this is true, then our universe is actually part of a much larger 'multiverse' of parallel universes, which is truly timeless.[7]

The cosmologist John Gribbin, co-biographer of Stephen Hawking, is probably representative of the majority of scientists, however. He asks,

> Did the universe really appear as a singularity bursting out from nothing at all? Or was there a previous cycle in which that singularity was created by the collapse of an earlier phase of the universe into a black hole? Will the universe expand for ever, or will it one day recollapse, forming a new singularity out of which a new universe might burst?[8]

He gives no answers, but merely concludes, 'With the Big Bang theory itself on a secure foundation, it is questions like those that now provide scope for cosmological speculation.' 'Speculation' is the right word for it. These varied statements, given in response to news that the 'Big Bang' was, apparently, a proven reality, bespeak much remaining uncertainty about the universe.

There are, as we have seen, those who still reject the Big Bang theory. Alternative explanations have been given for the phenomena of Red Shift and Cosmic Background Radiation that constitute its foundation. These include a shrinking universe (the 'Big Crunch'), the 'tired light' theory, weakening of gravity, spectral non-invariance, photon interactions, transverse Doppler Effect, decreasing speed of light, interaction of light with intergalactic dust, cosmic dust heating. More significant, perhaps, is the fact that the explosion of matter represented by the Big Bang would of itself – it is reasonable to suppose – have produced chaos not order, and this scarcely seems compatible with the Second Law of thermodynamics, which requires that the universe began in a condition of low entropy (high organisation). 'The Big Bang', writes Sir John Maddox, 'is an over simple view of how the universe began ...In all respects, save that of convenience, it is thoroughly unsatisfactory. It is an effect whose cause cannot be identified or even discussed.'[9]

The question, 'What came before the Big Bang?' is, of course, a disguised version of the question, 'What caused the Big Bang?' As the above writer points out, overt discussion of such cause is frowned on in most scientific circles. Defenders of the Big Bang theory tend to argue that the question is meaningless, as we have seen. Others, like Michio Kaku, are happy to discuss what amounts to a cause, yet in so doing they resort to largely meaningless assertions. The dictates of quantum theory may defy common logic, but it is linguistic nonsense, when you want to convey that something happened, to make the word 'Nothing' the subject of 'was unstable', or 'began to decay', or 'began to "boil"'. When people say, 'Nothing happened', we know perfectly well what they mean. Kaku defines his 'Nothing' as 'no net energy', because 'the positive energy found in matter is balanced against the negative energy of gravity', so that 'universes can literally spring from existence as a quantum fluctuation of Nothing', but this takes us no further. The phrase 'quantum fluctuation of Nothing' is semantically identical to 'no quantum fluctuation'. Of course, what Professor Kaku actually wants is to have his cake and eat it; this is shown by his use of the capital 'N'. His 'Nothing' is special; it can do things, even create universes; it is most definitely 'Something'. Yet by using the word 'nothing', which we all understand to mean non-activity or non-existence, Kaku is able to give the impression that there simultaneously was and was not a cause for the Big Bang; that is to say, non-activity or non-existence caused activity or existence. Quantum theory, he claims, demonstrates the truth of this contradiction in terms.

Not that Michio Kaku is alone in talking in riddles about the origin of the universe. 'Quantum theory is deeply implicated in the modern explanation of the Big Bang,' writes Max Wilkinson. 'One of the things it says is that empty space is not empty at all, but seething with particles popping into and out of existence in a tiny fraction of a second.'[10] Professor Carlo Rubbia, who prefers the term 'vacuum' to Kaku's 'Nothing' or Wilkinson's 'empty space', goes further, seemingly imbuing the state of nothingness with a form of intelligence: 'Contained within the vacuum is knowledge about all possible particles which can exist ...It is possible that the Big Bang occurred when the vacuum somehow "decided" to realise this potential.'[11]

On the basis of Einstein's theory, which postulates that both time and space only began to exist when matter began to exist, it is of course logical to say that nothing came before the Big Bang because only then did time begin. In the words of Professor Rowan-Robinson, there was 'no before'. The universe is a closed system, cosmologists tell us, which means it contains its own time; we can perhaps picture it as a disc, with time being the circumference. It is therefore meaningless to look for any of our own universe's time outside our universe. But is this the same as saying there is *nothing* outside it? The prevalence of theories about parallel universes – each presumably with its own matter, space and time – suggests otherwise. To go a step further, if our system is totally closed, does this mean we can only look for causes inside it, including its own cause? If so, it must have caused itself to come into being, which is really to say it had no cause? Can we not – must we not – when trying to find a cause for the very existence of this closed system look outside it? That is what we are doing when we posit God as the cause.

A greater logic

In Christian understanding, God is by definition outside our system; he is beyond matter and space (spiritual), and beyond time (eternal). He alone, therefore, has no need of a cause. People sometimes complain that the Argument from First Cause (for God's existence) is invalid because it does not explain what caused God. It is, they say, self-defeating. So it is, in terms of our closed system, in terms of the universe we know. But the whole point of postulating God as First Cause is to get round the problem of infinitely regressing causes by resorting to an original uncaused Cause.

Eminent scientists, as we know, are often prepared to talk of God as a reality, or at least as a genuine possibility. Arnold Wolfendale, for example, late Astronomer Royal, when commenting on the 1992 announcement of the new evidence for the Big Bang from the Cobe satellite, wrote, 'I see nothing to militate against the existence of God in any of the work that has been done; the reverse, perhaps.'[12] Others, like Albert Einstein and Stephen Hawking, readily use the name 'God', though it is not clear whether in so doing they mean what Christians and most other theists mean: a supernaturally existent Person, Eternal, Omniscient, Omnipotent. It often seems that they only mean a grand Principle underlying the universe, a Principle they seek to define in a Theory of Everything.

God, being by definition supernatural, is also by definition beyond proof in natural, or human, terms. But if the existence of God cannot be demonstrated (though by the same token it cannot be falsified) this does not mean that his existence is without pointers. There are paradoxes in life which demand explanation and if human logic cannot cope with them it is reasonable to conclude that a greater logic exists somewhere, based on data beyond our reach, that does explain them. Theists have in recent years been wont to cite the findings of quantum mechanics as evidence for the reality of this 'greater logic', this supernatural dimension, this parallel universe.

The mathematical theory of quantum mechanics, first put forward by Max Planck in 1900, describes a huge variety of empirical observations with precision and without anomaly. In simple terms, the theory proposes that energy travels in separate pieces, or *quanta*, and not in continuous form. In 1905, Einstein contributed the *photon*, a particle of light. He argued that light could act as a stream of particles as well as waves. In 1924, Louis de Broglie applied this wave-particle duality to electrons, with Erwin Schrödinger two years later developing an electron wave equation, similar to those of James Clerk Maxwell for light. The old idea of matter made up of solid particles, absorbing and emitting energy in continuous waves, had been replaced by a new physics that saw particles as waves and waves as particles.

The 'two-slit experiment' tells us something of how these quantum ideas arose. When a light source like an electric bulb is placed before a screen with two slits, a detector screen behind them will show an alternating set of bands of light and shade (interference fringes), resulting from the waves through the slits alternately reinforcing and cancelling each other out. This implies that light acts as waves; in corpuscular terms, it would mean that single particles of light were travelling through both slits at the same time. A similar experiment can be carried out with electrons. Electrons appear to behave like waves, interfering with each other in the manner of light waves, as they go through two small holes in the first screen, coalescing into particles when they hit the second detector screen. When electrons are fired one at a time at this apparatus, each one surprisingly behaves like a wave as well, 'interfering with itself', appearing to travel through both holes simultaneously. But this is not all. If additional detectors are placed to confirm the finding, it appears that each electron goes through one slit or the other, and when large numbers of electrons are fired together at the same apparatus, they also no longer behave like waves, but as particles. This strange behaviour has two possible implications: firstly, nothing 'solid' exists; secondly, the observer cannot be separated from the observed (observation of electrons appears to change their behaviour). Should we therefore accept that we cannot observe anything without changing it? Are we to conclude that we can never be sure what is happening? At the sub-atomic level, at least, it appears that we can talk about no more than probabilities. Werner Heisenberg, who said it is impossible simultaneously to assign to a particle both its position in space and its motion, implied exactly this with his 'uncertainty principle'.

The basic validity of quantum mechanics no one now disputes, though it took some years for Planck's work to be recognised. On the other hand, it has certain metaphysical characteristics that have not been fully explored, let alone agreed upon.

I have already referred to the notion of parallel universes, which Michio Kaku and others consider an implication of quantum theory. David Deutsch, professor of physics and an authority on quantum theory, is one of those others. He believes the idea of parallel universes provides a resolution to the basic paradox posed by quantum theory: observable physical quantities take discrete values, yet motion and change are continuous. (The 'bouncing ball conundrum', a version of Zeno's 'ad infinitum' paradox, is in some ways similar: how does a ball ever stop bouncing if each bounce is half as high as the last.) He writes,

> Within each universe all observable quantities are discrete, but the multiverse as a whole is a continuum. When the equations of quantum theory describe a continuous but not-directly observable transition

between two values of a discrete quantity, what they are really telling us is that the transition does not take place entirely within one universe. So perhaps the price of continuous motion is not an infinity of consecutive actions, but an infinity of concurrent actions taking place across the multiverse.[13]

There are other metaphysical interpretations of quantum theory. In 1952, David Bohm proposed that quantum effects were produced below levels of observation. While no evidence has been found for such sub-quantum forces, experiments predict that his theory must involve instantaneous connections across the universe. This suggests, contrary to human intuition, that everything is connected to everything else and is not reducible to parts.[14]

We do not, however, have to appeal to quantum theory if we want to find paradoxes; reasoning man has from the beginning been faced with the paradox inherent in the idea of infinity, whether of space or time. To put it simply, however far you go in space or time there must always be a 'beyond' – yet how can this 'beyond' go on forever? It is sometimes put less simply, though no less 'illogically', as by Adrian Berry, 'The universe is believed to have a definite edge, beyond which lies the same "nothingness" that originally characterised all. No spaceship could ever go there – any more than a traveller could go to Ruritania – because no such place exists.'[15]

Einstein refines the infinity paradox, but does not remove it. His ideas on gravity, described in his General Theory of Relativity, may indicate that mass can distort space-time, so that space and time are 'curved', and observation (like Eddington's measurement of the path of light from a star during an eclipse) may confirm some of his predictions, but his conclusions remain paradoxical. To dispense with the concept of infinite space or infinite time by postulating a closed or circular universe, as he does, may be demonstrable through mathematical equations, and even partially through scientific observation, but to human intelligence it seems little more than 'playing with words'. The average person has to ask, 'What is outside this circular universe?' – a meaningless question, no doubt, to Einstein the mathematician and those who understand his equations, as meaningless as the question, 'What came before the Big Bang?', but in no way meaningless to 'common sense'. Einstein's ideas become, if anything, even more difficult to conceive when we are told that the 'curved' trajectory produced by the effect of gravity from mass – as, for example, the path of starlight round the sun – is in reality a straight line, or the shortest path between two points, in curved space-time.[16]

In verbal contradiction, if no more, of Einstein's requirement that space-time is 'curved', is the requirement of an expanding universe (predicted by Einstein, let us recall) that space is 'flat' – a fact confirmed, most would say, by recent evidence that the Big Bang truly occurred. This idea of 'flatness' means that the early universe contained precisely the right amount of matter, so that, on the one hand, the pull of gravity was not too great, leading to the collapse of stars and galaxies into a 'big crunch', and, on the other, it was not too weak, resulting in the failure of primordial matter to condense into stars and galaxies. In a 'flat' universe, the process of expansion and star formation continues unimpeded along 'straight lines', instead of eventually 'falling back' somewhat like a display rocket. We have already referred to the extreme delicacy of the balance required for the Big Bang to be successful; despite this requirement, the giant explosion probably occurred. Alan Guth, in 1980, sought to explain how the achievement of the correct balance was not just a colossal fluke – or divine intervention – with his Grand Unified Theory, combining three elemental forces, previously considered separate, which may have amalgamated in the primordial furnace. This made the 'flatness' problem' seem less coincidental, but 'the theory is imperfect and the search continues'.[17] Such theories, perfect or imperfect, will come and go, but they are in any case of limited help to ordinary human intelligence, which finds it difficult to comprehend how space can meaningfully be considered both 'curved' and 'flat'.

We live with paradoxes and accept them as statements of truth because we have to, because, like Everest, they are there. The idea of God is also a paradox. Do we for this reason reject it?

Vacuous musings?

Many people today, especially scientists, dismiss God because they believe man has 'come of age', because science can now provide all the answers. Peter Atkins, professor of chemistry at Oxford University, is a notable example. Reviewing a book on the hoary old question of the relationship of science to religion, he concludes,

> This book is a testament to the delusion of theologians that they are contributing something useful to our understanding of the world and that they have something useful to say about: its origin (they do not, that is the job of the cosmologists); its sometimes painful unfolding (ditto, that is for evolutionary biologists); and its purpose (there isn't one). How much easier it is to accept the stark, clear-sighted view of right-thinking

individuals who see there is neither evidence nor need for God and that all the suggested answers in this book are but vacuous musings.[18]

The reader will decide whether Professor Atkins' verdict is well conceived; meanwhile, it is true that science has placed in man's hands an immense amount of data, on the nature of the universe and more generally about life. It is also true that as a result of computerisation this information can be processed and made accessible to all. The claim that man can now solve every problem, cross every horizon, conquer every enemy – death itself, perhaps – has apparent credibility. When we add to this the harm and suffering undeniably perpetrated in the name of religion, even in the name of Christ, it is hardly surprising that people have ruled out the very idea of God, let alone the call to worship him. Thus we find one polemic against the faith of Christ entitled *The Misery of Christianity*,[19] while a long and detailed chapter of Ludovic Kennedy's book *All in the Mind: A Farewell to God* (written, as he says on the fly-leaf, 'For Doubters Everywhere') is headed 'Christianity's Killing Fields'.[20] These authors, and many others, make much of the poor humanitarian record of religion – especially of the Church – as they mount their case against God.

But is religion, or even the institutional Church, much to do with God? My aim in Part III of this book will be to look in detail at a *person* – not a religion or church – whose message about life and about God continues to have universal appeal. I shall consider how much we can know about Jesus of Nazareth, then look at his life, his claims, his teaching. Before doing this, however, I will consider a rather different question.

What is sauce for the goose, they say, is sauce for the gander. Religion, the cry goes up, has done us no good. As for God, if he is not actually dead, he is either impotent or unfeeling; whichever way it is, he too has done us no good. Yet is today's science-driven world so very enlightened – a place of nobility, of peace, of joy? Put differently, are we, with our many scientific achievements, progressing in *wisdom*?

Chapter 7
Information, Information, Information

What name or epithet will best characterize the twenty-first century?

Fifty years ago everyone believed the third millennium would usher in a period of spectacular space travel. That grand endeavour has encountered problems, however, and after a tremendous spurt in the 1950s and 60s has progressed more slowly than expected. The unravelling of the human genetic code has led others, like Arthur C. Clarke, to suggest that the great new breakthroughs will come in genetic engineering and genetic-based medicine; mankind, Clarke believes, will develop techniques for living much longer – perhaps for ever. Yet despite the strides already made in this direction, a question mark hovers over the prospect of further major development. What may slow down achievement in this field is doubts about its morality. Humanity has a proven inability to cope ethically, or even practically, with quantum leaps forward in the sciences – nuclear power being a prime example. So we must look elsewhere for the overriding trend of the twenty-first century. Pope John Paul II, in seeking a suitable epithet, once cited André Malraux's dictum: 'The twenty-first century will be the century of religion or it will not be at all.'[1] Yet though religion (of an aggressive type) has revived in recent years, it is not the most prominent feature of the current era.

Knowledge of a kind

Bill Gates has said he wants a computer in every home worldwide; Tony Blair wants one on every pupil's desk in Britain. Why? To access information. The most dramatic – even astonishing – developments in recent years have been in the realm of communications: virtually anywhere you happen to be in the world today you can have access at the touch of a button to some personal or electronic source able to apprise you of almost anything knowable about anything – news, fact, opinion.

Our new century, surely, is par excellence the age of instant, universally accessible information.

Not that the Internet, or any other new communication superhighway, has initiated this age of information. We have been building up to it for a long time, the biggest previous step forward probably being the invention of printing in 1454 by Johann Gutenberg. More recently have come photography, the telegraph, the telephone (including, now, the mobile), the cinematograph, radio and television, each of which has added greatly to the swift dispersal of information. Indeed, it could be argued that the *twentieth* century represented the era of information, though less flattering titles are usually given it. But it is the Internet, capable of instantly transmitting vast amounts of data, including sound and moving pictures, that has catapulted us into what is essentially a new epoch.

'The Internet is ... a network without frontiers, without laws and with no one there to say that you cannot say that or you must not say this. Suddenly, governments are waking up to the realization that this is an information highway without any way to police its users.' So declared Dr Roger Burrows at the conference *The Governance of Cyberspace*, held at the Teesside University in April 1995, when the phenomenal growth in the number of users was becoming apparent. The Internet, he was telling us, had given individuals for the first time untrammelled freedom to forward to or receive from any quarter of the globe whatever kind of 'information' they desired.

Such information is not always savoury. Those attending the above conference were warned that among other things the new superhighway represented an unprecedented possibility for both propagating racism and allowing racists to access each other's ideas and resources. The fearful potential of the Internet in this direction was underlined when it was learned that the two Nazi-obsessed teenagers responsible for the Denver school massacre of 20 April 1999 (anniversary of Hitler's birthday) in Colorado, USA, had fed their violent fantasies via the Internet. And it is worth recalling that construction details of the bomb that destroyed the federal building in Oklahoma City on 19 April 1995, when 168 people lost their lives, were published on computer networks. Today's neo-Nazis, meanwhile, communicate on the Internet through an encryption system known as PGP ('Pretty Good Privacy'), the individual codes of which are extremely hard to crack.

The dissemination of pornography is another unpleasant use to which the Internet is put. Governments, police bodies like Interpol, social and religious organizations across the spectrum are wrestling with problems created by the fact that the Internet has become a heavily patronized red-light district, piping soft and hard porn into millions of homes worldwide. An early survey of a commonly utilized 'research engine' revealed that half the searches being made were aimed at locating pornography.[2] Particularly disturbing is the fact that international paedophile rings and child pornographers are known to make contact through the Internet using the PGP programme.

Of course, information dispersed through the Internet can focus on more wholesome matters. Edifying facts of history and life, inspiring tales of courage, ennobling literature and magnificent works of art, truths of science, philosophy and divinity are all available for those who want them. The 'net' is only the medium, morally neutral. The same is true of other mediums of communication – books, newspapers and journals, the telephone, the radio, television. It is the message that counts, not the means. Yet we all know that the media exhibit, in what they report, a 'bias to the bad'. The reason is simple: good news, which often simply amounts to a maintenance of the status quo, is not often salable news. We have only to scan our daily newspaper, or listen to any gossiping couple, to realise the truth of this. For some reason people like hearing and reading of war, disaster, tragedy, cruelty, crime, lust. And so, understandably in a way, the news we receive – and give – mostly concerns humanity's darker side.

This being so, the fact that bad news, provocative news, news of social unrest (quarrels, protests, defiance, insurrection) is now transmitted across the globe at the touch of a button, every problem instantly becomes a world problem. Nothing can now be contained, nothing can be restricted to a single locality, as was the case a couple of centuries ago when news travelled more slowly. Instant worldwide communication means instant worldwide reaction, and instant reaction is usually wrongheaded.

But this is being too negative, it may be argued. Why dwell on the bleaker features of the Internet revolution when there are so many benefits? Today, whether we like it or not, we live in an age of information technology, an age of instant access to data on every conceivable topic. Even if we wanted to, we can't put the clock back.

Which certainly rejoices the hearts of such as Bill Gates and Tony Blair. For to them and many others the more information is disseminated the happier and better people will be. The enemy of man, they seem to assume, is ignorance; the remedy to his ills is education, and that means more and more accessible data. If only people are *informed* about life in its beauty and fullness, *informed* about the wonders of modern scientific discovery, *informed* about the harm done by antisocial behaviour, *informed* about what is happening and, more importantly, what should happen in the world at large, they will come to their senses. They will start co-operating; they will stop killing, start loving. So the argument runs – and so it runs falsely.

Even if it were true that ignorance lay behind 'man's inhumanity to man', and that the remedy were the dispelling of that ignorance, what we have now – thanks to the Internet, especially – is an avalanche of information so immense that it is very difficult to assimilate, sift and interpret what is put before you. Eat too much food and you get indigestion; go on cramming food into your mouth and you choke. Too much information, like too much food, is harmful, counter-productive. To come to a sane conclusion about something, to create a good argument, to write a good speech, article or book, you need enough relevant information but only enough. Have too much data and – even with rigorous categorization (so often specious), even with the help of a computer (if the data is computer-compatible) – you become swamped. Susan Greenfield, professor of pharmacology at Oxford University and an authority on the human brain, says that 'information overload' is a problem of our time.[3]

'To come to a sane conclusion', I have said. The 'sane conclusion' is, of course, what matters, not the information that made a conclusion possible. And coming to a sane conclusion is not guaranteed even if you have a manageable amount of data and are intelligent. Other factors bear upon the issue, factors such as state of health, state of digestion, state of mind (happy, sad, contented, ambitious, frustrated, angry, resentful, vindictive), underlying personal circumstances.

Do people come to sane conclusions about the information they glean from the Internet? More pertinently, do they come to any conclusions? Let us consider more closely the uses to which the Internet is put.

We have already referred to some of the less edifying purposes for which the Internet is utilized – in one case extremely widely – by the public. At the other end of the spectrum are the millions who now use it for business, or 'e-commerce', including the buying and selling of shares. The type of information appropriate for this form of human activity is inevitably both limited and ephemeral, while opinions formed and conclusions reached are related only to the narrow field of money and the market-place.

What of your average computer buff? What lies behind his or her interest in accessing or, less often, imparting information through the Internet?

The motivation may be linked to pleasure derived from owning and mastering a sophisticated piece of electronic equipment. Beyond this, however, we find the avid user spending hour after hour – six, seven, eight, perhaps – clicking onto websites. Such 'browsing' does not spring from a wish to consider the weightier matters of life. Net specialists are not normally moved to think deeply about the snippets of information, endless facts and figures, unconnected items of news, beguiling travel opportunities they come across as they speed through cyberspace; on the contrary, the experience can induce a trance-like state, with viewers mesmerized by the range and variety of what they see and hear. Some become addicts, neglecting the real world of time and space as they explore this virtual world, inventing spurious cyber-personae for themselves and, in that guise, communicating with others similarly afflicted.

As noted above, the sheer volume of information currently available (not to speak of people's obsession with obtaining it) militates against reaching any conclusion, let alone a sane one. But in any case it is becoming unfashionable to have clearly defined views. We nowadays admire those who, having analysed a mass of data on some issue, sit primly on the fence. What matters is not having convictions but being well-informed, knowledgeable. And information technology certainly spreads knowledge.

Or does it? Information superhighways have imparted knowledge of a kind, what we might call head-knowledge; they have taught and can teach nothing in relation to heart-knowledge. The latter denotes understanding, which penetrates to the inner being of things, and it is clear that man's understanding of the deepest issues of life has not been improved by the current communications revolution; the plethora of facts available today on every conceivable topic tends rather to obfuscation.

Things fall apart

In February 2000, the Nigerian author Chinua Achebe was asked by the BBC to comment on the religious strife afflicting parts of his country, leading to hundreds of deaths and threatening to spark a new civil war. The response he made is instructive: 'Going out onto the streets with a machete is not the way to celebrate the twenty-first century. What we are witnessing is a loss of wisdom.' When asked what advice he could offer the authorities, he replied, 'The government must insist on law and order.'

'A loss of wisdom.' There has never been greater need for understanding, for *wisdom*. Professor Susan Greenfield, cited above, has made this point, stating that though we now possess vast amounts of information, 'we must be aware that knowledge, understanding, wisdom will not come from it'.[4] Her concern is that wisdom (with which she more or less equates knowledge and understanding) is not prized above information, as was once the case. She is surely right: the briefest glance round the world scene shows that wisdom is in drastically short supply.

Planet earth is threatened by forces – sometimes natural, but all too often man-made – that seem beyond his control. Of these, ethno-religious conflict is perhaps the most powerful and dangerous. The world is splitting asunder along ancient national, tribal or religious fault-lines. The poem by W. B. Yeats, *The Second Coming*, from which Achebe took the title of his best-known book,[5] depicts what is happening:

Turning and turning in the widening gyre
The falcon cannot hear the falconer;
Things fall apart; the centre cannot hold;
Mere anarchy is loosed upon the world,
The blood-dimmed tide is loosed, and everywhere
The ceremony of innocence is drowned;
The best lack all conviction, while the worst
Are full of passionate intensity.

Nigeria, of course, is but one of many countries where such a situation – incipient or actual civil war – appears to be normative. The international scene is even starker: as I write this, in August 2006, the Middle East has become a cauldron of such reckless, intractable violence that hope of any viable settlement has all but evaporated. Meanwhile, lawlessness of every complexion, whether representing terrorist or more traditional criminal activity, rises inexorably worldwide. Ugly incidents inspired by racial or religious hatred are endemic. Harrowing reports – in our newspapers, on the radio, on TV – assail us daily from every quarter: intimidation, beatings, barbarous mutilations, kidnappings, bombings, assassinations, murders, massacres, genocide.

What remedy is on offer? In the words of Achebe, 'the government must insist on law and order'. What else could he suggest for Nigeria, where action was imperative? But his response only reflects the attitude prevailing everywhere. 'They should do something' is the cry nowadays, whatever the problem. And where that problem involves criminal activity, let the solution be *imposed,* whatever the cost. Tighter government control appears the single option – except, perhaps, for 'better education'.

What, then, of education? It is at best a long-term solution, at worst no solution at all. If the root problem of violence and strife resides in a flawed human nature, education can scarcely be the answer. For human nature is 'unchanging', economic historian Graeme Snooks assures us,[6] so education *per se* will simply produce a cleverer breed of criminal. We are left, therefore, with our one strategy for dealing with human lawlessness: governmental action, a crackdown – or, in that chilling phrase, 'zero-tolerance'. With our jails running out of space for delinquents, we need no reminder of what this means.

Nigeria's problems of 2000 were more or less contained by government action, though similar outbreaks of unrest, needing similar action, have continued to occur in the country. What of the Middle East? What of the many other parts of the world characterized by hatred and violence? Who will impose 'solutions' in all these places? Hardly the USA. Spurred on by the events of '9/11', and gaining limited support from allies, the world's current superpower may have been prepared to play 'world policeman' in Afghanistan and Iraq (to what ultimate effect remains to be seen), but it is unrealistic to envisage her doing this on a permanent basis. Yet there is no other national or super-national entity – certainly not the European Union, nor the United Nations (unless developed and beefed up beyond recognition) – with the power or inclination to take on such a role.

Ethno-religious conflict is one uncontrollable force stalking the planet. A second, less spectacular yet in some ways as worrying, is economic turmoil.

Speaking to the US Congress on 15 September 1998, George Soros delivered this warning: 'The global capitalist system is coming apart at the seams.' The occasion for this apocalyptic assertion was a financial crisis in Russia. Soros described it as 'a complete meltdown ... frightening'. He was not alone in being concerned. President Clinton called for an economic summit to address 'the biggest challenge in half a century'. In *The Observer*, Will Hutton spoke of 'the risk of a world economic catastrophe ... growing by the day'. He declared,

> The importance of events in Russia is that they are taking the world financial system yet closer to the edge, and the system is now so structured that losses in one country are transmitted to another with the movements in financial prices vastly exaggerated by the speculative derivative markets.[7]

A further alarmed commentator was François Chesnais. Writing in *Le Monde diplomatique*, he saw the situation as recapitulating the 1930s, the financial crisis and global recession progressing simultaneously along three parallel, interdependent tracks. The first was deflation – the contraction in production, demand and trade, and the fall in prices – for which 'there is no known and easy remedy'. The second track was 'through the astronomical increase in bad debt, both public and private, held by the banking system'. He warned, 'When combined with political graft, the brutal spread of insolvency can bring the credit system to a halt, as in Indonesia and now in Russia.' The third track involved 'the close interconnectedness of the big stock markets and the transmission of funds from one to another by increasingly nervous investors'.[8]

As we know, the Russian economic crisis of 1998 constituted but a single feature of a wider scene of financial turbulence, namely, problems in Japan, then the sudden collapse of markets in Asia in the summer of 1997, this posing a serious threat to Latin America, where Brazil had to be rescued from financial collapse by a $41.5 billion loan package. We also know that by the summer of 1999 the economic situation in Russia had stabilized and that the Asian and Latin American economies had pulled back from the brink as world investors started buying back the stock they had previously off-loaded. What most people do not know is that a permanent descent into the economic abyss was on that occasion averted more by luck than judgement. As Ben Laurance wrote at the time in *The Guardian Weekly* in relation to the findings of the World Economic Forum held in Davos, Switzerland, in February 1999, 'There was no attempt to deny it: the world *is* facing an economic crisis …But that's where the consensus ended …There was absolutely no agreement about what might actually be done to deal with this crisis.'[9]

That nothing material was done became clear in the year 2000, when stock prices reached a peak with the Price/Earnings Ratio at its highest and most distorted on record – at which markets around the world collapsed, most dramatically in the technology field. Until late 2002 there was a classic 'bear market', with lower share prices and lower yields leading to tumbling interest rates and a huge increase in credit (especially in UK and USA). As a result of the latter two factors, however, something of a revival began in 2003. This lasted until May 2006, when investor nervousness returned and share prices again fell. The position seemed to stabilize, but very quickly analysts were advising that the three-year pick-up had been no more than a 'classic countertrend bear market rally', and that this had now run its course. They announced a 'return of the bear', warning that leading economic indicators were as negative as in the year 2000, and that falling share prices would on this occasion be against the backcloth of high consumer and corporate debt, so that recession could not again (as after the 2000 crash) be rescued by credit. They further referred to heightening tension in the Middle East, leading to record-level oil prices, which in itself created a negative environment for equities.[10]

Whatever the exact state of world markets today, heady talk of a 'new economic paradigm' is a thing of the past, with investor uncertainty caused by volatile markets fuelled further by currency fluctuation – the dollar first having soared, then plummeted, against the new euro. Financial turmoil is indeed a feature of our age.

Relative living standards is at the heart of today's economic problems. In September 1998, in its annual Human Development Report, the United Nations called for urgent action to raise the living standards of the world's poor. Gross inequalities were worsening, the Report said, with 20% of the global population accounting for 86% of consumption. Addressing the same theme, the economist Lester Thurow has argued that the West may be on the brink of a new Dark Age. In his book *The Future of Capitalism: How Today's Economic Forces Shape Tomorrow's World,*[11] he points out that past societies which have existed successfully with inequality were undemocratic: democracy and inequality just do not mix. This, he says, has been recognized in the West for the past two centuries, with governments seeking to reduce inequality. Now, with income inequality greater than at any time since records began, there are disturbing signs of social collapse.

Martin Van Crefeld argued in his book *On Future War* in 1991[12] that the Cold War was the world's last good time, when superpowers collaborated in forcing rogue rulers to come to heel and cracked down on terrorist movements that did not serve their interests. He predicted that state authority would atrophy as power passed from elected governments to the robber barons of drugs, computer banking fraud, religious fanaticism, extreme nationalism, or various forms of political crankiness. The social, political and economic turmoil we are witnessing in so many parts of the world today confirms, in many respects, the truth of that prediction. Far from being on the verge of a golden age of peace and prosperity, as some were suggesting only a few years ago, the world has seldom been so fragmented and unstable.

'Where shall wisdom be found?'

It is precisely this global fragility that has moved politicians in Europe and to some extent elsewhere (South-East Asia, for example) to push, often in the teeth of strong popular feeling, for confederation in some form. As the world fragments at the popular level, so leaders feel constrained to glue it together again at the political level. At the micro-level we have disintegration; at the macro-level integration, with each process encouraging the other.

Efforts made by world leaders towards confederation, towards integration, bespeak deep prevailing uncertainty. Ethno-religious conflict and market turmoil are just two among many global problems that confound those seeking answers, impelling them towards an overarching, one-world, imposed solution. Yet such a strategy is an admission of failure; it is a recognition that people in general are incapable of sorting out their own affairs and living and working together in harmony. The scientific fraternity, meanwhile, stands impotent in the face of this social fragmentation, its 'bright new world' a shattered dream.

'Where shall wisdom be found, and where is the place of understanding?'[13] Job's question echoes down the centuries.

Where today is the wisdom to curb mankind's folly, to cure greed, to check crime, to halt spoliation of the planet, to pacify fighting factions, to calm turbulent markets? We have information in super-abundance; there are hundreds – thousands – of informed specialists in every field; yet we remain incapable of solving problems we ourselves have created. To all this there appears to be a single 'solution', the one we have already noted – imposition of 'law and order' by Draconian government.

But what government? State authority will atrophy, Van Crefeld said in 1991. Four years later, at a News Corporation conference in Australia, Tony Blair explained how this was happening:

> Globalisation is changing the nature of the nation-state as power becomes more diffuse and borders more porous. Technological change is reducing the power of government to control its domestic economy free from external influence. Free movement of currency means free movement of capital, which seeks the highest return possible.

Philip Bobbitt, in his book *The Shield of Achilles*, has gone further. He says that the nation-state will be replaced by a 'market-state', dependent on 'the international capital markets and, to a lesser degree, on the modern multinational business network to create stability in the world economy'.[14]

Blair and Bobbitt argue in the context of economics, but as we know it is economics – more crudely, *money* – that largely if not entirely drives political agendas; economics is, in fact, simply an aspect of politics, probably the most important. The point the two are making, illustrated further by Mr Blair's penchant for the term 'world community', is that we live in an era of global inter-connectedness at all levels, so our problems – whether economic/political, social, religious – ultimately need global solutions. They are surely right. Which means that the 'Draconian government' will have to be global. The creation of a powerful, undemocratic, supranational authority, a kind of world government, cannot be far away.

Man in some representative form, proud and imperious, may one day achieve the worldwide dominion he aspires to. Science will be his handmaid, money his god, religion his creation, his conceit, his tool. Much knowledge, of a kind, he will possess; wisdom he will have forfeited; his soul – Life itself – he will irretrievably have lost.

T.S. Eliot had words for it:

Endless invention, endless experiment
Brings knowledge of motion, but not of stillness;
Knowledge of speech, but not of silence;
Knowledge of words, but not of the Word.
Where is the Life we have lost in living?
Where is the wisdom we have lost in knowledge?
Where is the knowledge we have lost in information?[15]

PART III: THE WORD

Chapter 8
Foundations

The 'Logos'

The ancient people of Mesopotamia celebrated their supreme God in terms of his absolute word of command: 'O Anu! Thy great command takes precedence, who could say no? O father of the gods, thy command, the very foundation of the heaven and earth, what god could spurn?' So too, centuries later, when they elevated the lesser god Marduk to a position of pre-eminence, they declared, 'Thy word is Anu.' That word, identified with Anu himself, cannot be disobeyed or countermanded; it underlies natural existence and order:

> Anu is the source of and active principle in all authority, both in human society and in the larger society which is the universe. He is the force which lifts it out of chaos and anarchy and makes it into a structure, an organised whole ... As a building is supported by, and reveals in its structure the lines of, its foundation, so the Mesopotamian universe is upheld by, and reflects in *its* structure, a divine will.[1]

What was true for Anu of the Mesopotamians was true also – as we learnt from the Memphite Theology (the oldest Egyptian text) – for Ptah, supreme God of the Egyptians: 'Great and mighty is Ptah ... It has come to pass that the heart and tongue control every member by teaching that he [Ptah] is throughout every body and throughout every mouth, of all gods, of all men, of animals, of all creeping things, and of what lives, by thinking and commanding anything that he wishes.' This, it has been said, is 'a creation in philosophical terms: the thought which came into the heart of a god and the commanding utterance which brought that thought into reality'.[2] Yet Ptah is not the Creator in a direct sense; in Egyptian tradition the 'creator-god' is Atum. But it is from Ptah, the Memphite Theology tells us, that Atum draws his being: 'Ptah, the Great One; he is the heart and tongue of the Ennead of gods ... There came into being in the heart, and there came into being on the tongue [something] in the form of Atum.' Atum here is not so much the creation of Ptah as a force or power proceeding from his mouth, his efficacious, creative speech.

111

The Hebrew concept of wisdom is similar. Job's question as to where it can be found, recorded in the Old Testament book bearing his name, is answered in the book of Proverbs:

> Does not wisdom call, does not understanding raise her voice? ... When he established the heavens, I was there, when he drew a circle on the face of the deep, when he made firm the skies above, when he established the fountains of the deep, when he assigned to the sea its limit, so that the waters might not transgress his command, when he marked out the foundations of the earth, then I was beside him, like a master workman.[3]

The Greek philosopher Heraclitus of Ephesus, living in the sixth century before our era, spoke of a 'Logos [or 'Word'] shared by all', to whom all men should hearken.[4] The early pagan sage Orpheus referred to 'the Logos divine ... the world's great ruler, our immortal king.'[5] Hermes Trismegistus described the Logos emerging from the oneness of God like a word or thought – the first thought of the Mind of God, through which he creates the universe. This Logos is, indeed, no less than 'the Son of God'.[6]

The opening verses of the gospel of John, in the New Testament, run as follows:

> In the beginning was the Word [*logos*], and the Word was with God, and the Word was God. He was in the beginning with God; all things were made through him, and without him was not anything made that was made. In him was life, and the life was the light of men. The light shines in the darkness, and the darkness has not overcome it.... And the Word became flesh and dwelt among us, full of grace and truth; we have beheld his glory, glory as of the only Son from the Father.[7]

What the Mesopotamians and Egyptians dimly perceived in the command of Anu and the speech of Ptah, what Job and the later Hebrews descried in the concept of divine wisdom, what the Greeks seemed to recognise in their philosophical principle of Logos or Reason, was declared by John the evangelist to have taken flesh in a particular man, in a particular place, at a particular time. That man was Jesus of Nazareth. It is an extraordinary – even ridiculous – claim.

Extraordinary or not, Jesus himself made claims that amounted to an assertion of divinity, as we have seen. Which raises a crucial question: Do the accounts of his life and teaching in the New Testament constitute a reliable record? In other words, did he truly make these claims, or were they – as many have argued – fabricated by the writers of the documents long after the events they describe?

I shall now turn to the sources underlying Christian teaching, looking first at some non-Christian documents, then considering the New Testament. I shall begin with Jewish sources.

Early Jewish sources

As we have noted, a new Jewish Sanhedrin, or Council, composed of doctors of the law, or rabbis, was constituted on a spiritual basis following the destruction of Jerusalem in 70 AD. The main function of this body was the organisation of religious law, a task which represented a first step towards codifying the 'Tradition of the Elders', the long accumulation of oral law. At the beginning of the second century, Rabbi Akiba began arranging codified tradition according to subject-matter, and following his death in 135 his disciple Rabbi Meir both revised what he had done and carried the work further. The work was completed by Rabbi Judah at the end of the second century and for the first time committed to writing (in Hebrew); it was referred to as Mishnah. A body of 'commentary', known as Gemara (in Aramaic), grew up around this code of religious jurisprudence in the rabbinical schools of Palestine and Babylonia, and this taken together with Mishnah was known as Talmud. The Palestinian or Jerusalem Talmud was completed in the fourth century and the Babylonian around 500 AD.

The Babylonian Talmud includes this entry: 'They hanged Jesus of Nazareth on the Eve of Passover because he practised sorcery and was leading Israel astray.'[8] It is a most interesting statement, not least because the reference to sorcery corresponds to the charge made against Jesus by contemporary Jewish leaders (as the New Testament records) of having performed miraculous signs through Satanic power.[9] There is no attempt here to contest the reality of such miracles; we have, rather, implicit testimony to the fact that these events occurred. But can we assume the integrity of this source? Can we trust a witness whose testimony was for many years transmitted orally? The answer is, 'Yes.' Oral tradition of this nature is extremely reliable – quite as reliable as written tradition, which depends on copying by scribes, who may be unfamiliar with the text they are working on. Such mechanical copying is susceptible to error induced by ignorance, tiredness, and even prejudice. The accuracy of oral tradition springs from the fact that the words involved are learnt by heart, and –

as anyone will know who as a child has committed to memory mathematical tables or nursery rhymes – you do not alter the content of what you have learnt in this way. If you remember it at all (and you usually do), you remember it accurately.

There are other Talmudic references to Jesus, or, in its original form, *Yeshu'a* (*Yeshu*) – a shortened form of the name *Yehoshu'a* (Joshua), adapted to *Iesous* (Jesus) in Greek. Some have argued that another person of that name is being denoted,[10] since 'Jesus' is a common name among first century Jews. This is unlikely, however, since the contexts in which the name is found are appropriate for the identification with Jesus of Nazareth. One entry has it that a rabbi 'was walking on the upper street of Sepphoris, and found one of the disciples of Yeshu the Nazarene'. Another entry reads, 'Our rabbis taught: Yeshu had five disciples – Mattai, Nakkia, Netzer, Buni, and Todah'. Yet another tells us that 'Rabbi Elazar ben Damah' was bit by a serpent and 'Jacob, a man of Kefar Soma, came to help him in the name of Yeshu ben Pantera'. The 'ben Pantera' is puzzling until we learn from the Jewish scholar Joseph Klausner (and others) that it is probably a corruption of the Greek *parthenos* ('virgin').[11] There is also the appellation Ha-Taluy, 'The Hanged One', which refers to Jesus, apparently, by the manner of his death. All in all, a fairly rounded picture of Jesus (from the point of view of orthodox Judaism) can be built up: he was a Nazarene teacher, whose followers healed in his name, but though he claimed to uphold the Law he was of questionable background, practised the black arts, led the people astray and was in consequence put to death at Passover-time. The outline given coincides with the New Testament account; furthermore, Klausner identifies other less obvious references to Jesus, as well as to early Jewish Christianity.

It is likely that Jesus is referred to obliquely in a Talmudic account of a discussion of a verse from the book of Daniel containing the words 'thrones were placed and one that was ancient of days took his seat'.[12] An early rabbinical school of thought held that the plural 'thrones' was used because, besides the throne placed for the 'Ancient of Days' (God), a second throne was placed for 'one like a son of man'. This figure is mentioned a few verses later in Daniel, 'Behold, with the clouds of heaven there came one like a son of man, and he came to the Ancient of Days and was presented before him'.[13] In the rabbinical discussion, Rabbi Akiba (see above) seems to have taken the view of the school of thought already mentioned: while one throne was indeed for the Ancient of Days, there was also, he suggested, 'one for David' – that is, for David's greater Son, Israel's Messiah. At which, we read, the other rabbis in the Council angrily protested, 'How long will you profane the divine glory, Akiba?'

Why was Rabbi Akiba so vehemently opposed? There is an obvious answer. This was the very passage of scripture to which Jesus referred in his reply to the High priest at his trial before the Sanhedrin. Having confessed that he was Messiah, 'the Son of the Blessed', he added, 'And you will see the Son of man sitting at the right hand of Power, and coming with the clouds of heaven.'[14] Jesus regularly used the title 'Son of man' to describe himself, as we have seen.[15] With these words, therefore, he was claiming a throne for himself, set alongside that of God. The view expressed by Akiba in the Council, though time-honoured, was no longer acceptable because it was an interpretation that would lend credence to the claim made by Jesus – as also, no doubt, made on his behalf by Christians living in Akiba's time. When Jesus had said the above, let us recall, 'the high priest tore his mantle, and said, "Why do we still need witnesses? You have heard his blasphemy. What is your decision?" And they all condemned him as deserving death.'[16] In view of this background, and in particular the Council's sentence of death upon Jesus for his 'blasphemy', the reaction of the rabbis as a whole to Akiba's interpretation is understandable.

Another interesting Talmudic entry concerns the extent of civil power granted by the Roman authorities to the Jewish Sanhedrin at the time of Jesus. Both the Babylonian and Jerusalem Talmud state that this Council of religious leaders had no authority to administer capital punishment, a statement that accords with the testimony of the writer of the fourth gospel.[17]

One other passage from the Talmud is worthy of note for its probable bearing upon early Christian history. According to the Talmud, the first century Rabbi Gamaliel, the greatest Jewish teacher of his day, had among his disciples one who displayed 'impudence in matters of learning'. The name of this recalcitrant student is not given; he is simply remembered as 'that pupil'.[18] Could this be a veiled reference to Saul of Tarsus – or Paul, in the English version of his Roman *cognomen*, Paullus? The apostle was, in his own words, 'brought up in this city [Jerusalem] at the feet of Gamaliel, educated according to the strict manner of the law of our fathers'.[19] The identification with Paul is likely, Klausner argues, the 'impudence' of 'that pupil' being a projection back to his earlier years of Paul's later course of life – from the perspective, of course, of Jewish orthodoxy.[20] If Klausner is right, we have further insight from an early rabbinical source into the first stage of Christian history, corroborating once again the account given in the New Testament.

Flavius Josephus was a Jewish historian who wrote from the Roman point of view. Born of a priestly family in 37 AD, he joined the Pharisaic party at the age of nineteen. At the outbreak of the Jewish War against Rome in 66 AD he was appointed leader of the Jewish forces in Galilee, where he defended the fortress of Jotapata against the Romans until resistance became useless. He and some forty others fled to a cave, but when it seemed that this refuge too would be taken by the Romans the group made a suicide pact. Josephus and one other were (by judicious management, perhaps) the last survivors, and the two agreed to give themselves up. On his surrender, playing his cards with great skill, Josephus predicted the elevation of the Roman commander Vespasian to the imperial purple, thus gaining favour with his captors. The prediction was fulfilled in the year 69, and during the siege of Jerusalem in 70 AD, conducted under the command of Titus, Vespasian's son, Josephus was attached to the Roman Headquarters. The city having fallen and the rebellion finally crushed, Josephus settled in Rome as a pensioner of the Emperor, assuming the latter's family name of Flavius. He died in around 100 AD.

Josephus was author of two works of special interest to us: *History of the Jewish War*, and *Antiquities of the Jews* (published in 93 AD). These contain a great deal of confirmatory background material for students of the New Testament, a vivid picture of John the Baptist, a reference to the stoning of James, 'the brother of Jesus the so-called Christ', and finally a passage about Jesus himself, usually referred to as *Testimonium Flavianum*.[21] The last mentioned reads as follows:

> And there arose about this time Jesus, a wise man, if indeed we should call him a man; for he was a doer of marvellous deeds, a teacher of men who receive the truth with pleasure. He led away many Jews, and also many of the Greeks. This man was the Christ. And when Pilate had condemned him to the cross on his impeachment by the chief men among us, those who had loved him at first did not cease; for he appeared to them on the third day alive again, the divine prophets having spoken these and thousands of other wonderful things about him: and even now the tribe of Christians, so named after him, has not yet died out.

This passage has been dismissed by some as a Christian interpolation, despite unanimous manuscript testimony to its authenticity, plus evidence of its existence in the fourth century through two quotations made from it by the Church historian Eusebius.[22] The argument against authenticity centres on the idea that the 'Christian' assertions in the passage would not have been made by a writer who, according to the early Christian theologian Origen, 'did not believe in Jesus as the Christ'.[23] However, a more likely scenario is proposed by Klausner, who instead of rejecting the whole passage as spurious suggests that only the sections implying Christian belief are interpolations.[24] This interpretation is supported by an Arabic version of the passage in a work by a tenth century bishop of Hierapolis, from which all the distinctively Christian references are absent.[25]

F.F. Bruce prefers to accept the whole passage as the work of Josephus, pointing out that it contains characteristics of his diction. He suggests, following other scholars, that certain words have been *omitted* from the original, such omissions being a feature of the textual tradition of *Antiquities*. (It is not difficult to imagine a Christian copyist wishing to eliminate the unbelieving stance of Josephus.) Thus the word 'so-called' could have been dropped before 'Christ' (bearing in mind the phrase 'the so-called Christ' in the passage about the death of James) and a phrase like 'as they said' or 'as they say' after the words 'for he appeared to them'. He is also inclined to believe that the word for 'the truth' (Greek *alethe*) has been corrupted from the original 'strange things' (Greek *aethe*), and also, following the Jewish scholar Robert Eisler, that the words 'a source of new troubles' originally stood between the words 'about this time' and 'one Jesus'. He sums up:

> This version of the *Testimonium* has got rid, by one or two very simple devices, of the difficulties of the traditional text ... The flavour of contempt is a little more marked as a result of the additions; it was always probably present in the parenthesis 'if indeed we should call him a man', and in the closing reference to 'the tribe of Christians', which is not inconsonant with a hope that though they have not yet died out, they soon may.[26]

Having looked at early Jewish writings that refer to Jesus, we will now turn to some early Roman writers – that is, to non-Christian Gentiles.

Early Gentile sources

Cornelius Tacitus, born between 52 AD and 54, was the greatest Roman historian in the days of the Empire. At around the age of sixty, while writing about the reign of the Emperor Nero, he described the great fire of Rome in 64 AD, rumoured to have been started by Nero so that he could rebuild the city and thereby win himself glory. Tacitus writes:

> To scotch the rumour, Nero substituted as culprits, and punished with the utmost refinements of cruelty, a class of men, loathed for their vices, whom the crowd styled Christians. Christus, from whom they got their name, had been executed by sentence of the procurator Pontius Pilate when Tiberius was Emperor; and the pernicious superstition was checked for a short time, only to break out afresh, not only in Judea, the home of the plague, but in Rome itself, where all the horrible and shameful things in the world collect and find a home.[27]

We cannot be sure from what source Tacitus gained his information about Jesus. Jewish informants would not have used the title 'Christus' ('anointed one', or Messiah), which Tacitus no doubt considered a proper name; Christian informants would certainly have sought to disabuse him of the idea that they were perpetrators of a 'pernicious superstition'. In around 112 AD, he was governor of Asia, where he would probably have been familiar with the new religious sect which at that very time, as we know, was causing problems for a certain Roman official in north-west Asia Minor. Christianity was in fact impinging more and more on Roman society, with believers being brought before the authorities; some facts about the sect's origin were probably becoming common knowledge from what Christians said in defence of their faith. Yet even if Tacitus had learned something of Christianity through casual contacts, it is unlikely that he would have named the Roman administrator responsible for Jesus' death without verifying his information from a reliable source. His own status, and the fact that he was son-in-law of Julius Agricola, governor of Britain from 80 to 84 AD, would have enabled him to gain access to official reports, so perhaps he confirmed in this way the truth of a story he had heard.

Besides his reference to Christians and to Jesus in relation to the great fire of Rome, Tacitus refers to Christianity in the context of the destruction of the Jewish Temple in 70 AD. The passage in question is preserved by Sulpicius Severus:

> Titus first took counsel and considered whether he should destroy so magnificent a work as the temple. Many thought that a building which excelled all mortal works in sacredness ought not to be destroyed ... Others, on the contrary, including Titus himself, expressed the opinion that the temple ought most certainly to be razed, in order that the Jewish and Christian religions might more completely be demolished; for

although these religions were mutually hostile, they had nevertheless sprung from the same founders; the Christians were an offshoot of the Jews, and if the root were taken away the stock would easily perish.[28]

This passage sheds light on the significant position Christianity had gained in Roman consciousness in Tacitus' day, as well as some forty years earlier. It was placed on the same level as Judaism, both religions being considered socially undesirable and worthy only of elimination. The Temple was of course destroyed, though not with the effect intended, since Judaism lived on in a more spiritual form, and Christianity was in any case not dependent on the temple sacrificial system. Jewish Christians had in fact left the city in 66 AD, before the outbreak of the war with Rome, and taken refuge in Pella, across the Jordan.[29] Josephus records that Titus wished to save the Temple, but this was probably because, as a grateful client of imperial generosity, he was publicising the view of things his paymaster wished people to believe.

The 'Roman official in north-west Asia Minor' mentioned above was C. Plinius Secundus, or 'Pliny the Younger', who in 112 AD, as governor of Bithynia, wrote to the Emperor Trajan seeking advice on how to deal with the Christians of his province. The problem arose because of the ban imposed on unlicensed *collegia* – clubs or secret societies – which the authorities feared (with some justification) were politically subversive. Christianity was not a recognised cult, so could not justify its meetings on religious grounds; it therefore fell under the ban. There was one group of people, however, to whom this general prohibition of *collegia* did not normally apply: members of burial clubs. It seemed sensible to Christians, therefore, so to organise themselves that they could as far as possible take advantage of the freedom in law enjoyed by such people. Having the semblance of burial clubs – by meeting (usually under cover of darkness) in cemeteries and catacombs, for example – to some extent alleviated the situation for Christians, but unfortunately there were those prepared to inform on them to government officials like Plinius Secundus. Early during his period of office, the latter ordered the execution of several Christians who would not recant. But in view of the large numbers of the sect in his province, as well as uncertainty about the precise legal situation, he wrote his letter of enquiry to the Emperor. After explaining the procedure he had been following and mentioning that he had acquitted some of those charged with being Christian who 'did reverence to your image and the statues of the gods and cursed Christ', Pliny reported what certain former believers had told him about the nature of Christian gatherings:

They were in the habit of meeting on a certain fixed day before it was light, when they sang an anthem to Christ as God, and bound themselves by a solemn oath [*sacramentum*] not to commit any wicked deed, but to abstain from all fraud, theft and adultery, never to break their word, or deny a trust when called upon to honour it; after which it was their custom to separate, and then meet again to partake of food, but food of an ordinary and innocent kind.[30]

Pliny's account of his contact with and treatment of Christians may constitute only indirect evidence of the faith's historical foundations, but it is powerful testimony to its appeal, high moral tone and the centrality of the figure of Christ. Believers included 'Roman citizens' and 'many of every age and class', and there is no reason to believe that such people were unusually credulous; they lived at a time when life was in some respects as sophisticated as ours, with the skills of reading and writing commonplace and communication within the Empire swift. It is worth quoting, in this connection, a sentence from Trajan's reply to Pliny: 'Anonymous documents which are laid before you [to inform on Christians] should receive no attention in any case; they are a very bad precedent and quite unworthy of the age in which we live'. In other words, the age in which Pliny and Trajan lived was in the latter's view an enlightened one, with written documents normative. Let us remember, further, that the two were corresponding no more than 80 years after the death of the man Christians honoured. So, while speaking of 'indirect evidence', we should keep things in perspective: we are talking about today's adherents of a movement that began in the 1920s – era of the flappers, era of the Charleston, era of silent films and Charlie Chaplin, era of my father's university days, of which he was wont to talk often until his death twenty-one years ago.

The Roman historian Suetonius, like Tacitus, also mentioned the Christians in the context of the great fire of Rome. In about 120 AD he wrote biographies of the first twelve Caesars, and in his *Life of Nero* he tells us, 'Punishment was inflicted on the Christians, a class of men addicted to a novel and mischievous superstitious.'[31] More interesting is his probable reference to Christ in his *Life of Claudius*: 'As the Jews were making constant disturbances at the instigation of one Chrestus, he expelled them from Rome.'[32] 'Chrestus' may conceivably have been a Jewish agitator (though it is not a name we would expect of a Jew), but as the name among Gentiles was a variant spelling of 'Christus' it is more likely that the troubles arose from the arrival in Rome of Christians whose preaching of the gospel of

Christ caused controversy among Jews. Suetonius, later finding a record of this quarrelling, wrongly inferred that 'Chrestus' was in Rome at the time. The New Testament confirms that Claudius in about the year 50 AD ordered all Jews to leave the Roman capital.[33]

A further Gentile writer who must claim our attention is Thallus, who around 52 AD composed a work tracing the history of Greece and its relations with Asia from the Trojan War to his own day. Josephus mentions a Samaritan of this name, a freedman of the Emperor Tiberius, and he has been identified with Thallus the historian.[34] We only have fragments cited by later writers of the latter's work, but a reference made to him by the Christian chronologist Julius Africanus in around 221 AD is of great interest. While discussing the darkness which, according to the New Testament, covered the land of Judea while Jesus was on the cross,[35] Africanus comments, 'Thallus, in the third book of his histories, explains away this darkness as an eclipse of the sun – unreasonably, as it seems to me.'[36] This dismissal is well founded, for there could have been no eclipse of the sun when Jesus was crucified, since it was at Passover-time, when the moon is full.

This reference to Thallus by Julius Africanus has a deeper significance for us, however. It tells us that the story of Jesus' death was current in Rome among non-Christian circles in the middle of the first century, as also that early opponents of Christianity did not deny the truth of this account but only sought to provide a natural explanation for its more unusual aspects. The latter point has a parallel in the writings of the second century philosopher Celsus who, when attacking Christianity, did not deny that Jesus had performed miracles but (like the rabbis) merely argued that he had done so through sorcery.[37] This general acceptance of the life-story of Jesus enabled Quadratus, writing a defence of Christianity to the Emperor Hadrian in 133 AD, to refer to the miracles of Jesus as facts that opponents did not dispute, adding that some whom Jesus had raised from the dead had survived to his own day.[38]

It is time now to examine our primary source for this story – chief witness to life of Jesus of Nazareth, known as the Christ or Messiah of Israel, Son of the Blessed, Word of God.

The gospel of John and an insecure edifice

Over the last thirty years or so there has been a quiet sea change in the understanding of Christian origins. It is, of course, impossible in a work like this to cover a wide range of modern scholarship. I will therefore focus on the work of three major investigators, scholars of unassailable stature, before offering my own interpretation of 'the Jesus of history'. The three writers in question hail from different backgrounds and approach the data from somewhat different angles. The first to concern us from this trio of scholars is a churchman whose name will be familiar to many within the Christian community and not a few outside it: the late John A.T. Robinson, formerly Bishop of Woolwich, in London.

Dr Robinson became something of a household name in Britain after his defence in court of D.H. Lawrence's controversial book, *Lady Chatterley's Lover*. From this novel the bishop cited passages describing sexual relationships which were, he claimed, analogous to the Christian doctrine of Holy Communion. In 1962, not long after this episode, he published a slim volume entitled *Honest to God*,[39] which caused a great stir among the orthodox because it seemed to be attacking the traditional view of God. In fact, the author's main thesis in this best-selling book was (as far as I could see) the well-worn and unexceptionable view that we should not conceive of the Almighty as an old man with a beard sitting 'up above'. Other well-publicised works followed, such as *In the End God*.

In due course John Robinson relinquished his bishopric and returned to his previous field of activity, that of academic teaching and scholarship as a member of the Faculty of Divinity at Cambridge University. In 1976 he published the work for which, as a scholar, he should chiefly be remembered, *Redating the New Testament*.[40] From one who had always been considered liberal rather than conservative in his views, this book came upon the theological establishment as a bolt from the blue. It represented a revolution: it questioned and then effectively demolished, at a stroke, the structure of New Testament theology laboriously erected over a period of more than a hundred and fifty years – a structure built on the assumption that most of the New Testament documents, including the four gospels, were written by second-generation Christians (even third-generation), *after* the fall of Jerusalem in 70 AD. There were no half measures for this liberal-turned-conservative; his was a root and branch approach.

Dr Robinson's primary concern was to give probable dates for the writing of each of the twenty-seven books of the New Testament handed down to us in Greek, not to expound their teaching or pronounce on the accuracy of historical and other statements contained in them. Yet it is obvious that the question of dating bears profoundly upon these other matters. Dr Robinson's conclusions, therefore, though tentative (as he modestly described them), have far-reaching implications.

The 'root and branch approach' adopted by Dr Robinson sprang in large measure from what he identified in the 1970s as a characteristic of the prevailing scholarly opinion. He explains this characteristic and his response to it in his opening chapter:

> Much more than is generally recognised, the chronology of the New Testament rests on presuppositions rather than facts ... What seemed to be firm datings based on scientific evidence are revealed to rest on deductions from deductions. The pattern is self-consistent but circular. Question some of the inbuilt assumptions and the entire edifice looks much less secure.[41]

The point here being made by Dr Robinson adds up to a justification of his root and branch approach. Precisely because the pattern of previous New Testament dating had been circular – the date assigned to one document depending on dates assigned to others, and *vice versa* – a piecemeal approach was inappropriate, if not impossible. What mattered was identifying and then examining the assumptions. If these were found to be false, it would clearly not be just one or two documents but the 'entire edifice' that would be up for reassessment.

The manner in which Dr Robinson's work turned assumptions upside down was too much for many theologians, who simply played the ostrich. This was especially the case among scholars in Germany, where the book did not appear until 1986, ten years after its publication in England. It was only then translated and printed through the combined offices of two religious publishers, one Catholic and the other Evangelical, which made it 'suspect' and unworthy of serious consideration in the eyes of the scholarly community. John Robinson's companion volume to this work was published posthumously in 1985, under the title *The Priority of John*,[42] described in a recent book on gospel dating as 'a minor masterpiece'.[43] The impact of this work in academic circles has been less than deserved.

Space does not allow a comprehensive explanation of how Dr Robinson challenges scholarly assumptions in these two books, but I will record key points.

It was the gospel of John that was the catalyst for the wide-ranging study made by Robinson and presented, with such sweeping conclusions, in *Redating the New Testament*. He explains how the gospel became significant for him in a crucial passage. He writes:

I have long been convinced that John contains primitive and reliable historical tradition, and that conviction has been reinforced by numerous studies in recent years. But in reinforcing it these same studies have the more insistently provoked the question in my mind whether the traditional dating of the gospel, alike by conservatives and (now) by radicals, towards the end of the first century, is either credible or necessary. Need it have been written anything like so late? As the argument *requiring* it to be set at a considerable distance both in place and time from the events it records began one by one to be knocked away (by growing recognition of its independence of the synoptists and, since 1947, by linguistic parallels from the Dead Sea Scrolls), I have wondered more and more whether it does not belong much nearer to the Palestinian scene prior to the Jewish revolt of 66-70.

But one cannot redate John without raising the whole question of its place in the development of New Testament Christianity. If this is early, what about the other gospels? Is it necessarily the last in time? Indeed, does it actually become the first? – or are they earlier too? And, if so, how then do the gospels stand in relation to the epistles? … And what about the book of Revelation, which, whatever its connection with the other Johannine writings, everyone seems nowadays to set in the same decade as the gospel?[44]

As well as revealing how Dr Robinson's thinking developed, this passage illustrates how individual books of the New Testament cannot be considered in isolation. As we saw above, previous generations of scholars had built up a self-consistent or 'circular' system of dating the various books. In one respect, these scholars were right: any attempt to date the whole corpus of documents has to be self-consistent. There is a 'seamless robe' quality about them; they stand or fall together, as Robinson realised. That is why it is so important to be careful about underlying assumptions. Robinson's challenge to presuppositions prevailing among scholars some thirty years ago began with doubts about assumptions relating to just one of the documents, albeit an important one. From those doubts grew his wider argument, which called in question their whole approach. As he put it, 'Disturb the position of one major piece and the pattern starts disconcertingly to dissolve. That major piece was for me the gospel of John.'[45]

We have seen, in the extended quotation above, some of Robinson's reasons for doubting the scholarly consensus about John's gospel. For the moment we must leave it at that; I will have more to say below about the fourth gospel. Let me now turn to another assumption he challenged – one that was even more seminal.

Generations of theological students have been taught that the prediction of the fall of Jerusalem ascribed to Jesus in the synoptic gospels (Matthew, Mark and Luke) cannot be genuine; it can only have been a prophecy *ex eventu*. In other words, it was not uttered by Jesus but invented by proposed second-generation Christian writers of the gospels after the fall of the city and then put into his mouth. This assumption, together with others related to the Hegelian view of historical development, lay behind the conclusions of the Tübingen School of biblical criticism, which dated most of the New Testament to the late first or early second centuries AD, and some of it (John's gospel and Acts, for example) even later.

John Robinson challenged the critical consensus on this matter of the fall of Jerusalem by turning the argument on its head. Following one or two other authors, he pointed out how strange it was, if most of the New Testament was written after the year 70, that nowhere in it do we find reference to that epoch-making event as having occurred.[46] He cites Professor C.F.D. Moule, one of the few to make the same point:

> It is hard to believe that a Judaistic type of Christianity which had itself been closely involved in the cataclysm of the years leading up to AD 70 would not have shown the scars – or, alternatively, would not have made capital out of this signal evidence that they, and not non-Christian Judaism, were the true Israel. But in fact our traditions are silent.[47]

There is another point to be made on this subject, however, one which in some ways argues even more tellingly against the consensus of the critics. The point is not made by Robinson and I have not seen it made explicitly by others.

It is clear from its content and language that the 'apocalypse' or outline of future Jewish history given by Jesus and recorded in the synoptic gospels reflects at many points Old Testament prophecies about coming judgement – to be directed, in particular, against Jerusalem. The book of Daniel is actually referred to by Matthew.[48] Jesus was not, therefore, simply speaking from his own perception or foresight but was quoting or echoing material from the prophets of old, especially Daniel. Now the book of Daniel – several complete scrolls of which were found among the Dead Sea Scrolls[49] – contains a prediction of the destruction of Jerusalem. Daniel learns from a vision, we are told, that 'seventy weeks of years' are decreed for the finishing of the divine purpose for 'your people' and 'your holy city'. After a given period, 'an anointed one' ('Messiah' means 'anointed') will come, but he 'shall be cut off, and shall have nothing'. The next words are these: 'And the people of the prince who is to come will destroy the city and the sanctuary'.[50] The words envisage the forces of a powerful ruler, due to appear after the coming and premature demise of this 'anointed one', overthrowing the holy city (Jerusalem) and its sanctuary (the Temple). Who can doubt that this passage from the book of Daniel was in the mind of Jesus when he predicted the destruction of the city in which, two days later, he was crucified?

On two weighty grounds, therefore, the critics' argument that the three synoptic gospels have to be dated after the fall of Jerusalem is shown to be baseless. There are further important reasons, however, for rejecting the assigning of the composition of these gospels to a date after the fall of Jerusalem. John Robinson deals with one of these at some length. It concerns the dating of the New Testament book known as The Acts of the Apostles, or simply as Acts.

No one doubts that Acts shares the same author as the book we know as the gospel according to Luke. The two commence, after the classical manner, with a dedication by the writer to a high-ranking figure, the 'most excellent Theophilus', presumably a Roman citizen of note. In Acts, the author refers in his opening words to his 'first book', in which he 'dealt with all that Jesus began to do and to teach, until the day when he was taken up'.[51] Besides this explicit claim within the text to common authorship, however, the two works are clearly the product of one mind, showing a unity of outlook and a common theology. It is therefore reasonable to assume that Luke (the gospel of Luke) was written before Acts.

The question of whether the author of the joint work was truly 'Luke the beloved physician', companion on his travels of the apostle Paul, need not detain us. On this question, Robinson says briefly, 'With the majority of English scholars, I see no decisive reason against accepting the traditional ascription'.[52] What is important for us is dating the book of Acts, because this bears crucially upon our dating not only of the gospel of Luke but also those of Matthew and Mark.

Apart from the predictions of the fall of Jerusalem in the gospel of Luke, which we have seen do *not* necessitate a post-70 AD date for that gospel, and apart from the criterion of the time taken for the development of the author's theology (a highly subjective means of measurement, depending in turn on other datings), there are two major considerations bearing upon a date for the composition of Acts: the literary dependence (as assumed by most scholars) of Luke on Mark, and the moment in history when the narrative of Acts ends. As regards the former, we are once again up against the problem of circular arguments. Mark is frequently dated 70 AD or later; if this were correct, Luke would have to have been written later and Acts later still. However, if we can establish an early date for Acts, that is, near in time to the last event it records, then of course the gospel of Luke has to be earlier and that of Mark earlier still.

Ancient Christian testimony tells us that Mark was the interpreter of Peter and used that apostle's memories of Jesus in writing his gospel, probably in Rome.[53] Other early traditions speak of Mark being the author of our second gospel, and that having written it he travelled to Egypt to found the church in Alexandria, where he died and was buried in the eighth year of the Emperor Nero (*c.* 62 AD).[54] Nothing in the content of the gospel itself offers grounds for disputing the essential accuracy of these traditions (see further below). Furthermore, a new piece of external evidence makes a dating as late as 70 AD for Mark's gospel impossible, and any dating after 50 AD highly unlikely. I shall say more on this crucial point below.

The story told in the book of Acts ends in 62 AD, two years after Paul has reached Rome as a prisoner of the Roman authorities. Arrested in Jerusalem for allegedly causing a disturbance in the Temple, Paul, who was a Roman citizen, appealed to Caesar. He was brought under guard to the capital in order to await the trial before the Emperor that was his right. The closing words of Acts read thus, 'And he [Paul] lived there two whole years at his own expense, and welcomed all who came to him, preaching the kingdom of God and teaching about the Lord Jesus Christ quite openly and unhindered.'[55] The obvious explanation for such an ending, both abrupt and anti-climactic, is that it reflects the situation appertaining when the words were written. As the eminent scholar Adolf von Harnack once put it,

> The more clearly we see that the trial of St Paul, and above all his appeal to Caesar, is the chief subject of the last quarter of Acts, the more hopeless does it appear that we can explain why the narrative breaks off as it does, otherwise than by assuming that the trial had actually not yet reached its close. It is no use to struggle against this conclusion.[56]

Notwithstanding that last sentence from Harnack, many scholars have tried to 'struggle against this conclusion', dating Acts anything from eight to eighty years later. It has been suggested, for instance, that Luke's apologetic purpose was served by ending on the positive note of Paul preaching 'openly and unhindered'. But, as Robinson points out,[57] there is no hint of the Neronian persecution, which, beginning in 64 AD, had soon wiped out 'a vast multitude' of Christians in Rome (as readers would well know if Acts was written later), winning them some sympathy among the populace,[58] nor of the death in Jerusalem in 62 AD of James the Lord's brother at the hands of the Jewish Sanhedrin – *against* the authority of Rome, a fact which would have suited Luke's apologetic stance. Nor is there the slightest indication that within four years the Jewish people had risen in revolt against Rome, culminating in the destruction of Jerusalem, in fulfilment of a dominical prophecy recorded by Luke in his earlier volume. Luke is careful to mention the fulfilment of a prophecy of famine;[59] it is most improbable that he would fail to mention an immeasurably more significant fulfilment of prophecy, had he known about it. Other explanations for the surprising conclusion of Acts – that the book was left unfinished, or that Luke intended a third volume – need scarcely be taken seriously. Even if Luke had planned another work on Christian history (for which there is no evidence, internal or external), his decision to break off the narrative of the second volume at such an unsatisfactory point demands explanation.

The truth, we are sometimes told, is simple and (usually) obvious. In the case of Acts, the simple and obvious explanation is that given by Harnack: Luke concluded his narrative when it had reached the present moment – the time in which he was writing. The completion of his second volume can therefore be dated 62 AD. This puts his first volume, the gospel of Luke, some years earlier, and implies that the other two synoptic gospels, those of Matthew and Mark, were earlier still.

It remains to say something more on the fourth gospel, which was for John Robinson, as we have seen, the catalyst for his reassessment of the dating of the whole New Testament.

Both those who follow ancient tradition in assigning the authorship of this gospel to the apostle John and those who reject apostolic authorship see it almost unanimously as having been written in the last decade of the first century. If John was the writer, he must have been writing as a very old man. On this dating of the gospel, Robinson writes, 'That the apostle *lived* to a great age, into the reign of Trajan (98-117), and that he was the last evangelist to *write* are both well attested in the tradition. But that he wrote as a very old man is an inference which only appears late and accompanied by other statements which show that it is clearly secondary and unreliable.'[60] As regards the view that John was the last to write, Robinson points out that the patristic tradition was based on the assumption that his aim was to write a 'spiritual' rather than 'bodily' gospel (thus Clement) or to supplement the other three with extra material from the beginning of Jesus' ministry (thus Eusebius).[61]

Robinson strongly inclines to the view that it was indeed John the apostle, son of Zebedee, who composed our fourth gospel. He writes, 'It is ... above all in Jerusalem and its environs that the distinctive topographical interest of the fourth evangelist is centred ...And here it seems to me that the evidence points strongly to the apostle John.'[62] He dismisses the oft-repeated argument that the gospel (indeed, the whole 'Johannine corpus' of gospel and letters, plus the book of Revelation) was the product of one of the apostle's disciples, 'the shadowy figure of John the Elder', for example, or of several disciples, with the words,

> I find it much easier to believe that the role of the disciples of John was basically confined to that of which we have direct evidence, namely their certificate in 21:24 that this disciple 'wrote these things', and that this certificate, given in his presence (*marturon*), is true.[63]

On the issue of dating, Robinson points out that the gospel nowhere suggests that Jerusalem and the Temple had suffered destruction. This, he argues, would be extraordinary if John were writing after the year 70, for his theme is, firstly, the rejection by 'metropolitan Judaism' of the one who came as 'Christ and King and Shepherd of Israel', and, secondly, the emptiness of Jewish religious observance and its ripeness for judgement, then replacement by the vital spiritual faith taught by Jesus.[64] There are, by contrast, indications that the city and Temple were standing when the evangelist was writing: for example, in a reference to the length of time it was taking to build the temple, and where John uses *the present tense* to refer to the existence in Jerusalem of the pool of Bethesda.[65] Asserting that material from the Dead Sea Scrolls 'has killed any dogmatism that the fundamental Johannine categories must be Hellenistic and must be late', Robinson concludes that the gospel was compiled in stages during a period between the 30s and mid-60s, a first edition being published between 50-55 and the final form, with prologue and epilogue, around 65 AD.[66]

As to how the apostle John (assuming he was the author) wrote the gospel, it is by no means certain that he knew or used the synoptic gospels; it is more likely that his sources were independent and that his own memories formed the chief source. It has been suggested that he made notes of Jesus' discourses immediately after hearing them, since in the gospel these show signs of first-hand reporting.[67] We can, at the least, assume that much of his material was communicated orally from an early date. Robinson comments, 'While not presupposing the synoptic gospels, John certainly presupposes the common oral tradition.'[68] This oral material would almost certainly have been in Aramaic; indeed, a strong case has been made for the view that our Greek form of the gospel was translated from an Aramaic original.[69] Vacher Burch argues that such an original was written 'near to the time of the crucifixion of Christ', with final editing taking place before 70 AD.[70]

The synoptic gospels

I shall now turn to the second of the trio of scholars who, as I mention above, have been key figures in the 'quiet sea change' in the understanding of Christian origins. This is John Wenham, who spent a lifetime in academic study, teaching and pastoral work. His first publication was *The Elements of New Testament Greek*, which became a standard work for university students. I corresponded with him on a point of theology while doing National Service in Cyprus many years ago and was enormously helped by his response, which was prompt, friendly and erudite.

John Wenham published his most important work, *Redating Matthew, Mark and Luke: A Fresh Assault on the Synoptic Problem*, in 1991.[71] In his Introduction, he writes, 'The title is of course a conscious echo of J.A.T. Robinson's *Redating the New Testament*, though in fact the two books are almost entirely independent in their treatment of the synoptic problem.' He then outlines his general approach, stating that his starting point is 'the strange ending of the Acts of the Apostles', which he explains in terms similar to those put forward by Robinson, whose advocacy of this and another point he gratefully acknowledges. He summarises his conclusions: that the gospel of Luke 'can be dated with some assurance in the early 50s', that 'the usual reasons for dating Mark around 70 have little weight' and that 'it can be placed more satisfactorily in the mid-40s', and that, in accordance with 'the universal tradition of the early church', the first gospel to be written, 'possibly ... in Hebrew or Aramaic', was that of Matthew, a work 'known to Mark'.[72]

Wenham's arguments leading to these conclusions cannot be rehearsed in detail here, but salient features of his thesis can be highlighted. As indicated, he shares certain views with Robinson, including the necessity of dating Acts in 62 AD, and the belief that Peter and Mark were together in Rome in 42-44 AD, making '*circa* 45' the best date for the composition of Mark's gospel.[73] He summarises his reasons for dating Luke's gospel in '*circa* 54' as follows:

Luke and Acts are separate works. The former could have been written during Paul's imprisonment in Caesarea, but 2 Corinthians 8:18 suggests an even earlier date. The 'brother whose fame in the gospel is throughout the churches' is evidently Luke, and his fame derives from his gospel-book. (This usage of *euaggelion* ['evangel', or 'gospel'] was to be expected any time after Mark 1:1 had been written.) It makes 55 the latest possible date for Luke.[74]

Wenham dates Matthew's gospel in '*circa* 40', 10 years after the death of Jesus (30 AD, though 32 is also possible). In so doing, he makes Matthew the first to be written, as we have seen. He gives detailed argument for seeing a dependence of Mark on Matthew rather than the other way round. Here it will suffice to say that material in Matthew not included in Mark looks more like Markan omissions than Matthean additions, there being indications in the text of Mark that the author is aware of the existence of material he is not using.[75] Wenham also argues that 'Matthew looks original', a point on which he quotes H.G. Jameson:

The elaborate and well-considered arrangement of the book ... [would] be more naturally found in an original composition than in an adaptation from other documents, while the masterly presentation of its subject, implying even in an original work an author of unusual skill, is very difficult to account for in a mere compiler, who is supposed ... to have conflated and interwoven these sources in a complicated patchwork of paragraphs and sentences.[76]

Wenham stresses the almost unanimous testimony of the early Christian fathers to the fact that Matthew the tax-collector, known also as Levi, was the author of the gospel bearing his name, that his gospel was the first to be written, and that he wrote for Hebrews in the Hebrew language and script.[77] While conceding that this tradition 'has been rejected in all its main particulars by most modern scholars',[78] he demonstrates the inadequacy of their reasons for so doing. He cites two statements from Eusebius: firstly, that Matthew wrote his gospel in the third year of the reign of Caligula, that is, in 41 AD; secondly, that he did so 'when he was on the point of going to others', and 'thus supplied by writing the lack of his own presence to those from whom he was sent'.[79] The latter suggests that the writing of the gospel preceded the departure of Matthew from

Palestine, which in turn fits in with the widespread belief that the apostles were dispersed from Jerusalem twelve years after the crucifixion. Wenham writes, 'Acts may perhaps hint that this had taken place by the time Peter was released from prison in 42, James the apostle having been killed and James the brother of the Lord having become head of the church there.'[80] Finally, Wenham looks at a passage from Irenaeus (quoted by Eusebius) which, he argues, has been misinterpreted to give a date for the writing of Matthew's gospel considerably later, in the 60s.[81]

Wenham believes there are good grounds for positing a Semitic (Aramaic or Hebrew) original for Matthew's gospel – known to us today, of course, in Greek. He identifies a number of Semitic idioms, including the sentence, 'You shall call his name Jesus, for he shall save his people from their sins.' He comments, 'The sentence makes good sense in Hebrew, but it makes no more sense in Greek than it does in English without further explanation. It looks as though a translator did not think to explain the meaning of the well-known name Jesus, although two sentences later he gave the translation of the more unusual Emmanuel.'[82] Wenham also follows other scholars in believing that Matthew (and probably others) made notes of what Jesus said at the time of speaking, the world of his day being highly literate, with many tax-collectors knowing shorthand. He writes, 'Matthew's livelihood was earned by interviewing tax-payers and discussing their affairs (usually in Aramaic) and then writing up his reports in Greek. He had a lifelong habit of noting things down and of preserving what he had written.'[83]

This brings us to John Wenham's view of how, in general, the three synoptic gospels were written, and what was their mutual relationship. The starting point for Wenham in investigating the composition of the synoptic gospels is the eagerness of the early church to pass on the words and deeds of Jesus to both Aramaic-speaking and Greek-speaking hearers. Aramaic was Jesus' mother-tongue, but there is every reason to believe that he also knew Greek, the *lingua franca* of the day, and he would have known Hebrew to read the Old Testament.[84] The teaching of local converts (mostly in Aramaic) and the many interested people visiting Jerusalem (mostly in Greek) would have involved some learning by rote, common practice in both Jewish and Greco-Roman education,[85] but written records would soon have become necessary, especially when the church became scattered. Matthew, as the first author, would have put in writing – initially, let us assume, in Aramaic or Hebrew – what he and his colleagues had been teaching orally.

He would have used his own recollections, the memories of his colleagues, and possibly his own first-hand notes. His order was not always chronological; the body of ethical teaching we call the 'Sermon on the Mount' and the section usually known as 'the mission charge to the twelve' were placed to the forefront of his book to emphasise their importance. When, later, the Semitic form of his work was translated into Greek, it would no doubt have been influenced by the Greek form of the early oral tradition.

Tradition tells us, as we have seen, that the content of Mark's gospel was substantially the teaching of Peter. Wenham points out that 'although Mark is not bad Greek, it is very informal, unliterary form of Greek, such as one might expect from an oral discourse';[86] this fits well with the patristic view of its Petrine origin. It is probable that Peter knew Matthew's gospel, either in Semitic form or Greek, but it is unlikely that he was dependent on it since he had his own memories of Jesus. Nor is it likely that Mark worked directly on the text of Matthew, which would have been in scroll form, making copying physically difficult. Verbal similarities between the two gospels are probably the result of Mark and the translator of Matthew's Aramaic or Hebrew original both drawing upon the Greek language oral tradition. Mark probably wrote as Peter and he were accustomed to teach, basing his order on Matthew's gospel and possibly checking his final draft against it.

Luke knew both the earlier gospels, it appears, and in his prologue was probably referring to them. He tells us that many before him had written narratives of 'the things which have been accomplished among us', basing their accounts on what had been 'delivered to us by those who were from the beginning eyewitnesses and ministers of the word'.[87] The from-the-beginning eyewitnesses would be primarily the apostles, one of whom was Matthew, who must have written his gospel in close association with the eleven others and with their approval. Mark would qualify as a 'minister' of the word, not himself an apostle, though acting as the 'interpreter' and having the authority of the greatest apostle. Interestingly, the word translated 'minister' (Revised Standard Version) is the word *hyperetes* ('minister, attendant, servant'), used in Acts specifically to describe Mark.[88] While having access to and apparently acknowledging the works of predecessors in the field, Luke had much material of his own, for which he must have had other informants. Tradition has it that he was himself a follower of Jesus in the flesh – his claim in the prologue to have 'followed all things closely' might seem to imply this[89] – but whether or not this is the case he seems to have been an experienced Christian teacher, well versed in the established corpus of oral material. He retains Mark's order, making some omissions and many additions from his own sources, plus a few additions from Matthew (as it appears).

The four gospels constitute our main New Testament sources for information about Jesus, but there is more information than most people realise in Acts and the letters of Peter, Paul and others. The letters of Paul, unlike the rest of the New Testament, are dated between 50 and 60 AD by most modern scholars, so their testimony is by common consent early – though some theologians, with little reason, consider them 'slanted' by Paul's desire to reinterpret Jesus and his message.[90] In the interests of brevity, I shall not attempt (except in passing) to assess the contribution of these and the other letters to our understanding of the historical Jesus. I simply record the fact that their contribution is significant.

The manuscripts and archaeological discovery

The third figure to whom I turn, another who has played a central part in bringing about the 'sea change' in our understanding of Christian origins, is Carsten Peter Thiede, Director of the Institute of Basic Epistemological Research in Paderborn, Germany. Born in 1952, Carsten Thiede studied at the Universities of Berlin, Geneva and Oxford, and at the latter two has held academic posts. He is a member of the International Papyrologists' Association and a board member of the History Department at Ben-Gurion University of the Negev, Israel. He specialises in the history, archaeology and manuscripts of the first century.

I mentioned above that there was a new piece of external evidence making a date as late as 70 AD for Mark's gospel impossible, and any dating after 50 AD unlikely. Carsten Thiede, following in the steps of an earlier scholar, has made a crucial contribution to the establishment and acceptance of this fact, so I will begin my assessment of his work on Christian origins with this matter.

In 1992, Thiede published a book entitled *The Earliest Gospel Manuscript? 7Q5 and its Significance for New Testament Studies.*[91] In this work he described in detail, with supporting photographs, his reasons for believing that a fragment from a papyrus scroll of the gospel of Mark had been discovered among the Dead Sea Scrolls. The scroll, he concluded, must have been delivered to the Essene community at Qumran in Palestine sometime before 68 AD, when it was sealed into one of the caves on the abandonment of the site by members of the community as the Roman legions were approaching.

Always interested in newly discovered material relating to Christian origins, though somewhat out of touch through living and working in developing countries, I had already read something vague and tentative about this development in a newspaper report. On seeing a notice of Thiede's book, I ordered it, and on its arrival began devouring it – with growing astonishment. Here was something sensational, surpassing all my expectations: hard evidence that a piece (albeit tiny) of one of the gospel manuscripts, copied by a Christian scribe perhaps five or ten years after the gospel had been written, was in our hands today.

I say 'five or ten years' advisedly, for apart from the fact of its Qumran provenance, fragment 7Q5 (as it is labelled: Cave 7, Qumran, Fragment 5) has features that make it likely that the scroll was produced fifteen to twenty years before the cave was sealed. Firstly, on grounds of orthographic style it has been assigned by a specialist in palaeography to a date no later than 50 AD, this dating being made *before the text was associated with Mark's gospel*.[92] Secondly, certain textual abnormalities, in particular the use of Greek 't' for 'd' (found also in the text of the famous 'temple barrier stone' unearthed in Jerusalem in 1871, and in a document precisely datable to 42 AD), require a very early date.[93] Thirdly, the fragment is not from a *codex* (the earliest form of book) but from a *scroll*, and though scrolls were used at the beginning of Christian history, as is witnessed by contemporary texts as well as early Christian art, they were quickly replaced by codices.[94]

With regard to the identification itself, that the text on the fragment came from Mark, the reader will have to turn for details to Carsten Thiede's marshalling of the evidence in his writings. I myself concluded, after careful study of the latter, that the likelihood of some other piece of Greek text of twenty-seven letters perfectly matching the verses from Mark (6:52-3) was so astronomically remote that the identification was beyond dispute. It was not, after all, just a matter of the matching text; there was the corroboration of the textual abnormalities. Papyrologists, at any rate, consider the matter settled – even if some theologians, for no obvious reason, continue to express doubts. Orsolina Montevecchi, professor of papyrology in Milan, former president and currently honorary president of the International Papyrologists' Association, confirmed in the specialist journal *Aegyptus* in 1994 that from the standpoint of papyrology the identification was certain.[95]

Carsten Thiede, as I have said, was building on the work of an earlier scholar. This was the Spanish papyrologist José O'Callaghan, who made the initial identification of 7Q5 as long ago as 1972, going on to identify other fragments from the same cave as being New Testament texts. The most significant of these – one which Thiede believes to be as certain as that of 7Q5 – is the identification of fragment 7Q4 with a passage from Paul's first letter to Timothy (3:16-4:1,3). The remaining seven identifications made by O'Callaghan consist of three more fragments from Mark, one from Acts, one from Paul's letter to the Romans, one from the letter of James and one from the second letter of Peter. Though the circumstances in which these seven fragments were found, alongside those from Mark and the letter to Timothy, might suggest that these further identifications are correct, they can never be finally confirmed as the fragments are too small.[96] It should be mentioned at this point that the scholarly community initially paid scant attention to O'Callaghan's findings; their implications were too revolutionary, especially for New Testament studies. It was left to later specialists, Carsten Thiede most notably, to inform and convince the world of their truth.

Also found in Cave 7 was a jar inscribed with Hebrew letters the sound of which when pronounced corresponds to 'Roma'. Joseph Fitzmyer, a Qumran scholar, adduced evidence in 1972 to support his view that this was a first-century way of writing 'Rome' in Hebrew letters. Inscriptions on other ancient jars refer not to the owner of the jar nor to its destination but to its place of origin. Thiede suggests that the Christian scrolls given to the Essene community at Qumran came from the church in Rome, though probably via the church in Jerusalem. This, as Thiede points out, is highly suggestive: Mark, himself originally from Jerusalem, probably wrote his gospel in Rome around 45 AD, as we have seen, and Peter wrote his first letter in Rome and perhaps his second. If members of the Jerusalem church sent the scrolls to Qumran, perhaps in 66 AD on the outbreak of the Jewish War with Rome, when Christians fled the city to take refuge in Pella, they or the recipients of the scrolls would have been likely to mark the jar in which the scrolls were placed for safe-keeping with their place of origin – none other than Rome, seat of the Empire *and* home to a vibrant Christian church where important Christian writings were composed.[97]

Thiede points to signs in the New Testament of a close relationship between the members of the first Christian disciples in Jerusalem and the Essene community. It is probable that Jesus was in touch with the Essenes (though not himself an Essene) and he may have used their calendar. The latter differed from others in circulation at the time, as discoveries at Qumran have revealed; employment of it by Jesus might explain apparent chronological discrepancies found in the gospels relating to the last few days of his life.[98] Jesus having died, the new Christian community tended to inhabit the south-western corner of Jerusalem, almost next to the Essene Quarter, according to both ancient tradition and the findings of recent excavations. Close links between the two movements may well have been forged when, as we read in Acts, 'a great many of the priests' became converts to the Christian faith; these may well have been members of the Essene sect, which was a priestly community. Such converts from the parties of the Pharisees and Sadducees are less likely: the former had very few priests, and were not led by them, and the latter, which included the chief priests, were violently opposed to the idea of resurrection. An interesting final question concerning the Essenes is whether their strict communal lifestyle provided the inspiration for the experiment in collective living conducted by the early church.[99]

Not long after he had published his findings on the papyrus fragments found in Cave 7 at Qumran, Carsten Thiede was embroiled in controversy over the redating of other papyrus fragments exhibiting text from one of the gospels. This is the Magdalen papyrus, labelled p64/p67 by scholars. It comprises three fragments, slightly larger than postage stamps, on which are inscribed, on both sides, incomplete Greek sentences from Chapter 26 of Matthew's gospel. These were first assigned to the late third- or early fourth-century. In 1953 they were redated to 180 AD, and in 1994 Carsten Thiede redated them again to around 66 AD. The story of these fragments – their acquisition by a one-time undergraduate of Magdalen College, Oxford, the Rev. Charles Huleatt, while working as a a chaplain of the English Church in Luxor, Egypt; his bequeathal of them to his college in 1901; his untimely death in the great Sicilian earthquake of December 1908, when any knowledge he had of the fragments also perished; the controversy surrounding the fragments among scholars today – is told in a book which quickly became a best-seller. Co-authored by Dr Thiede and Matthew D'Ancona, *The Jesus Papyrus*, published in 1996, takes its title from the fact that the person of Jesus is mentioned or implied seven times in the text of the fragments now comprising one of the most treasured possessions of the famous college.[100]

Carsten Thiede was visiting Oxford for a family celebration from his home in Paderborn in February, 1994, when, as an act of scholarly curiosity, he asked the Magdalen college librarian if he could take a look at the papyrus they kept stored in a cabinet with other college memorabilia. He was taken aback by what he found. 'I suddenly realised that some peculiar aspects of this papyrus had not been noticed at all by scholars,' he later told Matthew D'Ancona.[101] Following this initial viewing, Thiede made four further trips to the college to see the fragments and, in particular, to examine the precise form of the script employed. His work of investigation persuaded him that the distinctive script exhibited by the papyrus was used in the first century BC and into the first century AD, but was dying out in the second half of that century. Manuscripts from the early and mid-first-century AD with a similar form of Greek handwriting exist today, with one carrying the precise date of 24 July, 66 AD. Besides the form of the handwriting, however, other features of the text convinced Thiede that this gospel papyrus was older than most if not all others: the style of the language was sparse, without rhetorical embellishments, and there was a variant reading that was clearly original to the author, and not the 'improved' version of a later editor or copyist.[102]

Carsten Thiede's work on the papyrus fragments of Mark and of Matthew have helped to establish beyond doubt that those gospels were written before – if not well before – 70 AD. To be able to see with our own eyes, to be able to touch and handle (if they were not encased in glass) pieces of papyrus exhibiting text copied within a very few years of its composition by the author is remarkable. Not that these are the only very early New Testament manuscripts, as Thiede is quick to point out. There is the papyrus fragment p4 of Luke's gospel (3:32), which displays the same orthographic idiosyncrasy (putting Greek 't' for 'd') as the Qumran fragment of Mark, making a first century date likely. The famous papyrus fragment of John's gospel (18:31-33 and 18:37-38), labelled p52 and held in the John Rylands Library, Manchester, is commonly dated to around 125 AD but may, in Thiede's estimation, be thirty years older, thus falling within the lifetime of the evangelist. There is a near complete codex version of John's gospel, the p66 at Cologny, near Geneva, which is datable to around 150 AD. There is the papyrus codex p45, thirty leaves with much of the gospels and Acts, dated to the late second century, and also p46, eighty-six pages with most of Paul's letters plus Hebrews, dated to around 200 but believed by the papyrologist Young Kyu Kim to be from the late first century, some thirty years after Paul's death.[103]

All these, let it be remembered, are only the very earliest extant New Testament manuscripts; there are many, many others, from the early third century and later. Carsten Thiede writes, 'There is nothing quite like it in non-Christian literature of antiquity.' He points out that the world of classical scholarship was very excited when archaeologists discovered at the fortress of Masada, in Palestine, a papyrus fragment containing just one line of the *Aeneid* of Virgil. This, dated to around 73 AD, some 92 years after the poet's death, is now the oldest surviving papyrus of any work by Virgil. The oldest complete manuscript of Homer's *Odyssey* comes from the thirteenth century of our era, some 2,000 years after Homer wrote, and for the first six works of the *Annals* of Tacitus we also depend on a medieval manuscript.[104]

In his more general research into the first-century history of the Mediterranean region, Carsten Thiede stands on the shoulders of some illustrious forerunners. The most notable of these is probably Sir William Ramsay, the great archaeologist of Asia Minor, who began his work at the end of the nineteenth century. It is interesting to hear, in Ramsay's own words, how his discoveries changed him from being a sceptic about the historical value of what Luke wrote in the book of Acts to being profoundly respectful of its accuracy:

I began with a mind unfavourable to it [Acts], for the ingenuity and apparent completeness of the Tübingen theory had at one time quite convinced me. It did not then lie in my line of life to investigate the subject minutely; but more recently I found myself often brought into contact with the book of Acts as an authority for the topography, antiquities, and society of Asia Minor. It was gradually borne in upon me that in various details the narrative showed marvellous truth. In fact, beginning with the fixed idea that the work was essentially a second century composition, and never relying on its evidence as trustworthy for first century conditions, I gradually came to find it a useful ally in some obscure and difficult investigations.[105]

More recent historians specialising in Roman times have confirmed the judgement of Ramsay with regard to the reliability of Luke as a historian. A.N. Sherwin-White writes, 'For Acts the confirmation of historicity is overwhelming Any attempt to reject its basic historicity even in matters of detail must now appear absurd. Roman historians have long taken it for granted.'[106] A few examples of such points of detail will have to suffice: stone inscriptions corroborate Luke's use of the Roman title 'proconsul' in Cyprus and Greece (Achaia), for example, and his reference in the plural form to 'proconsuls' in Asia is confirmed by careful examination of the chronological data provided by Roman historians; inscriptions also confirm the accuracy of Luke's use of the title 'politarchs' for the chief magistrates at Thessalonica, his ascription of the title *Neokoros* to the city of Ephesus, and the description 'first man of the island' for the chief official in Malta.[107]

G.A. Williamson, translator for the Penguin Classics series of Josephus' *The Jewish War*, contrasts the speeches in Acts with those found in the work of the first-century Jewish historian:

> Very different are the addresses and conversations recorded in the Acts of the Apostles, in which the author shows a complete familiarity with the thought, expression, and habitual terminology of the speakers, and because he writes at so short an interval of time is able to draw on the memories of speakers or auditors – and what memories the people of that time possessed! – if not on written notes, which we have reason to believe were commonly made.[108]

Sherwin-White expresses his surprise that in the course of the twentieth century the attitude of many New Testament scholars to the gospels, to which they have applied the technique known as 'form-criticism', has hardened into the view that 'the historical Christ is unknowable and the history of his mission cannot be written'. He comments,

> This seems very curious when one compares the case for the best-known contemporary of Christ, who like Christ is a well-documented figure – Tiberius Caesar. The story of his reign is known from four sources ... These disagree amongst themselves in the wildest possible fashion, both in major matters of political action or motive and in specific detail of minor events ... But this does not prevent the belief that the material of Tacitus can be used to write a history of Tiberius.[109]

He concedes that the gospel narratives have not been confirmed by external witness to the same extent as the book of Acts, but he has an explanation for this that leaves their credibility intact: 'That the degree of confirmation in Graeco-Roman terms is less for the Gospels than for Acts is due to the differences in their regional setting. As soon as Christ enters the Roman orbit at Jerusalem, the confirmation begins.'[110]

These testimonials from modern archaeologists and secular historians to the historical worth of the gospels and Acts, as also, not infrequently, to other documents of the Christian faith,[111] underpin the evidence for their integrity provided by ancient non-Christian writers, by the text of the New Testament itself, and by extant early Christian manuscripts. Their confirmation of the worth of Luke as a historian is of crucial importance, since his work constitutes the primary source for the historical background of the life of Jesus; Luke alone sets his account clearly in the context of Imperial history, naming Roman emperors, governors, government officials and vassal kings. On this characteristic of Luke's account, F.F. Bruce comments, 'A writer who thus relates his story to the wider context of world history is courting trouble if he is not careful; he affords his critical readers so many opportunities for testing his accuracy.' It is in the light of the findings of scholars such as those cited above that Bruce continues, 'Luke takes this risk, and stands the test admirably.'[112]

In the next chapter I will attempt my own brief reconstruction of the life of Jesus. I will be depending much on the witness of Luke the evangelist. It seems appropriate, therefore, to conclude this chapter with a further quotation from the pen of Sir William Ramsay, in which he urges whole-hearted confidence in Luke's accuracy as a historian:

There is a certain presumption that a writer who proves to be exact and correct in one point will show the same qualities in other matters. No writer is correct by mere chance, or accurate sporadically. He is accurate by virtue of a certain habit of mind. Some men are accurate by nature: some are by nature loose and inaccurate. It is not a permissible view that a writer is accurate occasionally, and inaccurate in other parts of his book. Each has his own standard and measure of work, which is produced by his own moral and intellectual character ... The present writer takes the view that Luke's history is unsurpassed in respect of its trustworthiness ... Luke is a historian of the first rank.[113]

Chapter 9
The Real Jesus

'Seated before a stage built to resemble a giant Christmas crib, the Palestinian president, Yasser Arafat, earlier this month opened the millennium celebrations in Bethlehem, the town where tradition has it Christ was born ... But Bethlehem's claim to be the spiritual centre of the millennium is not unchallenged – for it is by no means certain Jesus was born there. Mark's gospel has his birthplace in Nazareth, while many historians suggest he was a native of Sepphoris, the largest town in Galilee at the time. For a figure who has exerted such a powerful influence on civilisation, Jesus as a historical figure remains remarkably elusive ...'

Thus Peter Stanford, in the New Year issue of *The Guardian Weekly*, 2000, began an article entitled, 'Will the real Jesus Christ please stand up?'

Which gospels was Peter Stanford reading and what authorities was he consulting to come up with such statements? They are not just tendentious; one of the assertions is demonstrably false. Mark nowhere says Jesus was born in Nazareth. He says at the beginning of his gospel that 'Jesus came from Nazareth of Galilee and was baptized by John in the Jordan', and he refers to the titles 'Jesus of Nazareth' and to 'Jesus the Nazarene', but that is all.[1] The words 'Jesus came from Nazareth' mean exactly what they say, that it was from Nazareth that he came to be baptized by John on that notable occasion. It can also be argued that they imply (but no more) that Nazareth was his hometown, where he was known and had been brought up. As to the titles, they refer to the town most commonly associated with Jesus. In neither case are we justified in inferring that Mark believes and is telling us that Jesus was born in Nazareth. It is, in fact, not at all unusual for infants to be born away from the normal home district of their parents; the latter (especially mothers) may want to be with relatives, or they may for any number of reasons be on the move at the time of a birth, which therefore occurs in a place of temporary domicile. I myself was born in a Wiltshire market town only because my parents, having recently returned from Africa, were staying there until moving on – which they did three weeks later – for my father to take up new employment.

142

Once in royal David's city

You my readers, I myself and a billion or two others know that in biblical tradition 'Bethlehem of Judea', not Nazareth, was the place of Jesus' nativity. That 'tradition' is preserved for us in the gospels of Matthew and Luke. From the fact that Mark appears to have known Matthew's gospel, we may infer that he also knew this tradition. If he did not refer to it, it was because it did not suit his didactic purpose, which was to witness to what Jesus said and did from his baptism onwards. He was content to let others fill in details of the birth and family background of Jesus – as also of his cousin John. Those details, however, have produced much scholarly controversy.

There are two main problems associated with the birth narratives of Jesus recorded in the first two or three chapters of Matthew and Luke. The first concerns his genealogies. The problem here is simple: each evangelist traces his genealogy back to David, and further, through Joseph the husband of Mary, yet the two genealogies are different.

It should at once be pointed out that neither Matthew nor Luke portrays Joseph as the natural father of Jesus. They both describe how Mary conceived her firstborn son through the operation of the Holy Spirit; in other words, Jesus was, in the time-honoured phrase, 'born of a virgin'.[2] The idea of a virgin birth, of course, troubles scholars – and many others. But this is not because of a textual difficulty, or lack of corroboration from other sources (as with other 'birth narrative problems'), but because they rule it out as intrinsically impossible. So, from the normal critical standpoint, there is nothing to discuss on this issue. Even if every detail of the circumstances surrounding the birth of Jesus as reported in the gospels were proved true, a large number of theologians – the majority, perhaps – would continue to reject the notion that Jesus had no human father.

Let us, therefore, return to the problem of the contradictory genealogies. Did one of the evangelists unwittingly include in his gospel an erroneous genealogy because he had not checked his source? Or, as some have suggested, did one (or both) wilfully fabricate a list of names, perhaps to 'prove' Davidic descent? The first suggestion stretches credulity to the limit: Luke, as we have seen, was a painstakingly careful historian and Matthew, by training and experience accustomed to being accurate, would have been most unlikely to include such an item without being assured of its authenticity. (He could easily have consulted James, the brother of Jesus.) The second suggestion is, frankly, beyond belief. If we accept the early dates of writing and integrity of authorship presented in the last chapter, the possibility of such duplicity must be discounted. Let us remember that among the Jews of Jesus' day genealogies were important; they would, indeed, often have been known and prized – as they were until a century ago in Ireland, or until more recently in northern Sudan, where people could repeat them from memory. Most significantly, Luke probably knew Matthew's gospel, as we have seen, and would thus have been aware that the genealogies were different. Assuming this to be the case, I cannot believe he would have published a work contradicting his predecessor unless he had known – and assumed others would know – that there was no actual discrepancy.

So how do we explain these genealogies?

The Davidic descent of Jesus 'according to the flesh' is considered crucial in New Testament theology.[3] This means, for those who (like Matthew, Luke and, presumably, the whole early church) consider Mary was a virgin when she gave birth to Jesus, that what matters is not Joseph's descent from David but Mary's. We might therefore expect to find Mary's genealogy recorded in the New Testament. J. S. Wright believes that it is – by Luke. This is not surprising in view of the fact that the early chapters of Luke's gospel are written from the point of view of Mary, who must have been, directly or indirectly, his informant, as the 'strong Hebraic features' of the language confirm.[4] Wright argues thus:

> In Luke, Joseph is the son of Heli, whereas in Matthew's gospel he is described as the son of Jacob. Let us suppose, then, that Mary's father was Heli. Mary had a sister; we are told that standing by the cross of Jesus were his mother, and his mother's sister. We are nowhere told of a brother. If, therefore, Heli had two daughters only, the line, which was always traced through the male line, would have died out. The regulations quoted in Numbers 27:1-11 and 36:1-9, were that, when daughters only survived, their possessions and their family name required a male relative, or at least someone of the same tribe, to carry them on. Even if Joseph was not a (near) relative of Mary, he was of the line of David, and, in marrying her, he carried on the line of Heli, thus becoming the son of Heli.[5]

There have been other explanations as to how the different genealogies of Jesus 'through Joseph' can both be purveying historical truth,[6] but Wright's interpretation is probably the right one.

The second problem associated with the birth narratives of Jesus concerns Luke's statement that his birth occurred at a time when Caesar

Augustus had ordered a census 'when Quirinius was governor of Syria'.[7] The census or registration would have been for tax purposes, as is clear from the Greek term, *apographe*, used to describe it. That periodic censuses of citizens and non-citizens took place during the reign of Augustus is well attested; it appears that they took place every fourteen years in Egypt.[8] Further, the requirement that people registering had to travel to their town of origin is illustrated by an edict of G. Vibius Maximus, Prefect of Egypt, in 104 AD.[9] Finally, early Christian apologists like Tertullian and Justin Martyr repeatedly appealed to the records of the census associated by Luke with the birth of Jesus; they claimed that these records, including the registration of Joseph and Mary, were preserved in the Roman archives and available to be checked by any who were interested. It is most unlikely that these writers would have laid themselves open to easy refutation by issuing a challenge of this nature without being sure of their facts.[10]

There are therefore no good grounds for believing that the census bringing Joseph and Mary to Bethlehem did not take place. Indeed, we know of one during the reign of Augustus that did take place – under Quirinius, too. This, however, was in 6 AD, the year in which Quirinius became governor of Syria, when he was immediately faced with a revolt led by Judas the Galilean. Both Josephus and, significantly, Luke (in his second volume of Christian history) mention this census and resultant insurrection.[11] The problem arises because both Matthew and Luke place the birth of Jesus squarely 'in the time of Herod king of Judea', who died well before 6 AD.[12]

Luke's wording in Greek about Quirinius and the census is slightly ambiguous, and there are variant manuscript readings; one reading, favoured by the Nestle Greek text of the New Testament among other authorities, is translatable, 'This census [for tax purposes] first was/ happened while ...' (*aute apographe prote egeneto*). In other words, Quirinius did not hold the census that took place at the time of Jesus' birth, but this census first took place when Quirinius was governor of Syria. There is evidence that Quirinius held such a post on a special basis around 10 to 7 BC as an extraordinary Imperial legate for military purposes attached to the regular legate in the province of Syro-Cilicia. Perhaps an earlier registration of the populace under the same general decree was held in that period.[13] Alternatively, Luke's wording might allow that the 'census', the registration or enrolment (which 'all', including Joseph and Mary, went to their towns to effect), was not *fully implemented* until the time of Quirinius in 6 AD, when for the first time payment of the tax to the

Imperial coffers was required. Such a requirement would, of course, understandably have led to the uprising under Judas.

Others have suggested that the name 'Quirinius' is an early misreading for Saturninus, regular governor of Syria from 9 to 6 BC, since Tertullian states that it was during his term of office that Jesus was born.[14] On linguistic grounds, it is easier to imagine a misreading of 'Quintilius'. Quintilius Varus was governor of Syria at the time of Herod's death, not long after which he had to put down a revolt in Judea, crucifying 2,000 people.[15]

The 'Quirinius' problem is clearly not insuperable. Luke's known integrity as a historian is perhaps the most powerful reason for believing that what he actually wrote and intended was historically correct. After all, according to ancient tradition he was a native of Antioch, capital of Syria;[16] it would be surprising if he made a major mistake in the chronology of the province's former governors. He knew about the census that led to the uprising under Judas, as we have seen, and we can assume he knew the true date of this significant Jewish event. He certainly knew that Jesus was born well before that date, as we shall shortly see. It is, on the face of it, most improbable that he confused the census of 6 AD with one taking place at the time of Jesus' birth, when, as he tells us, Herod was still king of Judea.[17]

When, therefore, was Jesus born? Our starting point, as intimated, must be Luke. The third chapter of his gospel opens thus:

> In the fifteenth year of the reign of Tiberius Caesar, Pontius Pilate being governor of Judea, and Herod being tetrarch of Galilee, and his brother Philip tetrarch of the region of Ituraea and Trachonitis, and Lysanias tetrarch of Abilene, in the high priesthood of Annas and Caiaphas, the word of God came to John the son of Zechariah in the wilderness; and he went into all the region about the Jordan, preaching the baptism of repentance for the forgiveness of sins.[18]

This list constitutes impressive testimony to the determination of Luke to anchor his account in history. The 'fifteenth year of Tiberius Caesar' has been calculated variously as 26/27, 27/28 or 28/29 AD, the main criterion being whether we reckon from the time that Tiberius was taken by Augustus as 'collega imperii', or from the death of the previous emperor Augustus in 14 AD.[19] There is therefore some ambiguity about the date for the commencement of John's ministry – though it should be pointed out that all the rulers and religious leaders Luke mentions were in office whichever dating is preferred.[20] Taking into account the sequence of the gospel narratives and various chronological clues given, the first dating seems preferable, with John's ministry of preaching and baptism commencing fairly early in 27 AD. This furnishes us with a date in the life of Jesus because Luke tells us he was among those baptized by John; this occurred later in the same year, most probably. Crucially, Luke adds that Jesus was 'about thirty years of age' at the time;[21] counting back thirty years from this date, we arrive at 4 BC, fairly late in the year, as the moment in history when Jesus was born.

Late 4 BC for the birth of Jesus constitutes a problem for most historians, because from what Josephus wrote they assume that Herod the Great died earlier in that year. The usual way round this difficulty is to say Luke was only intending to give Jesus' age approximately, or was simply wrong about it; either way, Jesus could have been older than thirty in 27 AD. Neither suggestion is attractive, in view of Luke's proven precision and reliability; it would be more acceptable to conclude that it was Josephus who had things wrong. (Too often scholars have assumed that where a discrepancy exists between a biblical and non-biblical writer the former must be in error; such an attitude is always dubious, but with regard to Luke it is especially so.) In this case, anyway, another explanation presents itself: Josephus mentioned that not long before Herod's death – exactly how long is unspecified – an eclipse of the moon occurred, visible from Jericho.[22] While most interpreters identify this with a partial eclipse that took place on March 13th, 4 BC, some have suggested the total eclipse of January 10th, 1 BC, as a more likely identification.[23] Statements in Matthew's gospel (referred to below) can be taken to imply that Jesus was born a fair time before Herod's death; the latter eclipse, therefore, could be the one in question. It is a suggestive possibility, which I will develop further. If the former eclipse is still favoured, it would seem necessary – assuming the general historical accuracy in their accounts of both Luke and Josephus – to see the birth of Jesus as occurring in the closing months of Herod's life, early 4 BC.[24]

Much has been written about the star which, Matthew tells us, led certain Magi, or 'wise men', from the east to the infant Jesus in Bethlehem. Efforts have been made to identify it with some astronomical happening of the last few years before our era. The most popular identification (first proposed in 1604 by Johannes Kepler) is probably that of the 'triple conjunction' occurring in 7 BC, when Jupiter and Saturn approached each other three times in the constellation of Pisces – Saturn being commonly identified with the God of Israel, Jupiter with the

Messiah, and Pisces reflecting Israel's role to 'water' the nations.[25] This interpretation of the 'star of Bethlehem' is scarcely compatible with a 4 BC date for the birth of Jesus, but there are other candidates for the star that would suit the later date. Chinese astronomers recorded the appearance of both supernovae and comets in 5 and 4 BC; one of these could have provided the sign that told astrologers of the birth of a great king.[26] I myself, however, while seeing no reason to dismiss the story of the Magi, would consider it best to admit that the exact nature of the 'star' that brought them to Judea still eludes us.

We can summarise the sequence of the birth narratives, giving *tentative* dates based on the date fairly late in 4 BC for Jesus' birth, on the assumption that the eclipse referred to by Josephus is that of 1 BC: Elizabeth, wife of Zechariah and 'kinswoman' of Mary, becomes pregnant with John, 'the Baptist' (5 BC); Mary becomes pregnant 'of the Holy Spirit' with Jesus (5/4 BC, six months after Elizabeth's conception of John); Elizabeth gives birth to John, in 'a city of Judah [Judea]' (fairly early 4 BC); Magi in the east see a heavenly sign (5/4 BC); Mary gives birth to Jesus, followed by his circumcision, in Bethlehem (fairly late 4 BC); ceremony of purification, in Jerusalem (late 4 BC, forty days after Jesus' birth); Magi arrive in Jerusalem, then go on to Bethlehem and identify 'the house' where they see 'the child with Mary his mother' (3 or even 2 BC); flight of Joseph and Mary with the child Jesus to Egypt (3 or 2 BC); massacre by Herod of 'all the male children in Bethlehem and in all that region who were two years old or under' (3 or 2 BC); death of Herod and return of holy family from Egypt to Galilee, avoiding Judea (early 1 BC).[27]

Commentators have been quick to point to differences between the birth narratives of Matthew and Luke. But as John Wenham points out, 'The one difficulty of harmonisation derives from Luke's omission of any reference to the flight into Egypt.'[28] Matthew included the Egyptian interlude in his account because he was keen to show Jewish readers how the story of Jesus, Israel's Messiah, reflected the history of his people. Luke knew and perhaps used Matthew's gospel, we have concluded (and it is generally assumed), so he must been aware of this event; however, he felt it unnecessary to include it in an account addressed primarily to Gentile readers. It fitted his purpose to speak only of a return to Nazareth, then of the visit to Jerusalem when Jesus was twelve, before moving on to the appearance of John the Baptist many years later.

We may assume that Luke did not consider anything in his account irreconcilable with that of Matthew. It is true that the latter's reference to the decision of Joseph not to enter Judea following the return from Egypt, so that 'he withdrew to the district of Galilee',[29] sounds a little strange beside Luke's statement, 'they returned into Galilee, to their own city, Nazareth'.[30] Matthew's wording reads rather as if Joseph had initially intended to settle in Judea, it being his home region. However, his language may simply reflect the fact that Mary, having just come through a traumatic refugee experience, wished to stay for a while with her 'kinswoman Elizabeth' in Judea[31] before going north to Galilee. The two were obviously very fond of one another, Mary having spent three months with Elizabeth during her pregnancy.[32] Alternatively, Joseph, whose family roots were in Judea, may (until sensing danger) have decided to settle there rather than go back to Galilee. Nazareth may not for very long have been his 'home town', but only that of Mary; he might have moved there from Judea for employment reasons before the events of which we speak, or perhaps gone there on a temporary basis to be near the girl he intended to marry. After the year or so in Egypt he might well have felt that he wanted to make a fresh start.

Two points in the birth narratives have intrigued people. The first is the fact that Mary, having given birth to her firstborn, 'laid him in a manger, because there was no room for them in the inn'. There is no mention of a stable, of course, nor of animals – though the 'manger' suggests their presence nearby, and the visit paid by shepherds conjures up a vision of sheep and lambs. It has, incidentally, been pointed out that shepherds would not have been out in the fields if the birth had been in mid-winter. We probably do well to envisage a crowded and rather chaotic scene, with large numbers of people visiting Bethlehem to register their names. Some could have been bivouacking in the open; others, Joseph and Mary among them, found makeshift shelter, such as a cave, used on occasions for animals. Tradition from Bethlehem itself tells us that the birthplace of Jesus was indeed a cave. If this is so, it need not have been too uncomfortable; it may have been provided by the inn-keeper, who suggested the cave, perhaps situated below the inn, as a place of some privacy – highly desirable in view of Mary's advanced state of pregnancy. It might, alternatively, have been offered by some well-wisher (an acquaintance or even a relative of Joseph), whose house was full but who owned or knew about a place which would provide rough shelter for the needy couple.

The second much-discussed point in the birth narratives concerns the timing of the Magi's arrival in Jerusalem and Bethlehem. From Matthew's gospel we learn that Herod's decision to kill male children *who were two years old or under* was based on information the Magi gave him about the time the star had appeared, the implication being that it had appeared up to two years before their arrival. This suggests, as mentioned above in relation to the eclipse question, that Jesus was born quite a time previously and well before the death of Herod. There are other indications that the Magi arrived when Jesus was past being a babe-in-arms. When the travellers finally found the one they were seeking, he was in Bethlehem, to be sure, but according to Matthew he was a 'young child' rather than a 'new-born babe', and he and his mother were in a 'house'.[33] It is very possible that the evangelist did not intend us to understand this as the time of Jesus' birth, or even as some weeks later (if Joseph had made Bethlehem his base while completing religious formalities), but as another occasion when Jesus was with his parents in Bethlehem. We know that the family went up to Jerusalem each year for the feast of the Passover;[34] perhaps it was on such a trip a year or so later, when they were again staying in Bethlehem (within walking distance from Jerusalem), that the Magi were able to pay homage and present gifts to the child born to be king.

The only other incident of Jesus' early life recorded in the gospels is that on which Jesus, when in Jerusalem at the age of twelve with his parents for their annual visit, confounded the Jewish scholars in the Temple with the depth of his understanding. From his remark to his parents about the necessity of being 'in my Father's house', responding to their surprise at his staying behind in the city, we may infer that he already had an inkling of his identity and mission. From this incident also, and from the brief reference to his obedience to his parents and his increase 'in wisdom and stature and in favour with God and man', we understand that Jesus was a sociable, sensible, intelligent and well-educated boy.[35]

I have dealt with these birth and childhood narratives in some detail not because they constitute an especially important part of the story of Jesus for us today (although they remain perennially popular) but because they usually attract negative critical attention. They also form something of a platform for the later narrative, and it is important that they are recognised as historical and not – as many scholars would have it – a mishmash of legend and invention.

Call, testing, and early ministry

Mark's gospel opens with John the Baptist calling men and women to repentance from their sins and to an act of baptismal cleansing in the waters of the Jordan. As we have seen, John probably began this ministry in the early summer of 27 AD. Jesus was among those who in due course came to be baptized, as we have also seen, and this event, recorded by all four evangelists, is depicted as his call from God, the signal for him to commence his own ministry.

At this point I must clarify the intention, from this point onwards, of this brief study of Jesus. The gospels, we must realise, are not biographies in the normal sense, so it is not possible to include the kind of material – people's personal appearance, their *obiter dicta*, descriptive background touches, amusing anecdotes – beloved of biographers. The main focus will be upon Jesus' role and mission, to which end I shall seek primarily to answer two questions: What was Jesus' teaching about, and what did he come to accomplish?

Let us return to that austere figure, 'clothed with camel's hair ...a leather girdle about his waist', who began preaching 'in the wilderness of Judea',[36] the barren, hilly area sloping down eastwards from Jerusalem towards the Jordan valley. Josephus calls John the Baptist 'a good man who commanded the Jews to practise virtue and to be just to one another and devout towards God'.[37] But John's message was much more dramatic than that. He spoke of 'the wrath to come', and of one coming after him who would baptize 'with the Holy Spirit and with fire', who would 'clear his threshing floor', gathering the wheat into his granary, but burning the chaff 'with unquenchable fire'.[38] This coming one turned out to be his own kinsman, who, having just turned thirty, joined those others who came to be baptized by him in the historic river.

The accounts of Jesus' baptism tell us much about the nature of his ministry, and of his role. His desire for baptism and the response he made when John sought to dissuade him from undergoing it suggest he already had a sense of mission, which included a wish to be identified with his people. John, it seems, was half-aware that his cousin was someone special, with a special role – perhaps the very one they were all waiting for. His reluctance to administer to Jesus a rite that presupposed the sinfulness and repentance of the recipient suggests that the carpenter from Nazareth possessed a nobility of character that had already deeply impressed him.[39] In any case, what happened at the baptism settled the matter: according to the gospel writers, 'the heaven was opened, and the Holy Spirit descended upon him [Jesus] in bodily form, as a dove', while a voice came from heaven, 'Thou art my beloved Son; with thee I am well pleased.'[40] John the Baptist as well as Jesus saw the dove. Indeed, we are told that it had been revealed to John that such a sign would identify the coming one, he who would baptize 'with the Holy Spirit'.[41] Jesus alone may have heard the voice, however, if we assume (as is likely) that the account of the event, or at least some of the details, emanated from him.

The words from heaven echo two Old Testament passages: Psalm 2:7, 'You are my son', addressed to the king of Israel, prototype of Messiah; Isaiah 42:1, 'Behold my servant, whom I uphold, my chosen, in whom my soul delights.' The heavenly voice, it would seem, confirmed to Jesus that he was truly Messiah of Israel, and that this messiahship was to be of the type described in Isaiah under the title 'servant'. Isaiah's 'servant of the Lord' was to be the true representative of Jacob/Israel; there is, indeed, some ambivalence in the prophet's oracles between a corporate or individual nature for the 'servant', that is, between an identity as the community of Israel or as an individual representing Israel. We need not understand this as a contradiction, however: the 'servant' is the community of faithful Israel until, finally, the community as a whole fails in its vocation, when the one remaining faithful member – Jesus, crucified Messiah – perfectly fulfils that long-foreseen vocation. The 'servant' is to be a blessing to his people, but also to the 'nations', the Gentiles.[42] Above all, he is to be one who suffers at the hands of wicked men, and for their sake.[43]

Immediately following his baptism, we read, Jesus 'was led by the Spirit for forty days in the wilderness, tempted by the devil.' The words closely echo some from the Old Testament book of Deuteronomy, referring to the forty years God kept the ancient Israelites in the desert of Sinai, 'that he might humble you, testing you', before entering Canaan, land of promise.[44] Further, Jesus parries all the specific temptations from the devil (which came after his 'forty days'[45] of fasting) by quotations from Deuteronomy. The account itself can only have come from the lips of Jesus. It may include a measure of symbolism, referring to temptations that, even if resisted before his ministry began, recurred from time to time later in that ministry. There is no need to doubt the reality of these mental battles, however, even if Jesus (a master storyteller) clothed them in vivid, pictorial language.

I believe this period of testing, following immediately after Jesus' call and his realisation of the true nature of his role, primarily concerns that role. Each temptation has something to say about his mission. We will briefly go through them, using the order given in Matthew.[46]

The first temptation, where Jesus declines to make stones into bread, stands for his refusal to see his mission in terms of being a social reformer, attending to people's physical, material needs. The second, where he will not cast himself off a pinnacle of the Temple, refers to his refusal to prove his messianic identity before the world by giving a 'sign', some extraordinary, perhaps miraculous, feat. The third, where he declares that he will not 'worship' Satan in return for worldwide dominion, represents his rejection of the idea of becoming a violent revolutionary, that is, of seeking a political kingdom by taking up arms against Rome.

After his call and time of testing, Jesus spent some time in Judea (southern Palestine), making occasional visits to Galilee (in the north). John tells us about this period, when 'John [the Baptist] had not yet been put in prison'.[47]

In Judea, early in 28 AD we may surmise, the brothers Andrew and Simon (Peter) became deeply interested in Jesus – Andrew already being a disciple of the Baptist. Then, on a trip to Galilee, Jesus called Philip to follow him, and Philip introduced him to Nathanael. John then describes the scene of Jesus' first 'sign' or miracle, at a wedding feast in Galilee.[48] Having stayed for a while in Capernaum, on the shores of Lake Galilee, with his mother, brothers and some disciples, Jesus returned to Jerusalem for the feast of the Passover. There he entered the Temple and cleared out the animals and moneychangers. Some have suggested that this is a misplaced account of what the other evangelists record Jesus as doing in the last week of his life. Yet what could be more natural or appropriate than that Jesus should repeat in that final week a dramatic action – a kind of enacted parable – with which he had commenced his ministry? Many people believed in Jesus following this first Temple-cleansing, John tells us, because 'they saw the signs which he did'; one such, it seems, was Nicodemus, a leading Pharisee.[49]

Jesus then remained in Judea, baptizing (through the agency of his disciples) alongside the Baptist. After some months, however, he became aware that a report had reached the Pharisees that he 'was making and baptizing more disciples than John'.[50] Partly for this reason, it appears, he decided to leave Judea and go back to his home territory of Galilee; the authorities were getting too interested in him. Matthew and Mark, however, imply another and more weighty reason – the arrest of John, which probably occurred in the fall of 28 AD.[51] John was arrested by Herod Antipas (son of Herod the Great) for reproving him for an adulterous relationship, and imprisoned in the fortress of Machaerus, near the Dead Sea across the Jordan. A few months later, Antipas had John beheaded.[52]

It would seem that Jesus construed this event as a sign that the period of quieter ministry, mainly to picked individuals (a sort of preparation to the real thing), was at an end. His proper campaign, a fully public ministry, should commence in Galilee. He was perhaps guided in this choice of Galilee not so much because it was his home territory as because Isaiah had long before prophesied that 'the land beyond the Jordan, Galilee of the nations' was to be the recipient of messianic blessing: 'The people who walked in darkness have seen a great light; those who dwelt in a land of deep darkness, on them has light shined.'[53] This, anyway, is how Matthew interprets it.[54] Neither Matthew, Mark nor Luke say anything about the earlier period in Judea. Mark, indeed, makes only the briefest of references to the preaching of John, the baptism of Jesus and his temptations (of which he gives no details), before confronting the reader with the dramatic words:

> Now after John was arrested, Jesus came into Galilee, preaching the gospel of God, and saying, 'The time is fulfilled, and the kingdom of God is at hand; repent, and believe in the gospel.'[55]

Focus on Galilee: teaching, healing, controversy
Luke commences his account of this period with a reference to Jesus preaching 'in their synagogues', and of his 'being glorified by all', before going straight to the occasion when he spoke in the synagogue of his home town of Nazareth. Having read a passage from the book of Isaiah, he applied the messianic prophecy to himself, then castigated the congregation on their unbelief. At this, 'all in the synagogue were filled with wrath'; they then 'led him to the brow of the hill on which their city was built, that they might throw him down headlong'.[56] This incident finds no mention in Matthew and Mark, who both commence their accounts of the Galilean ministry with the encounter of Jesus with Simon (Peter) and Andrew as they were fishing in the lake, and his call for them to leave their nets and follow him – which they promptly did.[57] The two brothers were included among the twelve appointed by Jesus a little later 'to be with him, and to be sent out to preach and to have authority to

cast out demons',[58] their number no doubt deliberately chosen to reflect the creation of a new Israel, superseding the nation of twelve tribes.

I want at this point to look generally at the scope of Jesus' ministry, focused as it was so strongly on Galilee.

C.H. Dodd, in his classic study of Jesus, divides his activities into three main strands: *teaching*, that is, his broad appeal to the public through addresses in synagogues, preaching in the open air, and quieter teaching and discussion with interested individuals; *healing*, which covers his ministering to human need, especially the sick in mind and body, and the renewing of people's faith by centring it upon himself; *controversy*, this being forced upon him for breaking minor rules of religious tradition, consorting with undesirable elements in society (tax-collectors, prostitutes, Zealots, and the like) and, finally, for raising questions – not necessarily sincere – about the source of his power.[59] The first two strands require closer attention; I shall therefore examine them further before concluding this section on a note of heightening controversy, prompting Jesus to a change of tactic.

A crucial point to note first about all Jesus' activities, both teaching and healing, is that they were directed at – and about – individuals, not corporate society. As Dodd puts it, 'The call is public, addressed to all who will hear; the response is necessarily made by individuals.' This appeal Jesus made to people was deeply compassionate. He declared on one occasion: 'Come to me, all who labour and are heavy-laden, and I will give you rest. Take my yoke upon you, and learn from me; for I am gentle and lowly in heart, and you will find rest for your souls.' The same compassion is evident from the words from Isaiah he took as his text and then expounded in the synagogue at Nazareth:

> The Spirit of the Lord is upon me, because he has anointed me to preach good news to the poor. He has sent me to proclaim release to the captives and recovering of sight to the blind, to set at liberty those who are oppressed, to proclaim the acceptable year of the Lord.[60]

Jesus carefully stopped short of the words that immediately follow in Isaiah's prophecy ('and the day of vengeance of our God'), underlining the fact that he was *not* (as some have suggested) publishing a political manifesto. On the contrary, he was deliberately drawing a line between his current messianic mission of preaching the good news of release to those in bondage, sight to the blind, liberty to the oppressed, on the one hand, and 'the day of vengeance', on the other. All the former tasks he fulfilled, in his own way, since he ministered to the 'poor' by proclaiming that they could find forgiveness and eternal life in him, healing many from their ailments (including blindness), releasing others from demonic possession, and even (witnesses assure us) raising one or two from the dead. What he refrained from doing – about which I shall say more below – was taking up a sword of vengeance against the foreign oppressor or against those from among his own people who opposed him.

Jesus insisted that his kingdom (for the time being, at least) was inward and spiritual, not outward and political. One of his sayings is particularly clear on the issue: 'The kingdom of God is not coming with signs to be observed; nor will they say, 'Lo, here it is!' or 'There!' for behold, the kingdom of God is within you.'[61] This 'inwardness' of the kingdom is put across in a number of other ways. The kingdom's ethics, for example, outlined in the 'sermon on the mount',[62] are concerned less with the outward act of sin than with the inner and sinful motive. The parables of the kingdom[63] seem to stress the inwardness, privacy, almost secrecy of the kingdom: it is 'seed' that is sown; it is 'a field' in which 'good seed' and 'bad seed' are scattered; it is 'a grain of mustard seed'; it is 'leaven'; it is 'treasure hidden in a field'; it is 'a merchant in search of fine pearls'. True, the final parable, where the kingdom is likened to 'a net', as well as the parable of the 'field', point to a final judgement, suggesting an 'outward' dimension, but this judgement is nothing to do with men on earth; it is effected by the 'Son of man' and 'his angels'.

The teaching of Jesus more generally about life's meaning stresses the fact that outward and material welfare and success are secondary and of no ultimate significance. The 'beatitudes' heap blessing on the 'poor', on the 'meek', on those who 'hunger', on those who 'weep'. Jesus counsels his followers not to 'fear those who kill the body, but cannot kill the soul'. He tells them that 'he who finds his life will lose it, and he who loses his life will find it'; that 'unless a grain of wheat falls into the ground and dies, it remains alone, but if it dies, it bears much fruit'; that 'he who loves his life loses it, and he who hates his life in this world will keep it for eternal life'. Finally and unforgettably, he takes a little child and says, 'Whoever humbles himself like this child, he is the greatest in the kingdom of heaven'.[64]

All the normal values of our material world Jesus reverses: poverty may be more blessed than riches, weakness than strength, sorrow than joy, death than life. Why? – because his kingdom is not outward but inward; because his call is not for 'society' to be reformed but for souls to be transfigured; because what matters is not success but sincerity, not power but purity, not gain but God.

This concentration on the spiritual rather than the physical in Jesus' teaching raises a question in relation to his acts of healing, and to other of his 'mighty works', since these were mostly performed – it would seem – in response to people's material needs, especially their need for bodily health or wholeness. We could conclude from such actions that earthly issues and values were primary for Jesus.

Before considering this question, however, I must say something on the reality of these 'mighty works' or 'miracles'. I shall allow F.F. Bruce to make my main point:[65]

Early non-Christian writers who refer to Jesus at any length do not dispute that he performed miracles. Josephus calls him a wonder-worker; later Jewish references in the Rabbinical writings attribute his miracles to sorcery but do not deny them, just as some in the days of his flesh attributed his powers to demon-possession. Sorcery is also the explanation given by Celsus, the philosophic critic of Christianity in the second century. The early apostles referred to his miracles as facts which their audiences were as well acquainted with as they themselves were; similarly the early apologists refer to them as events beyond dispute by the opponents of Christianity. Justin Martyr says that an account of them is given in Pilate's official report.

As far as we today are concerned, the miracles as a whole stand or fall by whether or not we accept the greatest miracle of all, the resurrection of Jesus from the dead. If we accept this as true, confirming his claim to divinity, then the rest follows as night follows day. In my final chapter I shall discuss the circumstances of the supreme Christian 'miracle'.

I now return to the question raised above about Jesus' miracles, whether of healing or the so-called nature-miracles – creating wine from water, walking on the lake, stilling the storm, multiplying the loaves (all of them, incidentally, performed in response to people's needs).

What is significant is that Jesus was highly selective about performing such deeds. Only a tiny proportion of the world's needy was blessed by him in these ways. And although these acts were manifestly not divorced from his feeling of compassion for people, it is made clear in the gospels that they were, when meeting people's physical needs, conceived as signs of a deeper and spiritual concern – signs addressed, moreover, to those who were already in some measure responding to him, not to those who were unbelieving. One of the ways in which Jesus demonstrated this selective approach and requirement for a degree of prior faith was his tendency to wait for people to take the initiative in coming to him for healing. Indeed, where there was no prior faith, as at one time in his home territory, he could not or did not perform any miracles. But above all, underpinning his whole approach to performing 'mighty works' was a guiding principle: there was to be no question of forcing belief on anyone; to do so would be to succumb to the second temptation.[66]

I will conclude this overview of the way in which Jesus ministered to human need, particularly in Galilee, by referring to one great 'nature miracle'. John's gospel, like the other three gospels, records the feeding of some five thousand people from the meagre resources of five loaves and two fish.[67] John, however, unlike the other three evangelists, records an incident that followed immediately after that event, an incident crucial in two ways: it underlines how Jesus perceived his role; it led to a falling away of some of Jesus' followers and, indirectly, to a hardening of opposition to him.

The crowds, John tells us, realising that something quite abnormal had occurred, exclaimed, 'This is indeed the prophet who is to come into the world'. John then continues, 'Perceiving then that they were about to come and take him by force to make him king, Jesus withdrew again to the mountain by himself.'[68] C.H. Dodd comments thus:

> In that brief phrase John passes over what must have been a gravely critical situation. It was no less than an attempted rising against the government with Jesus as leader. If he had been a 'Messiah' of the common sort it was a golden opportunity; but that sort of messiahship he had long ago rejected as a temptation of the devil. It remained for him to put an end to a situation which threatened to compromise his whole mission. First, the disciples must be isolated from dangerous contacts. He 'compelled' them, Mark says (as if they were reluctant to leave the exciting scene),[70] to take to the boat and cross the lake – and that at nightfall and with a storm brewing. Then he used his remaining influence with the crowd to induce them to disperse peaceably, and retired to solitude to the hills.[69]

So we see that when Jesus was confronted with the real possibility of casting himself in the role of a political leader – indeed, a revolutionary – he spurned the idea. Yet his action on this occasion only illustrated what he consistently taught about the spiritual nature of his kingdom, as we have seen.

John goes on to tell us that the day after this incident Jesus gave a long dissertation on himself as 'the bread of life'. This was in Capernaum, where he was teaching large numbers of people, some of whom were his followers, in the synagogue. We read, however, that 'the Jews murmured at him' and 'disputed among themselves' about his teaching. Many of his own disciples were offended at his words, and John concludes by saying, 'After this many of his disciples drew back and no longer went about with him.'[71] Jesus may intentionally have given them a 'hard saying'[72] to discourage them from wrong ideas about his being a political leader.

This feeding of the multitude and attempt to make Jesus king, which probably occurred around April 29 AD, brings us to Dodd's third strand in Jesus' ministry, that of controversy. Controversy presupposes opposition and, as we have just seen, opposition at this time was intensifying.

It seems that Jesus took this development as a signal that his very public Galilean campaign should come to a close; it had lasted some six months. He would now have a period of more private instruction for his closest disciples. This would best be served by moving into foreign territory, away from the synagogues, where the murmuring and disputing about him was most prevalent, encouraged as it was by 'scribes' (doctors of the law) who came down from Jerusalem.[73]

In the gospels of Matthew and Mark we read of Jesus withdrawing to the region of Tyre and Sidon, Phoenician territory, and of his return south to the region of the Decapolis, or Ten Cities, on the far side of the Jordan. Then, a little later in the far north of Galilee, at Caesarea Philippi, Jesus put a crucial question to his disciples, 'Who do you say that I am?' Peter gave the uncompromising reply, 'You are the Christ, the son of the living God.'[74] Jesus commended Peter for having recognised the truth about him, but having done so 'strictly charged the disciples to tell no one that he was the Christ'. He then went on 'to show his disciples that he must go to Jerusalem and suffer many things … and be killed, and on the third day be raised'.[75]

What Jesus claimed; who he was

Peter's ringing declaration that Jesus was 'the Christ', that is, 'Messiah' or 'anointed one', raises the question of our own attitude to Jesus – to his teaching, to his deeds, but above all to his remarkable claims. Before moving on to the final stage of his ministry, therefore, let us look at the claims Jesus made about his authority and power, and thus about his identity. I will then examine a title he regularly applied to himself, not least when making his various claims, that of 'son of man'. The significance of this title is crucial for any investigation of who Jesus was and what he came to accomplish.

Jesus claimed to be lord of the Sabbath; he claimed to have control over nature; he claimed the right to forgive sins; he claimed authority over the powers of evil; he claimed the right to judge and condemn in an ultimate sense; he claimed to have God as his Father, and even to be 'one' with Him – in other words, to be Son of God, a notion that was bound up with his acceptance of the title of 'Christ', or 'Messiah'.[76]

All these claims amount, implicitly or explicitly, to assertions of divinity – as indeed Jesus' contemporaries usually took them. No one else in history has dared to make them, except perhaps a few who have been branded lunatics. How is it that millions – billions – have been prepared to take such claims perfectly seriously in the case of Jesus, while even those who have rejected them have (with few exceptions) honoured the founder of Christianity as uniquely noble and wise rather than brushed him aside as deluded? Of course, nobility and wisdom are the two qualities of the Nazarene that immediately strike any reader of the gospels; yet his self-exalting claims scarcely lack prominence. It is, on the face of it, strange that so many people revere him for the former qualities while ignoring or dismissing his claims. Jesus was at times reticent about publishing his identity or the nature of his role. Has this feature of the story confused some who have read it superficially, failing to penetrate beyond the broad outline of his life and ethical teaching, skating over 'difficult' theological passages or discounting them as irrelevant pieces of hyperbole? A brief consideration of the title 'son of man' as used by the carpenter from Nazareth in relation to himself will go some way towards resolving these and other questions.[77]

In Aramaic, the phrase 'son of man' is an ordinary way of saying 'man' in the sense of an individual of the human species – 'a man' or 'the man'. Further, in the Aramaic of Palestine it was quite common for the speaker to substitute 'son of man' for 'I' or 'me' (rather as in English the impersonal 'one' is used) out of diffidence or to leave doubt about whether the speaker was referring to himself or to someone else. Jesus may well have used the title for the latter reason, since some of his sayings were so bold. He wanted people to ask what 'son of man' he was talking about, and then to become aware that he was referring to his role as the Servant described by Isaiah. Many occasions on which he used the title are associated with the functions of this Servant figure.

We must also take account, however, of the figure described in a passage from the book of Daniel: 'With the clouds of heaven there came one like a son of man'.[78] (We have already referred to this passage, originally written in Aramaic, when discussing the rabbinical attitude to it;[79] it is crucial to an understanding of Jesus.) The passage continues: 'And he came to the Ancient of Days [God] and was presented before him. And to him was given dominion and glory and kingdom, that all peoples, nations, and languages should serve him; his dominion is an everlasting dominion, which shall not pass away, and his kingdom one that shall not be destroyed.' Daniel, it is recorded, sees this sequence in a dream, which is then interpreted for him by a celestial being. The interpretation tells us that 'the kingdom shall be given to the people of the saints of the most high'.[80] Some commentators have seen here an ambivalence between an individual 'son of man', and a corporate 'son of man' (i.e. a community). If so (though the sense of the passage does not demand it), it would parallel the Servant figure in Isaiah, who sometimes represents Israel considered corporately and sometimes seems to be an individual.

Most significant for us, however, is the fact that during his trial Jesus referred to this 'son of man' figure from Daniel, applying it to himself. In Mark's gospel we read: 'The high priest asked him, "Are you the Christ, the Son of the Blessed?" And Jesus said, "I am; and you will see the Son of man sitting at the right hand of Power, and coming with the clouds of heaven."'[81]

This exchange between Jesus and the high priest constitutes the final public and unequivocal claim by Jesus to be the Messiah of Israel – a Messiah, moreover, who enjoyed divine status as 'Son of the Blessed [God]'. Having accepted the latter title, Jesus (as so often) used scripture to reinforce his claim. He interpreted the 'one like a son of man' in Daniel, with whom he identified himself, as being on a par with God, since he described him as sitting at the latter's right hand.[82] The divinity of this figure is, indeed, scarcely less clear in the book of Daniel: he is given 'dominion and glory and kingdom'; all peoples serve him ('worship' him, as the NIV has it); his dominion is 'everlasting' and his kingdom 'shall not be destroyed'. The high priest's reaction to the words of the prisoner before him constitute final confirmation, if such were needed, that Jesus was claiming equality with God: tearing his mantle, the Jewish prelate proclaimed, 'You have heard his blasphemy.'[83]

I mention above that readers of the gospels may sometimes be confused by the hesitance displayed by Jesus towards publicly revealing his identity as Messiah. This trait, certainly, must lie behind the suggestion made by some that he never made such a claim.[84] What we should understand is that in some respects the title was an embarrassment to Jesus; it was associated too much in the public mind with the political and military role of 'Son of David'. He did not want the title to be used of him openly until his hand was forced and he had to declare himself. By then, he must have hoped, his close followers, if not the public at large, would have learnt that he had come to be a different kind of Messiah.

The question at issue, therefore, is not *whether* Jesus claimed to be Messiah for the Israel of his day but *what kind of* Messiah he claimed to be. As we have seen, the role he cast himself in was that of the Servant Messiah of Isaiah's prophecy. C.H. Dodd sums the matter up:

> Jesus set himself to constitute the new Israel under his own leadership; he nominated its foundation members, and admitted them into the new 'covenant', and he laid down its new law. That was his mission. If it did not entirely agree with any of the contemporary ideas of what the Messiah should do, there was no other term available which came near to covering it. He could not deny his mission; he could not disavow the authority that went with it; and therefore, if the question was posed, he could not simply repudiate the title 'Messiah'.[85]

Road to Jerusalem

Let us now, having jumped ahead of our narrative, turn back to the point at which Peter made his confession of faith in Jesus as Messiah and Son of God,[86] this dramatic declaration probably occurring in the early summer of 29 AD, after Jesus had concluded his high-profile campaign in Galilee. How did the story develop from that moment to the final, fateful week in Jerusalem? We turn first to John's gospel.

We learn from John that in the fall of that final year Jesus visited Jerusalem for the Jewish Feast of Tabernacles, going up quietly on his own.[87] After a few days in the capital, however, he began teaching publicly, mostly in the Temple area. He also confronted his Jewish opponents with some plain speaking about their evil motives and intentions, particularly towards himself, and this provoked controversy. John records the following sequence:

> Some of the people of Jerusalem said, 'Is not this the man that they seek to kill? And here he is, speaking openly, and they say nothing to him! Can it be that the authorities really know that this is the Christ?' ... The Pharisees heard the crowd thus muttering about him, and the chief priests and Pharisees sent officers to arrest him ... Jesus stood up and proclaimed, 'If any one thirst, let him come to me and drink. He who believes in me, as the scripture has said, "Out of his heart shall flow rivers of living water."' ... When they heard these words, some of the people said, 'This is really the prophet.' Others said, 'This is the Christ.' But some said, 'Is the Christ to come from Galilee?' ... So there was a division among the people over him. Some of them wanted to arrest him, but no one laid hands on him. The officers then went back to the chief priests and Pharisees, who said to them, 'Why did you not bring him?' The officers answered, 'No man ever spoke like this man!'[88]

Jesus stayed in Jerusalem or its environs, it appears, till the Feast of Dedication when, as John says, 'it was winter'.[89] The authorities tried to trap him into declaring himself during the feast, and it was on this occasion that Jesus made the statement, 'I and the Father are one.' 'The Jews,' we read, 'picked up stones again to stone him', but the Nazarene's ironic response, asking for which of his 'many good works' they were taking this action, deflected their efforts. Instead of launching their missiles, his opponents were stung into making the clearest statement we have of Jesus' unpardonable 'sin' in the eyes of the religious establishment: 'We stone you for no good work but for blasphemy; because you, being a man, make yourself God.' Jesus then worsted his enemies in further argument, again using Old Testament scripture ('the word of God') in support of his teaching, and having thus bought himself time managed – as so often before – to elude their grasp.[90]

Following this incident, Jesus went away, across the river Jordan. Here he remained, and here people visited him, many becoming believers.[91]

John's gospel then moves rapidly on. We read of the raising of Lazarus, and of renewed consternation among the religious authorities, who convened a meeting of the Council to discuss a situation that was becoming critical. 'If we let him go on thus,' they protested of Jesus, 'every one will believe in him, and the Romans will come and destroy both our holy place and our nation.' The high priest, Caiaphas, then admonished his colleagues with words that revealed his criminal intentions but also contained deeper truth than he realised: 'You know nothing at all; you do not understand that it is expedient for you that one man should die for the people and that the whole nation should not perish.'[92]

It may be asked how inside information about the proceedings of the Jewish Sanhedrin became known to John the evangelist.

John was, according to his own testimony, 'known to the high priest'.[93] It was this personal connection with the highest religious authority (possibly a family link, through marriage) that enabled him to enter the courtyard of the high priest's house, then bring in Peter, when Jesus was arrested and sent to Annas, father-in-law of Caiaphas. John, it thus seems, had access to reports on what the nation's religious leaders were planning and plotting, even behind closed doors. There is another possible source of his information, however. Both Joseph of Arimathea and Nicodemus, disciples of Jesus, were members of the Jewish Council.[94] John, and indeed the other evangelists, could have obtained information from either of them about the Council's activities in private session.

The heat was now on for Jesus, as John makes clear in words concluding his account of the Council meeting. 'From that day on,' he tells us, 'they took counsel how to put him to death.' Jesus accordingly withdrew to a town on the edge of the Judean desert, Ephraim, staying there with his disciples until shortly before the Feast of the Passover.[95]

How do the accounts of these days given by the other three evangelists fit in with what we have learnt from John? I will let Mark, for the most part, inform us about this.

Moments after Peter at Caesarea Philippi had proclaimed his faith in Jesus as Messiah, he was reproaching his master for talking plainly about suffering and even death at the hands of the religious authorities. Jesus rounded on the impetuous apostle, seeing in his words Satanic temptation to follow the counsel of men rather than that of God. He now began in earnest to teach his followers what the call of God entailed: self-denial and the taking up of a cross – the reversal of all normal worldly values, as noted above. We go on to read of the visionary experience of Peter, James and John, when Jesus 'was transfigured before them', his garments becoming 'glistening, intensely white, as no fuller on earth could bleach them' (a first-hand description, if ever there was one); of the healing of a boy who was possessed, moving Jesus to rebuke his disciples for faithlessness because they had not been able to help him themselves;

and of a journey through Galilee when Jesus 'would not have anyone know it' because he was still trying to teach and convince his followers about his coming death – and resurrection. Mark, or more accurately perhaps his informant Peter, comments: 'They did not understand the saying, and they were afraid to ask him'.[96]

Jesus and his disciples passed through Capernaum, then came to 'Judea and beyond the Jordan', with crowds following him everywhere and Pharisees turning up once again 'to test him' with a question on divorce. Having dealt with this, and having yet again had to remonstrate with his disciples, this time for trying to stop people from bringing children to him, we come to the words, 'And as he was setting out on his journey ...' This would appear to refer to Jesus' final, purposeful, almost relentless march up to Jerusalem with his disciples for the Passover of 30 AD. What actually happened as he was setting out was the sudden arrival of a rich young man to question him on how to 'inherit eternal life'; as we all know, the man was told by Jesus to sell his possessions and follow him, but he went away sorrowful. Jesus then uttered one of his best-known sayings: 'How hard it will be for those who have riches to enter the kingdom of God!'[97]

Following this incident, Jesus once again emphasised to his followers the sacrificial nature of true discipleship, so that 'many that are first will be last and the last first', but he had now reached a very late stage in his ministry. Mark's next reference to the journey they were making is striking: 'And they were on the road, going up to Jerusalem, and Jesus was walking ahead of them; and they were amazed, and those who followed were afraid.'[98] It is as if the scene had been etched on someone's memory – Peter's, no doubt. It takes little imagination to fill out the details: the lonely figure of the master striding out in front, eyes fixed on the way ahead; the group of his closest disciples following wearily behind with eyes cast down, occasionally turning to each other to say something in muted tones; then some other walkers, including the women who, we are told, followed Jesus everywhere; finally a few stragglers, only half-convinced they should be there at all.

Yet again, we read, Jesus made an effort to explain what was happening. He stopped abruptly, took the twelve aside – under a convenient tree, perhaps – and tried to explain what they were witnessing: a 'dead man walking'. In Jerusalem the 'Son of man' was to be delivered up, mocked, scourged, killed; yet 'after three days he will rise'. The task was still beyond him; even his closest followers were unable to take in the terrible, wonderful message. Luke says of this occasion, 'They understood none of these things; this saying was hid from them, and they did not grasp what was said.'[99] Even as he finished speaking, the two sons of Zebedee, James and John, came forward to ask if they could be granted special seats of honour, 'one at your right hand and one at your left, in your glory'. Patiently Jesus responded, 'You do not know what you are asking.' He then called his disciples together for a discourse on true greatness, concluding with a statement that summed up his mission: 'For the Son of man also came not to be served but to serve, and to give his life as a ransom for many.'[100]

References to the passing of time during this period in Mark and the two other synoptic gospel writers have been vague, but we can date this final journey up to Jerusalem with some confidence to the spring of 30 AD. In fact, all three synoptists move quickly over the period from Peter's confession in the early summer of 29 to the point we have now reached. Mark, indeed, appears to cover the period filled in by John from the Feast of Tabernacles (fall 29) to the Feast of Dedication (winter 29/30), when Jesus was in and around Jerusalem, with a single sentence: 'And he left there [Galilee; specifically Capernaum] and went to the region of Judea and beyond the Jordan.'[101] The reference to crossing the Jordan is probably paralleled by John's reference (mentioned above) to Jesus going 'across the Jordan to the place where John at first baptized,' following the attempt to stone him for blasphemy.[102] Of course, Jesus probably moved to and fro across the Jordan quite often.

Returning to our narrative, the little party of disciples, resignedly following their leader up to the Jewish capital, passed through Jericho, then wound up through the rolling Judean wilderness as far as 'Bethphage and Bethany at the Mount of Olives'.[103]

The next event in the story is known by those who have only the most casual knowledge of the life of the teacher from Galilee: the 'triumphal entry' into Jerusalem, a few days before Passover, with Jesus astride a donkey's foal, its mother trotting alongside. Jesus' preparations were no doubt made intentionally to fulfil the words of Zechariah recorded by Matthew, 'Tell the daughter of Zion, Behold, your king is coming to you, humble, and mounted on an ass, and on a colt, the foal of an ass.'[104] In the book of Zechariah the messianic prophecy continues, 'I will cut off the chariot from Ephraim and the war horse from Jerusalem; and the battle bow shall be cut off, and he shall command peace to the nations.' Dodd comments:

As we might put it, he [Messiah] will carry out a programme of disarmament and, instead of declaring war on the Gentiles ... he will make overtures of peace to them. If we suppose Jesus to have had this prophecy in mind, then his decision to enter the city in this guise is explained. He was challenging the people to rethink their ideas and their hopes for the nation.[105]

A breathtaking view confronts you as you round the spur of the Mount of Olives just beyond Bethany and look across the deep Kidron valley towards the Holy City. In front of you lies the Temple area, on which today stands the Dome of the Rock and the Al-Aqsa Mosque, with other domes and pinnacles creating a glistening backdrop. Set in the massive wall of both the city and Temple area is the eastern gate, bricked up until Messiah comes, as some would have it. In the time of Jesus you would have been looking straight at the magnificent Temple itself, rebuilt on a lavish scale by Herod the Great, though still – after some fifty years of work – incomplete.

Crowds of bystanders, many of them no doubt pilgrims, greeted the small group – teacher and disciples – on that spring day nearly two thousand years ago as it wound down into the valley before climbing up again to enter the city. There were certainly plenty of people around; Josephus tells us that up to three million would flock to Jerusalem from the provinces for the Feasts of Tabernacles and the Passover.[106] Spreading their garments or branches from the trees in the road before the approaching figure, they raised their voices in joyful acclamation: 'Hosanna to the Son of David! Blessed be he who comes in the name of the Lord, even the king of Israel! Blessed be the kingdom of our father David that is coming! Hosanna in the highest!'[107]

There was little doubt in the minds of those present what the strange procession signified: a religious revival, certainly, but also political revolution. Indeed, for many a pious Jew the former included the latter, since the true king of Israel could only be God or his viceroy. There was no room in the nation's religion as originally conceived for foreign government, the settlement under Moses having been theocratic. So ordinary Jews (but not their 'quisling' religious leaders) believed that the nation must break free, achieving what Judas the Galilean had attempted but failed to achieve a quarter of a century earlier. No doubt, too, some of those supporting Jesus from among the pilgrims thronging the route were from Galilee – centre of the Zealot movement, which proposed violent revolution against Rome.[108] Zechariah's portrayal of a humble, peaceable leader was far from the thoughts of those welcoming this prophet from Galilee, despite the clear visual allusion he was making to it. It was the conviction that the long-awaited deliverer from Roman dominion had at last arrived that lay behind the people's excited cries of 'Son of David', 'king of Israel', and that spurred them to shout provocatively about 'the kingdom of our father David that is coming'.

Death of a king

Within six days the people's hero was dead.

I suppose no death has so fascinated and perplexed thinkers of every generation. Book follows book and theory follows theory as to what exactly happened in Jerusalem – and why – during that last week of Jesus' life. Some go so far as to argue that in reality he did not die,[109] while others conclude that we can never know what happened, let alone understand why, because the records we have are insufficient or unreliable.[110]

I am as fascinated as anyone by the last days of Jesus and by the circumstances of his death – as by the immediate aftermath of that death. But I am not perplexed. In my judgement, the records we have in the gospels (and to some extent elsewhere) of the dramatic sequence of events, far from being inadequate are full and plainly authentic. Of what other character in ancient history do we have a fraction of the data relating to his or her final days on earth? I can think of no one. Yet we readily accept as historical the relatively meagre information available from ancient authors about, for example, the events leading up to the death of Socrates, or of Julius Caesar, or of Nero.

So let us turn to the records of the last days of the charismatic Galilean and see what we discover.

The first point to make is that Jesus really did die. Apart from the testimony of the four evangelists, of Paul in his many letters, of Peter, John, James, Jude (the last two being brothers of Jesus) in their letters and of John in Revelation, plus the writer of the letter to the Hebrews, we have Tacitus speaking of Jesus' death under Pontius Pilate, Josephus and the Talmud likewise referring to it, plus the witness of other slightly later non-Christian and Christian writers. It is not credible that such a host of authorities should have been mistaken. There is also an important piece of evidence, often overlooked, confirming the fact that death really did take place on the cross. John records in his gospel that the soldiers responsible for the execution of the three men at Golgotha broke the legs of two of them (to hasten death) but refrained from breaking the legs of the Nazarene hanging between them when they 'saw that he was already dead'. Instead, one of the soldiers pierced the latter's side with a spear, at which 'at once there came out blood and water'. The evangelist then notes, 'He who saw it has borne witness – his testimony is true, and he knows that he tells the truth'.[111] John is clearly anxious to assure his readers that he received the information about this occurrence from an impeccable source. It thus constitutes powerful corroboration that the crucified man from Galilee actually expired: firstly, evidence of an eyewitness that the Roman soldiery confirmed death in their own crude but effective manner; secondly, the backing of medical science, which confirms that the effluence of blood and water (or a watery substance) could well occur from such a spear thrust following the development of an internal complication inducing death.[112]

Jesus died, as he had predicted, in Jerusalem – or rather, just outside its walls. 'It cannot be that a prophet should perish away from Jerusalem,' he had once said, the bitter thought moving him to a lament: 'O Jerusalem, Jerusalem, killing the prophets and stoning those who are sent to you! How often would I have gathered your children together as a hen gathers her brood under her wings, and you would not! Behold, your house is forsaken.'[113] Yet during those last crowded days this prophet did all he could to bring truth and sense to the tragic city, once described as 'joy of all the earth'.[114] Commencing with a dramatic enacted parable to follow up and complement the one he had given in his manner of entering the city, he went on to instruct, exhort, admonish and warn in a series of discourses.

Jesus went straight to the Temple having received the rapturous acclaim we have described. He looked round briefly, it being already late, but from what he saw determined on a plan; the next day he took action. Driving out vendors and customers alike and overturning the stalls of those changing money (to facilitate payment of Temple dues) or selling pigeons (for sacrificial purposes), he proceeded to bar the way to those wishing to carry merchandise through the sacred precinct. 'My house shall be called a house of prayer,' he proclaimed, echoing the prophets of old, 'but you make it a den of robbers.'[115] There was apparently no popular resistance to his action, nor any protest from the priests, who had their own police force and whose special domain the Temple was. Further, the Roman military, whose garrison overlooked the area, did not intervene. The whole exercise must have been carried through with remarkable speed and efficiency by the sheer power of his personality.

Having achieved this initial objective, the Galilean prophet gave himself to healing those who approached him (still in the Temple) and to teaching, with people hanging on his words. The religious authorities lamely interposed when they heard children in the Temple calling out to him as 'Son of David!', but Jesus countered, as so often, with a word from their scriptures – 'Out of the mouth of babes and sucklings thou hast brought perfect praise' – then retired for the night with his disciples to Bethany.[116]

The incident in the Temple has been seen as an attempted *coup d'état*,[117] yet nothing could be further from the truth. Jesus chose the Temple for this second enacted parable precisely because he was concerned about people's relationship with God, not with Caesar. He was telling his people to reform their religion, their pattern of worship, not their politics, and certainly not to seek the overthrow of the existing ruling power. The next day the authorities had a go at him on the latter issue, hoping to trap him into an answer that might impugn his loyalty to Rome; they asked whether he considered it lawful to give tribute to Caesar – the very point on which the revolutionary Zealots stuck out, arguing that to pay such a tax constituted treason towards God. Jesus neatly avoided criticism by showing them a Roman coin bearing the image of the Emperor, then giving the impeccable answer, 'Render to Caesar the things that are Caesar's, and to God the things that are God's.'[118]

The question of whether or not Jesus was politically motivated, even to being a would-be revolutionary, is frequently aired in both Christian and non-Christian circles. A whole school of teaching, 'liberation theology', is based on the assumption that Jesus was himself a Zealot, or at least had strong sympathies with Zealot aims.[119] I will therefore run briefly through some of the arguments used by supporters of this thesis: certain sayings of Jesus are adduced, such as the one about his coming 'not ... to bring peace but a sword', or a more obscure one about the kingdom of heaven suffering violence, and 'men of violence' taking it by force; the entry into Jerusalem astride a donkey is seen as the first stage in an attempted armed insurrection, while Jesus' action in the Temple is reinterpreted as the occupation of this key institution by force; emphasis is laid on the fact that when the Jesus and his disciples left for Gethsemane following their final meal together in the upper room they were carrying two swords, and on the action of Peter a little later in the garden itself in striking out with a sword and removing the ear of one of those who came to arrest his master.[120]

None of these arguments is compelling. As regards the two sayings mentioned above, Professor Alan Richardson concludes that 'alternative explanations are more probable':[121] the reconstruction of the 'Palm Sunday' entry and Temple incident to make them into an attempted insurrection has no support from the text itself, which is all we have to go by, and the reference to just 'two swords', and Peter's lone action in Gethsemane (which, we read, Jesus immediately reversed by healing the unfortunate man), do not provide evidence that Jesus intended forcibly to resist the authorities' attempts to seize him – rather the opposite.

There is no evidence in the gospels or anywhere else that Jesus attempted to resist the various stratagems of his opponents by force; everything points in the other direction. We have already fathomed the reason: the kingdom he preached was spiritual; it was, as he told Pilate, 'not of this world'.[122] As he went on to explain to the governor, its non-worldly nature was specifically demonstrated by the fact that his servants had not resisted his arrest. Had his kingdom been of this world, in other words, had his agenda been political, they would have fought to prevent his being handed over to the Jewish authorities.

On this whole question of Jesus as a 'political revolutionary', one modern work stands head and shoulders above others. *The Trial of Jesus*, by David Catchpole,[123] goes exhaustively into every facet of the events leading up to Jesus' crucifixion at the hands of the Romans. It is beyond the scope of this work to examine his argument in detail, though I have done this elsewhere.[124] His conclusions, however, can bring this brief excursus into the subject to a close. On the issue of the relationship of Jesus with the Zealot party, Catchpole writes, 'Jesus was no Zealot, nor was he close to the Zealots. It is altogether in excess of the evidence to regard his movement and Zealotism as parallel or in sympathy with one another.' On the wider issue of what exactly it was about Jesus that caused the Jewish authorities to seek his death, and the Roman governor to implement it, and whether or not Jesus was executed as a political offender, Catchpole's verdict is very much in line with what we have already seen of Jesus' activities and the reaction they provoked. He concludes, 'The one place where Jesus can be shown to have caused offence is in matters religious. It is here he was both different and dangerous, and it would be surprising if his end should take up something he had not done and completely bypass something he had done.'[125]

I will now turn back to the course of events during this week in early April, 30 AD, that ended with three barbaric Roman executions. We noted above that over these few days Jesus continued with his teaching, giving a number of discourses aimed to instruct, exhort, admonish and warn. Was there something distinctive about his message at this time, contrasting with his earlier teaching?

I think we can see, not surprisingly, a new urgency in what Jesus was saying to people in these final hours. He was more confrontational, as if (almost in relief) throwing caution to the winds, and there was a greater tendency to speak in judgemental terms. Yet this was partially in response to the increasingly aggressive attacks he himself was sustaining. For example, there was the delayed response of the religious authorities to his action in the Temple. It came the day after the dramatic incident in the form of a carefully phrased question, 'By what authority are you doing these things, or who gave you this authority to do them?' This was a tricky one: if Jesus gave 'God' as his answer his opponents would take it as a confession of messiahship (or try to force from him an explicit confession) and Jesus still did not want to make an unambiguous public declaration of his identity; if, on the other hand, he spoke about acting on his own authority, they would denounce his action as improper. So he had better not answer at all; he had more to do, even now, before submitting to the death he knew to be his destiny. So he met their question with another question, asking on what authority John the Baptist had been acting. Now it was the religious leaders who could not answer: if they said 'from God', Jesus would ask why, therefore, they had not believed in him; if they said, 'from men', that is, he was acting on his own authority, the common people would be in uproar, since they were sure the Baptist was a prophet. Jesus accordingly declined to answer his questioners, sidestepping 'a crisis too soon', and simultaneously eliciting from the priests tacit recognition of John's God-given role – and, indirectly, of his own, since it had followed directly on from that of John.[126]

Jesus then moved onto the offensive, challenging his interrogators with a story – a parable, with its usual allegorical message – about a man who owned a vineyard, then departed, leaving it in the hands of tenants. The man sent servants to collect the produce, but the tenants abused or killed them; when he sent his own son, they killed him too. Jesus now turned to his audience (astute public speaker that he was) and made them deliver the punch-line. 'When therefore the owner of the vineyard comes,' he asked, 'what will he do to those tenants?' Some of his listeners were only too ready to respond: 'He will put those wretches to a miserable death, and let out the vineyard to other tenants.' You can almost see them rubbing their hands with satisfaction as they spoke, sensing the discomfiture of the authorities. Jesus then rounded off the proceedings with a pithy saying about a stone rejected by builders that ended up as the cornerstone. The 'chief priests and Pharisees' can have been in little doubt about what the story and saying signified – their evil treatment of God's messengers, especially Jesus (God's 'son', in the allegory, though his hearers may not immediately have made the connection), and the judgement to be visited upon them. They tried to arrest Jesus, we are told, but 'feared the multitudes, because they held him to be prophet'.[127]

Representatives of the various religious and political groups and parties – scribes and Pharisees, Sadducees, Herodians – tried other ploys to trap the elusive Nazarene into saying something on which they could fasten to accuse him of heresy or blasphemy, but each time he defeated them in argument. They finally decided the strategy was pointless, and desisted. Jesus, meanwhile, was openly denouncing them to the common people who flocked to hear him – within the very precincts of the Temple. 'Beware of the scribes,' he told the crowds, 'who like to go about in long robes, and to have salutations in the market places and the best seats in the synagogues and the places of honour at feasts, who devour widows' houses and for a pretence make long prayers.' He then called down a series of 'woes' upon such 'hypocrites! ... blind fools! ... blind guides, straining out a gnat and swallowing a camel!' He concluded with the words: 'You serpents, you brood of vipers, how are you to escape being sentenced to hell?'[128]

Jesus had at last come fully into the open, speaking his mind without reserve, clearly aware of what he was doing. He was facing his opponents with the truth about themselves, as well as propagating the fact to the world. It would provoke a response, he knew, but not the one his heart desired, not the one that would have allowed him to gather Jerusalem's children together 'as a hen gathers her brood under her wings', not the one thing needful: repentance and a fresh covenant with God. That response would only come in due course from the few, the very few who had always followed him and to whom he must now turn his attention to give final instruction, warning and encouragement.

Having delivered himself of his verdict on the authorities, Jesus left the Temple. His disciples accompanied him and one of them, as they were leaving, remarked on the magnificence of the complex of buildings.

This, we are told, prompted Jesus into predicting the Temple's destruction.[129] Minutes later they were asking him when this event would occur and when, further, they could expect his 'coming' and 'the close of the age'.[130] He responded with an outline of future history from a Jewish perspective, culminating with 'the Son of man coming on the clouds of heaven with power and great glory'.[131] The latter words allude to the verse from Daniel already referred to in relation to Jesus' trial before the Sanhedrin, when he declared himself Messiah and Son of God.[132]

Jesus' closest followers had by this time, it appears, accepted his claim to be Messiah of Israel and, further, were aware that the establishment of an earthly kingdom under him was not to be immediate. On the other hand, they seem still to have been confused about the reason for such delay; there is little to suggest that even at this stage they properly understood the 'Servant' aspect of his messiahship, that it involved suffering and death. Yet perhaps the truth had begun to take root in one or two: we read, for example, how Thomas, not long after the Jewish leaders in Jerusalem had wanted to stone Jesus for blasphemy, had accepted his master's determination to return to the environs of the city to minister to his friend Lazarus. 'Let us also go,' he said to his fellow-disciples, 'that we may die with him.'[133] (It was Thomas, of course, forever the 'realist', who later disbelieved his colleagues' report that Jesus had risen from the dead.) At all events, there can be little doubt that the inner ring of Jesus' followers was by now extremely uneasy about the way events were moving; it did not need an ingrained pessimist to see how disastrously things might end.

Having concluded his discourse about the future, to which he appended several stories stressing the importance of faithful service,[134] Jesus yet again warned his disciples of his impending death: 'You know that after two days the Passover is coming, and the Son of man will be delivered up to be crucified.'[135] The blunt, almost brutal wording gives the impression that at last Jesus assumed some understanding in his hearers.

The narrative in all three synoptic gospels now shifts to the activities of the enemy.

The religious authorities, not surprisingly in view of the words of condemnation Jesus had just directed against them, as well as their own impregnable pride, from this point concentrated all their efforts on a single purpose: arresting this unendurable teacher and engineering his death – quickly and quietly.[136] Passover celebrations were no more than two days away and it was imperative to get him out of the way before the Feast began. Pilgrims were continuously streaming into the city, many of whom would be generally sympathetic to Jesus' stance; an attempt to arrest him publicly, especially during the Feast itself, could lead to a popular demonstration in his favour, which in turn could prompt a nervous Roman governor to send in the military. Such a development, the religious leaders knew, would rob them of any genuine power and, at worst, spiral downwards into a situation where their very security was at risk. This had to be avoided.

The chief priests can scarcely have believed their luck when one of Jesus' closest followers came to them secretly and asked what it was worth for him to give information about his leader's movements. Here was the opportunity they had been looking for to seize their man with the minimum of fuss and rid themselves once and for all of his opposition and the deadly threat it posed.[137]

What exactly impelled Judas Iscariot to perpetrate this treachery we will probably never know, though John tells us in another context that he 'was a thief, and as he had the money box he used to take what was put into it'.[138] We cannot ignore this verdict of a contemporary; John was, after all, a close associate of Judas. Yet it is hard to dismiss the thought that Judas – even if fundamentally dishonest – had another motive besides money. An idea some have put forward is that Judas' act of betrayal was intended to force his master's hand, to compel him into taking violent action, into becoming, in fact, a political revolutionary. There is no warrant for such a view in the text, however, and both it and other reconstructions remain pure speculation.

The stage was now set for the final act in the drama.

Jesus, realising his death was imminent, made arrangements to eat a final meal with his twelve closest followers. He chose the venue for this occasion with care, reserving a 'large upper room' (being above street level would make for quietness and privacy) in the house of a friend, who would see that it was suitably prepared. There is some indication that the friend may have had a connection with the Essene sect, members of which could well have been sympathetic to Jesus' aims.[139] In the synoptic gospels we are told that the arrangements were made on the first day of Unleavened Bread, when the Passover lamb was sacrificed, and that the meal Jesus had with his disciples that same evening was a celebration of this Feast. John in his gospel implies that the 'supper' took place 'before the feast of the Passover', in line with the Talmudic entry that Jesus died 'on the Eve of Passover'.[140]

As already suggested, differing calendars may explain the discrepancy, John basing his chronology on the calendar used by the authorities and the synoptists following the one used by Jesus – perhaps that of the Essenes, with whom, as we have seen, he may have associated. 'Everyone had to conduct his ritual practices according to one of the current calendars,' Carsten Thiede concludes, 'and the one used by the Essenes would be as convenient and plausible (or implausible) as any of the others.'[141]

During this intimate session with the group he had chosen to educate and commission as his heirs for the task he had undertaken, Jesus gave some crucial final teaching. In the three synoptic gospels we read how Jesus gave his disciples instructions to remember him, after his death, by the simplest commemorative action, that of recalling him and his sacrifice on their behalf (about to be consummated, as he was in no doubt) whenever in future they shared bread and wine together. The bread stood for his body, 'given' for them; the wine stood for his blood, 'poured out ' for them.[142] John records a long discourse given by Jesus on this occasion, the emphasis of which was upon the need for them to stay close to him by obeying his 'word' or 'commandments', and to serve one another in humility, living together in unity and love. He promised that they would be supported and upheld in this by the 'Counsellor' or 'Spirit of truth', who would come to them. Beyond this, he stressed that he had to leave them, at least in a physical sense, but that one day he would return to take them to a heavenly home.[143]

The little group sang a hymn in the upper room once Jesus had concluded his valedictory message. The master then led his disciples out and, 'as his custom was', made for the mount of Olives, across the Kidron stream to the east of the city. On the lower slopes of the hill, in an enclosed garden called Gethsemane, where he had often retreated with his disciples, Jesus stopped and told them to wait while he moved off a few yards with his closest friends, Peter, James and John, to pray. It must have been the latter three who recorded what now transpired – or perhaps just Peter, the informant of Mark (though the latter himself may also have been present[144]). Mark describes how Jesus 'began to be greatly distressed and troubled', telling his friends that he was 'very sorrowful, even to death'. So disturbed was he that he 'fell on the ground', praying that 'if it were possible, the hour might pass from him'. Yet in all his agony he was able to conclude the prayer to his Father with the words, 'Not what I will, but what thou wilt'.[145]

Jesus prolonged his time of prayer and when he had finished found his followers 'sleeping for sorrow'.[146] It is a vivid touch: great emotion and tension induce sleep – sleep 'that knits up the ravelled sleave of care'.[147] This slumber, however, could not last long. Even as Jesus was gently rebuking his friends for not watching with him, Judas (who had slipped away during the meal in the upper room to give the nod to the authorities) was approaching with an armed gang, carrying lanterns and torches. The betrayer, as the world knows, identified his leader with a kiss – though this proved unnecessary, for John tells us that Jesus, 'knowing all that was to befall him', was already coming forward. Yet even at this stage the power of the Galilean's presence was enough to check the mob's advance. When Jesus confirmed that he was the one they were seeking, the crowd 'drew back and fell to the ground'. The wanted man was the one in control: restraining his followers from offering resistance and ordering the soldiery to let them go free, he allowed himself to be seized and bound. Matthew and Mark tersely add that the disciples (all of them) forsook Jesus and fled.[148]

Jesus was led away to the house of the high priest, where he was mocked and abused by those holding him, then handed over to Annas, former high priest, father of five later high priests and father-in-law of the current one, Caiaphas. Though elderly, the one-time supreme religious leader wielded considerable influence. Indeed, though the Romans sometimes deposed and appointed new high priests, the Jews considered the office life-long, so that the title was retained until death. Annas, therefore, may in practice (even legally, according to the strictly orthodox) have shared power with Caiaphas.[149] So it was that, in the early hours of the morning, first before Annas and then before Caiaphas and the assembled Council (the Sanhedrin), Jesus faced his opponents. He was questioned 'about his disciples and his teaching', then, when various 'witnesses' had failed to bring consentient evidence substantiating charges against him, he was adjured by the high priest (incensed by his prisoner's silence) to say whether or not he was Messiah and Son of God.[150] We have already noted his affirmative response and the Council's verdict that he was guilty of blasphemy and deserving of death. The authorities thus fulfilled their aim of finding 'testimony against Jesus to put him to death'[151] – yet not in the way they had intended. Since no accusation had stood up to scrutiny, not even that of his having threatened to destroy the Temple and rebuild it in three days (a perversion of what he had actually said),[152] the only damning testimony they could come up with was from his own lips.

Meanwhile, we read in all four gospels of Peter's threefold denial of his Lord while in the high priest's house, to which he had gained access through the good offices of John, an acquaintance of Caiaphas. It is a moving piece of narrative and, like much else in the accounts we have of the last days of the Nazarene, includes touches of detail that ring true.[153]

The Jewish Sanhedrin had no authority to administer capital punishment, though under the liberal policy of the Empire it exercised wide jurisdiction as a court of justice in other matters arising from Jewish religious practice. In bringing Jesus to trial, therefore, it needed to do two things: firstly, to discredit him in the eyes of the Jewish public by demonstrating that he was, from a religious point of view, guilty of a capital charge; secondly, to find an equally serious charge against him that could be brought before the Roman court, which could then pronounce the death sentence. In eliciting from Jesus the confession that he was Messiah and Son of God the authorities succeeded in achieving both these aims. The claim to messiahship may not in itself have been blasphemous in the eyes of the religious establishment, but the associated assertion of divine status most certainly was, as we have seen. So his 'blasphemy' fulfilled the requirement for a capital religious offence. As to a comparable crime against Rome, the messianic claim provided an ideal ground on which to bring Jesus before the governor because it could be cited as treason, the offence of setting yourself up as king and therefore as rival to Caesar.

Their way ahead clear, early on Friday morning Caiaphas and his colleagues took Jesus over to the palace, or praetorium, to face Pontius Pilate. They immediately began accusing him: 'We found this man perverting our nation, and forbidding us to give tribute to Caesar, and saying that he himself is Christ [Messiah] a king.'[154] Pilate then inquired of the prisoner whether he himself made such a claim, to which Jesus gave an ambiguous response – though readily confessing to a non-worldly kingship.[155] This seemed to convince the governor of Jesus' innocence before the law so he told the Jewish leaders what he felt and sought a way out of the impasse. Having discovered that Jesus was from Galilee, he sent him off to Herod Antipas, who had limited jurisdiction over the region; his aim was probably that of seeking advice from a local ruler. Herod, however, after allowing his soldiers to revile and ill-treat the man in their charge, sent him back again.[156]

Pilate, therefore, insisting to the Jewish authorities that both he and Herod considered the accused innocent, suggested that after being scourged Jesus should be released, in accordance with the regular Passover custom. The authorities would not entertain the idea, immediately demanding that another prisoner be released – one Barabbas, arrested for insurrection and murder. According to John, the governor made yet further efforts to have Jesus released, encouraged in this both by his wife, who had been troubled by a dream, and the disturbingly quiet demeanour of the man before him. Yet once the Jews began to accuse him of disloyalty to Caesar, Pilate's resistance crumbled. 'Shall I crucify your king?' he asked. 'We have no king but Caesar,' they replied. The Roman procurator, in a sadly pathetic gesture, proceeded to 'wash his hands' of the matter; then, having released Barabbas, he had Jesus flogged before handing him over to his soldiers for the sentence of death to be implemented. It was now between six and seven in the morning.[157]

The Imperial troops – a whole battalion, we read – spent some time inside the palace making fun of their prisoner and knocking him about before leading him out, with two criminals, to be crucified. He was by then too weak to carry the heavy timber crosspiece all the way to the place of execution, so a passer-by was pressed into this grim service. The procession to Golgotha, 'place of a skull', just outside the city walls, must have taken some time as people thronged the route, many of whom were women bewailing the fate of one they had days before welcomed as prophet and deliverer. Even now Jesus found the resources to turn to them and tell them not to waste their tears as worse was to befall the people of Jerusalem.[158]

Arrived at Golgotha, the soldiers impaled the condemned men on the wooden frames, with Jesus crying, 'Father, forgive them.' The crosses were then erected, Jesus hanging between the two felons with Pilate's inscription (in three languages) fastened above his head: 'Jesus of Nazareth, King of the Jews'. It was about nine in the morning. Few words came from the Nazarene's lips, and those he uttered – saving for the single statement, 'I thirst' – concerned the needs of others (including that of the robber hanging beside him), his mission, or his Father. He died quickly, by most standards; crucified men could linger half-alive for days. This meant, as we have already seen, that unlike the men on each side of him he did not have to be dispatched by the soldiers so that his body could be removed before sunset and the onset of the Sabbath. Following his death, at about three o'clock on a strangely dark afternoon, the officer-in-charge of the proceedings declared that the man hanging limp before him must have been innocent – more, that he was 'Son of God'.[159]

Chapter 10
'He is always there'

The Ashanti tribesman whom we met at the outset of this study was in no doubt that there was a Supreme Spirit who existed from eternity to eternity. 'The sun falls in the evening time, but He is always there.'

The witness of Jesus of Nazareth is in essence no different. His life comprises the most eloquent statement of the reality of an all-powerful, all-knowing, all-loving Creator. By common consent the noblest and wisest of men, he suffered rejection, vilification, death by torture – yet his faith did not waver. Those dying words epitomise his attitude from first to last: 'Father, into thy hands I commend my spirit!'

Could such a human have been wrong on the ultimate question? Who are we, so frequently wrong on issues great and small, to dismiss his testimony?

One of the last things Jesus said to his followers in the upper room was this: 'Do you now believe? The hour is coming, indeed it has come, when you will be scattered, every man to his home, and will leave me alone; yet I am not alone, for the Father is with me. I have said this to you, that in me you may have peace. In the world you have tribulation; but be of good cheer, I have overcome the world.'[1] Jesus knew about suffering and deprivation, and he predicted it for his disciples. His own faith had been refined in the furnace of affliction and his friends must expect the same. Yet for them the way of suffering had already been pioneered, so their task was correspondingly lightened. Jesus was the forerunner, who had blazed the trail; they had only to trace his steps, enjoying an inner peace whatever the circumstances because he had already defeated evil in all its forms. While they remained 'in' him, they too would defeat every kind of evil.

Jesus had 'overcome the world'; he had defeated evil. In what sense had he done so? The question brings us to the biggest mystery the world has seen or will see – or else to history's most remarkable hoax. I refer to the Christian claim that Jesus rose from the dead. One writer puts it thus:

> The story told in the gospels does not end with Jesus dead and buried. They go on to say that he had risen again. That this was so is a conviction that runs through the whole of the New Testament. It is not a belief that grew up within the church; it is the belief around which the church itself grew up, and the 'given' upon which its faith was based.[2]

To the first Christians, then, the way Jesus had 'overcome' was clear enough: he had overcome man's 'last enemy', which is death.[3] This meant he was alive and able to succour and assist them in their journey through this world. As he told them (after his resurrection), 'I am with you always, to the close of the age.'[4]

We may or may not share the conviction of those early followers of Jesus that he is still alive. It is, however, an issue of immeasurable significance. What, we may therefore ask, made the first Christians so sure that their master had risen again, and what convinces those who hold that belief today?

The disciples' claim that Jesus had risen rests on two assertions: firstly, that the tomb in which his body was laid by Joseph of Arimathea late on Friday afternoon was unaccountably empty on Sunday morning; secondly, that on that same Sunday and for several weeks afterwards he appeared in risen form to many of his disciples. I say 'assertions', as if those first followers of Jesus were trying to convince both themselves and the world of something that contained an element of doubt. Yet for the women and then men who came to the tomb early on that first day of the Jewish week there was, according to our records, no uncertainty. The condition in which they found the tomb, described in detail, admitted of no doubt.

Mary of Magdala, followed closely by some other women who, together with her, had seen their master's linen-wrapped body laid in the tomb two days previously, was the first to find the grave empty. Greatly distressed, she hurried back to tell Peter and another disciple (he 'whom Jesus loved': almost certainly John) that someone had managed to roll back the stone blocking the entrance to the sepulchre and gone off with the body of their master. The two immediately ran off to verify this troubling news. They found the tomb empty of the body, as Mary had said, but to their astonishment the linen cloths that had enclosed it were lying in position, with the smaller piece of material that had been placed around the head also in position, a little apart from the other cloths and still rolled up. It could only mean one thing: Jesus had risen from the dead. John, in describing the reaction of 'the other disciple' on his arrival at the tomb, simply says: 'He saw and believed'.[5]

What made this disciple so sure? Sheer logic. No one had taken the body away, for who on earth would have removed the linen cloths from a corpse and then carried it away naked? Even if for some incredible reason the cloths had been removed from the body, they would have been left in a disordered pile, or, if robbers had been involved, haphazardly strewn around; they would certainly not be lying collapsed where the body had been, with the head-cloth looking as if it should be wrapped round something. There was just one explanation for what they were looking at: the body had somehow *passed through* the cloths. They were also aware, of course, that the stone at the entrance to the sepulchre had been rolled back, but this was a small matter to explain beside the phenomenon of the linen cloths. Anyway, they may very well have felt the earthquake earlier that morning, and so concluded that the stone had as a result become dislodged.[6]

The fact of the empty tomb was unquestionably a cornerstone of belief for the first disciples. Peter referred to it obliquely in his first public address in Jerusalem in defence of his faith.[7] No one tried to refute what he said by producing the body of Jesus, or pointing to another tomb, official or otherwise, in which the body was said to lie. This fact effectively precludes any theory based on the removal of the body by human agency or the notion that the women, and others later, went to the wrong tomb. The suggestion that the disciples themselves removed the body of their master and went on to propagate a colossal lie is not worth considering, on psychological grounds alone. And we have already refuted the idea, sometimes advanced, that Jesus merely swooned on the cross, revived in the tomb and then somehow escaped from it.

Complementing the evidence of the empty tomb for the resurrection of Jesus, and at first sight more significant, is the claim made by the first disciples that they had met him in risen form after his death – talked with him, ate with him, touched him. It is not always appreciated how extensive these claims are. Mary of Magdala was the first to say she had seen the resurrected Lord, followed by the other women who came with her to the tomb early on Sunday morning. Later that day, we are told, Jesus appeared to Simon Peter. Cleopas and another disciple then recounted how, during an afternoon walk on the same Sunday to a village outside Jerusalem, they had been joined by a stranger whom they suddenly recognised as their master. Towards evening on the same day, when the disciples – minus Thomas – had assembled in Jerusalem behind closed doors 'for fear of the Jews', Jesus 'came and stood among them'; he invited them to 'handle' him to make sure he was 'flesh and bones', then demonstrated his physical nature by eating some fish before them. He appeared to the disciples eight days later when they had again come together – this time including Thomas, whom Jesus mildly rebuked for not having earlier believed his colleagues. He also met the disciples in Galilee, appearing to Peter, Thomas, Nathanael,

John, James and two others after they had been fishing in the Sea of Tiberias, when he talked with them and partook of breakfast, and then to the eleven (and probably others) on a mountainside. Paul tells us, finally, that on one occasion Jesus appeared 'to more than five hundred brethren at one time', most of whom were still alive when he was writing (around 55 AD), that he made a personal appearance to James, his own brother, and that 'last of all, as to one untimely born, he appeared also to me'.[8]

Simply listing these appearances of the risen Jesus does not, of course, add up to proof that they occurred. Yet the careful and often detailed documentation of these putative events by the four evangelists, Paul, and others, clearly establishes that they and the first Christians were wholly persuaded of their historicity – indeed, were in many cases convinced as a result of personal encounters. There is not a hint in the accounts of contrivance or extravagant embellishment; they constitute sober, descriptive reports. And there is one feature that is artless in the extreme, something that would never have been included in a concocted story: the references (implied if not stated) to a slight strangeness in Jesus after his resurrection, so that people had to reassure themselves that the man before them really was the master. The following examples can be cited: Mary of Magdala did not recognise him immediately but thought he was the gardener (she had, of course, been weeping); Cleopas and his friend did not know the stranger as Jesus until he broke bread before them in the house; the disciples to whom Jesus appeared late on the first Sunday in Jerusalem were at first 'startled and frightened, and supposed that they saw a spirit'; after their fruitless night's fishing in the Sea of Tiberias, the disciples did not know it was Jesus on the shore calling out advice until, on doing what he said, they netted a huge catch; some of those to whom Jesus appeared on the Galilean mountainside 'doubted'.

No more need be said about the remarkable aftermath of Jesus' death except to point out that as a result of what happened the disciples were transformed. Frightened outcasts, cowering behind locked doors, became fearless ambassadors of a new Way of love and forgiveness. Those who confess the same conviction, the same faith in the carpenter from Nazareth, can expect a like transformation. For if Jesus truly rose from the dead, all is changed: we have a new reality, shedding light on every facet of experience, every aspect of being; we have a 'greater logic'; we have the Word made flesh; we have God himself – everlasting Love – revealed.

'He is always there.'

Notes and References

Biblical quotations, unless otherwise stated, are from the Revised Standard Version (RSV). Other versions occasionally used are the Authorised Version (AV), the Revised Version (RV) and the New International Version (NIV). Abbreviations used for the gospels Matthew, Mark, Luke, and John are Mt,, Mk, Lk, and Jn.

Chapter 1: In the Beginning

1. e.g., Frazer, J.G., *The Golden Bough: A Study in Comparative Religion*, London: Macmillan, 1890; Vol. I, pp. 348-9; Otto, Rudolf, *The Idea of the Holy*, Penguin, 1959 (German original, 1917), pp. 28-31; Kennedy, Ludovic, *All In The Mind*, London: Hodder and Stoughton (Sceptre Paperback), 1999, pp. 29-30, 33-35. Kennedy refers also to 'some evidence' for 'some primitive tribes' having 'fashioned a Supreme Being who existed conjointly and had power over lesser gods' (see Notes 8 and 9, below). *Cf.* Armstrong, Karen, *A History of God*, London, Heinemann, 1993; Mandarin paperback, 1994, pp. 9-10. Armstrong refers to the book *The Origin of the Idea of God* by Wilhelm Schmidt (first published in German in 1912; published in English [transl. by H.J. Rose] in 1931, with the title *The Origin and Growth of Religion*), who argues that there had been a primitive monotheism before men and women started to worship a number of gods. She concludes: 'It is impossible to prove this one way or the other. There have been many theories about the origin of religion. Yet it seems that creating gods is something that human beings have always done.'

2. Frankfort, H. and H.A., Wilson, J.A., and, T. Jacobsen., *op. cit.*, Penguin, 1949, pp. 12, 14-15; originally published as *The Intellectual Adventure of Ancient Man*, University of Chicago Press, Chicago, 1946.

3. *Ibid.* pp. 17-18; also Frazer, *op. cit.*, Vol. I, p. 301.

4. *Op. cit.*, p. 17.

5. Rattray, R.S., *The Tribes of the Ashanti Hinterland*, Oxford: Clarendon Press, 1932, Vol. I, p. 42.

6. *Op. cit.*, London: Longmans, Green and Co, 1955, p. 57.

7. Meek, C.K., *Tribal Studies in Northern Nigeria*, London: Kegan Paul, Trench, Trubner and Co., Ltd., 1931; Vol I, p.191.

8. Kennedy, L., *op. cit.*, p. 33.

9. *Ibid.* p. 32.

10. *Op. cit.*, p. 58.

11. 'Primitive Monotheism', in *The Sociological Review*, XXVII, pp. 337 f. (1935); cited by Oesterley, W.O.E. and T.H. Robinson, *Hebrew Religion: Its Origin and Development*, 2ⁿᵈ ed., London: S.P.C.K., 1937, p. 5; New York: Macmillan, 1930.
12. Frankfort, H., *et al.*, *op. cit.*, pp. 140-1.
13. *Ibid.* p. 153.
14. *Ibid.* p. 152.
15. Cited by Wiseman, P.J., *New Discoveries in Babylonia about Genesis*, 6ᵗʰ ed., London: Marshall, Morgan and Scott, 1953, p. 25; 1ˢᵗ ed., 1936.
16. Handcock, P.S.P., *Mesopotamian Archaeology: An Introduction to the Archaeology of Babylonia and Assyria*, London: Macmillan, 1912, p. 375.
17. *Ibid.* p. 386.
18. *Ibid.* p. 387.
19. Cylinder of Cyrus, inscription on baked clay, c. 536 BC; from Babylon; see Wiseman, D.J., *Illustrations from Biblical Archaeology*, London: Tyndale, 1958, p.74; *cf.* (in the Bible) Ezra, Chap. 1.
20. Frankfort H., *et al.*, op. cit., p. 65.
21. *Ibid.* p. 60.
22. *Ibid.* p. 67.
23. *Ibid.* p. 65; John 1:1.
24. *Ibid.* p. 68; Genesis 2:2.
25. *Ibid.* p. 107.
26. *History of the Near East*; cited by Wiseman, P.J., *op. cit.*, p. 28.
27. Frankfort H., *et al.*, *op. cit.*, pp.105-6.
28. *Ibid.* p. 115.
29. *Sumer and Akkad*, p. 3; cited by Wiseman, P.J., *op. cit.*, p. 28.
30. *The Sumerians*, p. 37; cited by Wiseman, P.J., *op. cit.*, p. 29.
31. Frankfort, H., *et al.*, *op. cit.*, p. 107.
32. *Ibid.* p.119.
33. Frazer, J.G., *op. cit.*, Vol. I, pp. 301-305; concerning a resurrection of Osiris celebrated at his mysteries, Frazer cites Plutarch, *Isis et Osiris*, 35.
34. Ross, J., *The Original Religion of China*, London: Oliphant, Anderson and Ferrier, 1909, pp. 19-20; cited by Kang, C.H., and Ethel R. Nelson, *The Discovery of Genesis: How the Truths of Genesis Were Found Hidden in the Chinese Language*, St Louis: Concordia Publishing House, 1979, p. 2.
35. Couperie, T. De La, *The Language of China Before the Chinese*, Taipei: Ch'eng-wen Publishing Co., 1966, p. 114; cited by Kang and Nelson, *op. cit.*, p. 2.

Chapter 2: Out of Ur

1. Genesis 12:1. The designation of Ur in Genesis 11:31 as 'Ur of the Chaldeans' has been considered anachronistic, since the Chaldeans are not mentioned in extra-biblical texts until the eleventh century BC. Lack of extra-biblical evidence does not in itself prove the presence of an anachronism, but, if there were one, the biblical designation could be readily explained as a gloss by a later editor.

2. *Op. cit.*, p. 19.

3. 'Jehovah' is the traditional biblical rendering of the Hebrew four-letter divine name more properly transcribed in English 'YHVH' or 'YHWH', sometimes known as the Tetragrammaton. The ancient Hebrew script, like that of Arabic, did not indicate short vowels, so the original pronunciation of the name is unknown. Jews today, when reading aloud, simply pronounce the Hebrew word 'Adonai' (meaning 'Lord') if they encounter the Tetragrammaton, impelled mostly by reverence for this holiest of divine names. Early Protestant translators inserted the vowels from 'Adonai' between the letters of the Tetragrammaton (using J and not Y for Hebrew 'yodh') to come up with 'Jehovah'. Theologians today usually render the Tetragrammaton 'YHWH' or 'Yahweh' (using W and not V for Hebrew 'vav', or 'waw'). See further, pp. 23-4, below.

4. *Old Testament Theology*, 1893, Vol. I, p. 25; cited by Wiseman, P.J., *op. cit.*, p. 11.

5. *The Stones and the Scriptures*, New York: J.B. Lippincott, 1972; London: Inter-Varsity Press, 1973, p. 24; *cf.* Harrison, R.K., *Introduction to the Old Testament*, Grand Rapids: Eerdmans, 1969; London: Tyndale, 1970. Harrison (1970) writes, p. 59, 'The Graf-Wellhausen school mostly ignored the possible effect which extra-Biblical sources might have as a control over the more extravagant use of purely theoretical speculations.'

6. *Cf.* Harrison, R.K., *op. cit.*, pp.21 and 65. Harrison cites H.F. Hahn and J. Pedersen, theologians who have noted (and, in Pedersen's case, repudiated) the Hegelian overtones of the Wellhausenian analytical scheme.

7. *New Discoveries in Babylonia about Genesis*, London: Marshall, Morgan and Scott, 6th ed., 1953 (1st ed., 1936), p. 10; for Wiseman's arguments in detail, *passim* in the quoted work.

8. *Cf.* Wilhelm Möller, who in 1912 argued that the two names were indicative of two different functions; cited by Harrison, R.K., *op. cit.*, p. 39; *also* Gordon, C.H., *Christianity Today*, IV, No. 4, (1959), pp. 131ff. A veteran Near Eastern archaeologist, Gordon draws on parallels in ancient Near

Eastern literature to show the complete inadequacy of using the divine names in the Pentateuch as a criterion for analysis. His is, in effect, a criticism of the Graf-Wellhausen method.

9. e.g., G.T. Manley, *The Book of the Law*, London: Tyndale, 1957. Arguing that topographical and geographical data in Deuteronomy show every sign of being original, he rejects the view that the book was written in the time of king Josiah in the seventh century, at a time of reforming zeal for the Law.

10. e.g., Albright, W.F., 'Historical and Mythical Elements in the Story of Joseph', *Journal of Biblical Literature*, XXXVII (1918)' pp. 112-143; and Martin Noth (1948), who regarded it as a late scholastic reconstruction; cited by Yamauchi, E., *op. cit.*, p. 34.

11. Albright, W.F., 'Abram the Hebrew: A New Archaeological Interpretation', *Bulletin of the American Schools of Oriental Research*, No. 163 (1961), p. 49; cited by Yamauchi, E., *op. cit.*, p. 19.

12. 'Archaeology and Scripture', *The Westminster Theological Journal*, XXXIII (1971), pp. 151-2; cited by Yamauchi, E., *op. cit.*, p. 13.

13. e.g., Karen Armstrong, *op. cit.*, p. 24.

14. *Op. cit.*, p. 8; *pace* Karen Armstrong, *op. cit.*, p. 77.

15. *Cf.* Lambert, W.G., 'A New Look at the Babylonian Background of Genesis', *Journal of Theological Studies*, XVI (1965), pp. 287-300; cited by Yamauchi, E., *op. cit.*, p. 26.

16. Frazer's 'larger collection' of flood traditions is referred to by Nelson, Byron C. (1931), p. 170; Nelson himself gives a 'small portion of existing traditions' (Appendix II, pp. 170-190), covering 39 distinct traditions from Assyria-Babylonia, Persia, Syria, Asia Minor, Greece, Egypt, Italy, Lithuania, Wales, Scandinavia, Lapland, Russia, China, India, North America, Central America, South America, and the Pacific Islands. For the Gilgamesh Epic, see Mallowan, M., 'Noah's Flood Reconsidered', *Iraq*, XXVI (1964), pp. 62-82; cited by Yamauchi, *op. cit.*, p. 28.

17. Genesis 22:1-19.

18. Hebrews 11:17-19.

19. Micah 6:7b.

20. See Note 3, above.

21. Wiseman, P.J., *op. cit.*, pp. 109-118, explains this in detail.

22. The book of Joshua, *passim*.

23. e.g., R. de Vaux and André Parrot; cited by Yamauchi, E., *op. cit.*, p 48.

24. e.g., Armstrong, K., *op. cit.*, p. 65; *cf.* Oesterley and Robinson, *op. cit.*, p. 196.

25. Exodus 15:11; 20:3; Deuteronomy 5:7; 10:17; II Chronicles 2:5; Psalm 82 (*cf.* Psalm 86:8); Genesis 6:2,4; Job 1:6; 38:7.
26. e.g., Deut 32:16-21; 37-39; I Samuel 4,5; II Kings 19:17-19; Psalm 97:7,9; Isaiah 41:21-24; 44:6-8; Jeremiah 5:7.
27. Isaiah 6:1-5; 9:6,7; 11:1-5.
28. The weaknesses, in particular the subjectivity, of the arguments used by scholars to establish the existence of this 'Second Isaiah' have been demonstrated by O.T. Allis in *The Unity of Isaiah*, London: Tyndale, 1951.
29. Isaiah 52:13 - 53:12.
30. Hosea 6:6; *cf.* Matthew 9:13.
31. Facts confirmed by archaeological discovery, especially that of the Babylonian Chronicle; see Yamauchi, E., *op. cit.*, pp. 79-81.
32. Jeremiah 31:31,33.

Chapter 3: New Era

1. e.g., Armstrong, K., *op. cit.*, p. 95; *or* Kennedy, L., *op. cit.*, pp. 53-4; *or* Kahl, J., *The Misery of Christianity*, London: Penguin, 1971, pp. 103-21 (German edition: Hamburg, 1968).
2. *The Empty Tomb*, London: Panther, 1963, p. 143.
3. Mark 12:29.
4. Mark 1:15.
5. Matthew 9:13; 12:7.
6. Mark 10:14,15.
7. A.N. Wilson, for instance, discussing in his book *Jesus* (London: Flamingo, 1993, p. xvi [Sinclair-Stevenson, 1992]) the question of whether Jesus thought himself to be divine, writes that he had not been able to find 'the smallest evidence that Jesus had ever entertained such beliefs about himself'. It is difficult to know what gospel Mr Wilson can have been reading in order to reach this conclusion.
8. Mark 1:17; 2:5,23-28; 5:7; 8:34-38; 14:61-2. For Jesus applying the title 'Son of man' unequivocally to himself, *see* Mark 2:5-11 (*cf.* Luke 5:20-34 and Matthew 9:2-8); Lk 22:48; John 9:35-37.
9. John 10:31,33.
10. *Cf.* Fox, R.L., *Christians and Pagans in the Mediterranean world from the second century AD to the conversion of Constantine*, London: Penguin, 1988, p. 422. He affirms, 'Christians are not known to have attacked their pagan enemies; they shed no innocent blood except their own ... never rebelling against the Emperor's temporal rule.'
11. *Christianity in European History*, London: Collins, 1952, p. 11.

12. Cited by Toynbee, A.J., *A Study of History*, [abridgement of Volumes 1-6 by D.C. Somervell], London: Oxford University Press, 1946, p. 435.

13. In 'Defining Judaism: Some Ground-Clearing', *Jewish Journal of Sociology* (London), No. 2 (December 1965), pp. 166; cited by Neusner, J., *The Way of the Torah*, Belmont, California: Wadsworth, 1988, p. 27.

14. *Ibid.*, p. 28.

15. This teaching about Jesus comes from three of the chapters in the Koran: the chapter (or *sura*) entitled 'Mary', another entitled 'Women', and a third entitled 'The Table'. Quotations are taken from the English translation from the Arabic by N. J. Dawood (London: Penguin, 1956).

16. From the Koran: 'Women'.

17. The summary of Hinduism given in these paragraphs is indebted to the book *Hinduism*, by R.C. Zaehner, London: Oxford University Press, 1962, pp. 1-11.

18. *Buddhism: The Path to Nirvana*, New York: Harper & Row, 1987, p. 17. The summary of Buddhism given here is indebted to this work.

19. *Op. cit.*, p. 56.

Chapter 4: Death of Divinity

1. Romans 1:17b (AV).

2. Cited in Armstrong, K., *op. cit.*, p. 352.

3. *God's Funeral*, London: Abacus, 2000, pp. 35-6 (John Murray, 1999).

4. Hume, David, *Dialogues Concerning Natural Religion*, ed. Kemp Smith, Edinburgh: Nelson, 1935, pp. 76-9; cited by Wilson, A.N. (2000), pp. 24-5.

5. Cited by Kennedy, L., *op. cit.*, pp. 176-7.

6. Cited by Armstrong, K., *op. cit.*, p. 393.

7. See Lyons, J., *Language and Linguistics*, Cambridge: Cambridge University Press, 1981, p. 232.

8. Cited by Cragg, G.R., *The Church and the Age of Reason*, London: Penguin, 1960, p. 142.

9. Cited by Wilson, A.N., *op. cit.*, p. 57.

10. See Cheyne, T.K., *Founders of Old Testament Criticism*, 1893, pp. 13, 21; cited by Harrison, R.K., *op. cit.*, p. 14.

11. *Komposition des Hexateuchs*; cited by Harrison, R.K., *op. cit.*, p. 21.

12. *Geschichte Israels*, I, 1878, pp. 3ff; cited by Harrison, *op. cit.*, p.21, Note 8.

13. *Op. cit.*, p. 22.

14. e.g., P.C. Hodgson, *The Formation of Historical Theology: A Study of F.C. Baur*, New York: Harper and Row, 1966.

15. *The Sea of Faith*, London: BBC, 1984; SCM, 1994, p. 275.
16. *Op. cit.* (2000), pp. 58-9.
17. Dr Benjamin Jowett, Master of Balliol, commented on one of his addresses: 'Well, all that I could make out was that today was yesterday and this world is the same as the next.' Sir Mountstuart Grant was more sweeping: 'I must have heard him, first and last, some thirty or forty times, and never carried away one clear idea, or even the impression that he had more [than] the faintest conception of what he himself meant.' Both quotations are cited by Stephen Pile, *The Book of Heroic Failures*, London: Routledge & Kegan Paul, 1971, p. 21. For information on Coleridge, Maurice and others of the period I am also indebted to Alec R. Vidler, *The Church in an Age of Revolution*, London: Penguin, 1961.
18. Cited by Armstrong, K., *op. cit.*, p. 403.
19. Cited by Hamilton, K., *Earthly Good: The Churches and the Betterment of Human Existence*, Grand Rapids, Mich.: Eerdmans, 1990, p. 62.
20. *Theology of Metaphysics*, 2nd ed., Bonn, 1929, p. 29; cited by Armstrong, *op. cit.*, p. 406.
21. Cited by Wheen, F., *Karl Marx*, London: Fourth Estate, 1999; paperback, 2000, p. 53.
22. Marx was essentially a pragmatist: philosophy must give way to action; the philosopher must serve the revolutionary. As he wrote in *Theses on Feuerbach* (1845), 'The philosophers have only *interpreted* the world, in various ways: the point is to *change* it.' Cited by Wheen, F., *op.cit.*, pp. 54-5.
23. Cited by Wheen, F., *op. cit.*, p. 364.

Chapter 5: A Question of Substance

1. 'The Desanctification of Nature', in *Sanctity and Secularity: the Church and the World*, from 'Studies in Church History', ed. Derek Baker, Vol. 10, Oxford: Blackwell, 1973, p. 10.
2. *Op. cit.*, London: John Murray, 1859.
3. *The Selfish Gene*, Oxford: Oxford University Press, 1976; paperback, 1989, p. 1.
4. The problem of the development of such attributes is not just the complexity of those attributes, making their acquisition through random mutation and natural selection extremely difficult to envisage. It is also that many organs of today's living creatures would have been no help at all while they were in the process of evolving, but would, possessed in an imperfect state, have been a destructive hindrance in the struggle for existence. It is, indeed, hard to see how the transition of life from water

to land can have happened at all without one monster mutation occurring in a single creature (or perhaps in two, for sexed creatures), allowing it (them) to make the critical jump from one environment to the other – and survive.

Richard Dawkin's idea (*The Blind Watchmaker*, London: Longman, 1986; Penguin, 1988) that inherently improbable mutational developments like that of the human eye are rendered less improbable by postulating an enormous number of tiny mutations occurring over vast ages, falls into the error dubbed the 'Statistical Fallacy' by Francis Crick (*Life Itself*, London: MacDonald, 1981). This is explained by Richard Milton (*The Facts of Life: Shattering the Myth of Darwinism*, London: Fourth Estate, 1992, pp. 144-5): 'What Dawkins is saying with his cumulative evolution argument is that the probability of each single step in a cumulative process must be less than the whole probability of leaping straight to the finished result, simply because each step itself is less than the whole. But this is simply wrong. The improbability of step number 2 correctly following step number 1, correctly followed by step number 3 and so on for 100 mutations, is as great as leaping to the 100th step in one go. What is more, the greater the number of steps into which we break up the overall leap, the more improbable it becomes that they will all take place in the right order.'

5. e.g., Kennedy, L. *op. cit.*, pp. 209-14; Wilson, A.N., *op. cit.*, p. 226.
6. *The Blind Watchmaker*, Penguin ed., 1988, p. 6.
7. *The Selfish Gene*, paperback ed. 1989, p. 330 (Note to p. 198, on 'faith').
    Philip Sherrard (see Note 1, above) has written, 'There is one particular fallacy from which we must free ourselves, and this is the idea that contemporary scientific theories are somehow neutral, or value-free, and do not presuppose the submission of the human mind to a set of assumptions or dogmas in the way that is said to be demanded by adherence to a religious faith.' (Cited by Jonathon Porritt, *The Guardian Weekly*, 8-14 June 2000.)
8. This seems to be his position, as witnessed by his remark in a speech at the Edinburgh International Science Festival, 15 April 1992 (reported in *The Independent*, 20 April 1992): 'The more you understand the significance of evolution, the more you are pushed away from the agnostic position and towards atheism.'
9. *The Selfish Gene*, p. 1.
10. From his article, 'Professor Dawkins' atheism requires an act of faith', *The Daily Telegraph*, 12 April 1996.
11. In the Edinburgh speech cited, Note 8, above.

12. *Ibid.*
13. e.g., Schwartz, J. H., *Sudden Origins: Fossils, Genes and the Emergence of Species,* London: John Wiley, 2000; *cf.* Jones, S., *Almost Like a Whale: The Origin of Species Updated,* London: Doubleday, 1999.
14. Cited by Prof. Phillip E. Johnson, University of California, Berkeley, in a public lecture sponsored by the Faculty of Law of the University of Cardiff, 18 September 1997; reported in the form of an article, 'Time's up for the comatose watchmaker', in *The Times Higher Education Supplement,* 21 November 1997.
15. Cited by Tom Bethel, contributing editor to *Harper's Magazine,* in an article, 'Creation and Evolution', in that magazine, February 1985.
16. *Ontogeny and Phylogeny,* Harvard University Press, 1977; also, London: John Wiley.
17. From his review of Schwartz's book (London: John Wiley, 2000) in *The Times Higher Education Supplement,* 14 April 2000.
18. Hennig's principal work was *Phylogenetic Systematics,* published in English (an updated edition) by the University of Illinois Press, 1966.
19. Cited by Tom Bethel, February 1985 (*see* Note 15, above).
20. Cited by Nelson, B.C., *After Its Kind: The First and Last Word on Evolution,* Minneapolis: Augsburg Publishing House, 2nd ed., 1952, p. ii.
21. *Almost Like a Whale: The Origin of Species Updated,* London: Doubleday, 1999.
22. Cited by Kam Patel, in an article, 'Aping Darwin', in *The Times Higher Education Supplement,* 10 September 1999.
23. From *Yahoo News/Reuters*; report by M. Fox, Health and Science Correspondent, 11 February 2001; also BBC news, 12 February 2001.
24. Professor Scott, University of Princeton, *The Theory of Evolution,* p. 163; cited by Nelson, B.C. (1952), p. 106.
25. See the journal *Nature,* 15 July 1922; cited by Nelson (1952), p. 8.
26. See Punnet, R., *Mendelism,* 6th ed., 1922, p. 182. He writes, 'It is not visible attributes that constitute the essential difference between one species and another. The essential difference, whatever it may be, is that underlying the phenomenon of sterility. There is little doubt that numbers of well recognised species (i.e. systematic species) will eventually fall to the ground as soon as we are in a position to apply the test of breeding.' Cited by Nelson (1952), p. 8.
    Crossing similar but distinct species (such as bison with domestic cattle) results in many progeny being born dead and live progeny usually being sterile, while 'the progenies of partially fertile hybrids run back to the parental condition'; see Babcock, E.B. and Clausen, R.E., *Genetics in Relation to Agriculture,* 1927, p. 324; cited by Nelson (1952), p. 11.

27. Cited by Nelson (1952), pp. vi, 104.

28. In *Science*, January 1922.

29. See Linton's review of Eldredge's book, *The Triumph of Evolution and the Failure of Creationism* (Basingstoke: Freeman, 2001), in *The Times Higher Education Supplement*, 20 April 2001.

30. *The Guardian Weekly*, 14-20 February 2002.

31. Nelson, B.C., *The Deluge Story in Stone: A History of the Flood Theory of Geology*, Minneapolis: Augsburg Publishing House, 1931, pp. 100-2. As regards the periodical deposition of sediment through an 'ebb and flow' of waters, Nelson writes (pp. 109-10), 'Were there a Deluge which produced the strata by a continued ebb and flow of its waters, individual and characteristic layers should exhibit a gradual thinning out until they disappear. The thin edges of different layers should wedge into one another, the thin edge extending over or under the thick part of another. Such is exactly the situation in the earth as it is laid open in many places.' He illustrates the point (p. 75) with a diagram of coal strata, themselves containing seams of fireclay, pebbles and gypsum, the strata interspersed with strata of sand, clay and/or soft sandstone, as seen on the face of Pulpit Rock, Colorado Springs, USA.

32. *Ibid.*, pp. 111-12. For forty-foot trees in vertical position in coal seams, see Broadhurst, F.M., 'Some aspects of the palaeontology of non-marine faunas and rates of sedimentation in the Lancashire coal measures', in *American Journal of Science*, Vol. 262, 1964, p. 865.

33. *Ibid.*, p. 112.

34. See *The Sunday Times*, 5 August 2000.

35. Nelson (1931), pp.107-8, 113 (fish and cuttle-fish); 44 (shark); *cf.* a BBC report on 29 November 2000 of fossils in which even soft tissues were preserved, found in a Brazilian mountain range.

36. *Ibid.*, pp. 120-31, citing H.H. Howorth, F.S.A., M.R.A.S., *The Mammoth and the Flood*, 1887. *Cf.* Stone, R., *Mammoth: The Resurrection of an Ice Age Giant*, Fourth Estate, 2002, who refers to a frozen mammoth found in 1900, the meat of its shoulder fresh and grass and buttercups in its mouth and stomach.

Howorth, though defending the idea of an immense flood, was not motivated by a wish to confirm Judaeo/Christian scripture (which, he said, had 'no authority whatever') but simply treated the biblical account as one flood tradition among many others worldwide. He drew his information about Siberian conditions from the reports of explorers and travellers, as well as from official documents of the Russian government. One explorer, Wrangell (hence Wrangell Island), recorded that two islands off the coast north of Siberia (one fifty miles square and the other a hundred miles long by fifty miles wide) were 'almost composed of fossil bones', and, of Bear Island, 'mammoth bones seem ... to form the chief substance of the island'. Whenever there was a storm, he noted, fresh supplies of bones appeared on mud-banks, suggesting that the strata forming the bottom of the sea off Siberia is also full of bones. Nelson (1931, p. 125) concludes, 'Considering the vast area over which the remains of elephants are scattered, and the numbers in which they are known to exist in many places, it does not seem improbable that five millions or more of these great animals perished in Siberia.'

37. See reports in *The Daily Telegraph*, 17 August 1996, and *The Guardian Weekly*, 24-30 July 2003.

38. See report in *The Guardian Weekly*, 13-19 May 2005, by Tim Radford, who writes: 'Dr Kirkland [of the Utah Geological Survey] estimates that thousands of dinosaurs are preserved at the site, south of a town called Green River. Nobody knows why so many creatures died at the same place: drought, fire and poisoning have been suggested.'

Nelson (1931), p. 99, gives a photograph showing 'bones of rhinoceroses, camels, giant wild boars and others buried at Agate Springs'. He cites the estimate of the excavators that 'the bones of 9,000 complete animals are buried in one hill', and their conclusion that 'the bone-layer once extended over a very wide area'.

Howorth (Note 36, above), refers to Tuscany, Italy, where 'immense numbers of elephants are entombed in a stratum beneath another of entirely different fossil content', and where also in 'a chalk cliff overhanging the sea, the remains of elephants, hippopotami, rhinoceroses, hyena and other species are exposed'. Arguing for the sudden, violent deaths of animals represented by frozen carcasses and mass collections of bones in the strata of Siberia and elsewhere, he writes, 'Animals do not usually die naturally in crowds when young, and yet we find remains of quite young animals abounding in all classes from mammoths to mice. How are we to account for this fact, save by summoning an abnormal cause? How again can we account for the fact that the mummied [*sic*] animals found in Siberia seem to have been in robust health, stout and strong?'

39. See *The Daily Telegraph*, 9 December 1995.

40. *Cf. The Daily Telegraph*, 17 May 1996, which records the discovery of *Carcharadontosaurus saharicus*, perhaps 'the biggest meat-eating dinosaur yet discovered', in the Kem Kem region of the Morrocan Sahara, 'once a vast flood plain.' Also *The Times*, 21 December 1995, recording the finding

in the Gobi desert, Mongolia, of a well-preserved skeleton of an 'oviraptor' dinosaur apparently trying to protect its eggs as it was probably 'overwhelmed by a sandstorm'; its 'brooding' attitude led to speculation that dinosaurs were warm-blooded creatures.

41. See the article by Robert Matthews in *The Sunday Telegraph*, 19 November 1995.

A simple explanation for the sudden extinction of dinosaurs is that terrestrial conditions were markedly different before the universal deluge. It has been pointed out that dinosaurs must have needed extraordinarily strong hearts and lungs to pump the required oxygen round their colossal frames. Evidence from fossils has cast doubt upon the capacity of the organs they possessed to achieve this if conditions were such as prevail today. Antediluvial conditions, however, appear to have been different: vast fossil fuel deposits – coal or oil strata, for example – suggest phenomenal vegetable fecundity, which in turn suggests a higher level of oxygen in the atmosphere than now appertains. High atmospheric oxygen density greatly improves bodily function and healing, and may even increase longevity. Dinosaurs were able to thrive in such conditions; however, following the deluge, those that had not already drowned were unable to survive the lower level of oxygen. *Cf.* K. Prince in 'Notes and Queries', *Guardian Weekly*, 15-21 August 2002, who cites the fact that during the age of the dinosaurs 'the atmosphere was considerably richer in oxygen than it is now'.

42. Nelson, (1931), p. 98.

43. Cited by Milton, *op. cit.*, p. 71. In 1903 Geikie published a massive *Textbook of Geology*.

44. *Op. cit.*, p. 71.

45. The material summarised or quoted from Milton in this and the previous paragraphs can be found on pp. 71-76 of his cited work.

46. From *The Independent*, 30 April 1993; report on microbe fossils found in Australia, plus 'geological column' showing 'The story of life on earth'.

47. Nelson (1931), p. 107; citing George Young, nineteenth century author of *A Geological Survey of the Yorkshire Coast*.

Nelson further cites Young: 'In the marlstone bands, occurring in the lias of Yorkshire, there is a seam composed chiefly of oyster shells, about four or five inches thick, extending for many miles along the coast, being found where the marlstone beds appear, and reaching far into the interior, where it is seen in front of the Cleveland hills. The shells of this seam are chiefly single shells, many of them are water-worn, all of them appear to have floated to their present positions, their flat sides being laid in the plain of the bed. No unprejudiced observer can affirm that this is an ancient oyster bed, in its original place and form; its contents must have been *drifted together* to produce this extensive and singular stratum.'

48. A good example of circular dating relates to the famous dinosaur discovery site at Como Bluffs, Wyoming, USA; see Milton, *op. cit.* pp. 28-9. As regards radioactive dating, Milton explains (pp. 29-36) how the radiocarbon dating method developed by Willard Libby in the 1940s can be questioned because of evidence that the amount of carbon 14 in the world may have varied. He cites (pp. 32-3) Melvin Cook, Professor of Metallurgy at Utah University, who using Libby's own methods has come up with anomalous results, suggesting the age of the earth's atmosphere can be measured in thousands rather than billions of years; see Cook's article, 'Do radiological clocks need repair?' in *Creation Research Society Quarterly*, Vol. 5, October 1968, p. 70.

49. *Op. cit.*, p. 839; cited by Nelson (1931), p. 143.

50. See Nelson (1931), p. 143, who made a special study of the 7,000 square mile 'reversed' strata; he illustrates the phenomenon with photographs from both the U.S. and Canadian Geological Societies.

51. *The Sunday Times*, 20 August 1995.

52. Writing in *National Geographic* magazine, March 1996, Donald Johanson questions the authenticity of this 'hominid', found in fragmented fossilised form by Professor Tim White of California University. Johanson concludes, 'It has many chimp-like features.' Cited by John Capon, *The Sunday Telegraph*, 31 March 1996.

    French anthropologists made the dating of the twelve bones from 'the world's oldest known upright hominid', found in Kenya, to six million years ago (BBC report, 7 February 2001). For the fossilised skull of *Sahelanthropus tchadensis*, or 'Toumaï', discovered on the southern edge of the Sahara in Chad, see *The Guardian Weekly*, 18-24 July 2002, or *The Times Higher Education Supplement*, 25 October 2002, which mentions that some experts consider the skull to be that of a female gorilla.

53. See 'Changing face of human evolution', by Tim Radford in *The Guardian Weekly*, 29 March – 4 April 2001; he quotes Henry Gee, who, in the journal *Nature* in March 2001, reported the discovery at Lake Turkana, Kenya, of the fossil skull, and the interpretation put upon it by researchers. Gee writes: 'This single fossil destroys current pictures of human ancestry with the casual abandon of an Exocet colliding with an egg. This new creature ... is not very much like *Australopithecus*, or anything else, and suggests that the ancient humans diversified much earlier than had been suspected, and the diversity was greater ... The flat face adds to the list of features

once thought distinctively human, that are found in the non-human fossil record.' Radford also quotes Louise Leakey, from Kenya, who said, 'It revolutionises the way we look at human ancestry ... It doesn't simplify the picture at all.'

54. See *The Times*, 4 June 1992; an article by Nigel Hawkes.

55. For China/East Asia, see article by James Pringle in *The Times*, 16 August 1995; for Georgia, see 'Made in Savannahstan' by Marek Kohn in *New Scientist*, 1 July 2006.

56. See *The Times*, 4 June 2002 (Anglia Man); *The Times*, 8 September 1995 (Boxgrove Man).

57. *Human Diversity*, Scientific American Library, 1982, p. 163; cited by Bethell in *Harper's Magazine*, February 1985 (see Note 15, above).

58. Cited by Bethell (see Note 15).

59. *Ibid.*, *i.e.*, all the quotations in this paragraph.

60. *Ibid.*

61. From his article cited; Note 14, above.

62. Cited by Roy Peacock, late Visiting Professor in Aerospace Sciences at the University of Pisa and an authority on thermodynamics, in *A Brief History of Eternity*, Wheaton: Crossway, 1990, p. 69.

63. In *The Daily Telegraph*, 11 August 1990. Bailey's article was prompted by the publication of a book co-authored by Dr Roger Highfield, the newspaper's science editor, and Peter Coveney, *The Arrow of Time*, London: W.H. Allen, 1990.

64. *Ibid.*

65. Cited by Peacock, R.E., *op. cit.*, p. 75.

66. From his article, in which he acknowledges *The Arrow of Time*, by Highfield and Coveney, as his source for this information (Note 63, above).
Further to this, the Nobel laureate Ilya Prigogine has shown through his study of dissipative (far from equilibrium) structures that order can arise out of apparent chaos. M.A. Corey, however, points out, 'Molecules may be able to adopt spontaneous positions of order out of apparent chaos when the circumstances are right, but this type of chaos doesn't qualify as genuine disorder, because the physical molecules themselves represent a higher degree of order than could ever be expected to be found purely "at random." Indeed, atoms and molecules, along with the subatomic particles of which they are made, seem to have been constructed in such a way as to make their spontaneous assembly into higher and higher degrees of order virtually inevitable.... Nevertheless ... they still tend to lean in the opposite direction: namely, towards returning to the lowest energy state possible (which also qualifies as the most disordered state

possible).... It is a physical fact that the natural inclination of all atomic particles is to reach thermodynamic equilibrium. Indeed, the only way this relentless push towards equilibrium can be forestalled is if a higher degree of order is somehow imposed upon a group of molecules. In this case, the anti-equilibrium effects of the externally contrived system act to oppose the natural tendency of matter to become thermodynamically equilibrated.' (*God and the New Cosmology*, Lanham, Maryland: Rowman and Littlefield, 1993, p. 142)

67. From his article cited; Note 14, above.

68. Cited by Alan Linton, reviewing Eldredge's book; see Note 29, above.

69. In an article on evolution entitled, 'Cosmic comets enliven the primal stew', in *The Daily Telegraph*, 10 December 1995.

70. His Edinburgh speech cited; Note 8, above.

Chapter 6: Biggest Bang

1. Op. cit., *p. 106.*

2. *J. D. Barrow and F. J. Tipler,* The Anthropic Cosmological Principle, *Oxford: Oxford University Press, 1988; cited by R. Peacock, op. cit., pp. 119-20.*

3. Superforce, *London: Simon and Schuster, 1984; cited by Peacock, op. cit., pp. 120-21.*

4. *See the article, 'Big Bang marks start of time', by Adrian Berry, science correspondent, in* The Daily Telegraph, *25 April 1992.*

5. *'Life, the universe and nothing',* The Times, *30 April 1992.*

6. *See 'Ripples in space hold key to the universe', Susan Watts, technology correspondent,* The Independent, *25 April 1992.*

7. *From, 'Welcome to the next world',* The Daily Telegraph, *11 October 1995.*

8. *From, 'And there was in the beginning ... Proof positive for the Big Bang believers',* The Sunday Times, *26 April 1992.*

9. Nature, *10 August 1989; cited by Amnon Goldberg, in a letter to* The Independent, *24 April 1992, to whom I am indebted for information given in this paragraph. Fred Hoyle, together with Geoffrey Burbidge and Jayant V. Narlikar, in* A Different Approach to Cosmology, *Cambridge: Cambridge* University Press, 2000, argues that cosmic microwave background radiation is not a relic of the Big Bang but starlight that has been thermalised by graphite and iron 'whiskers' formed and ejected by supernovae. This fits in with his 'quasi-steady state model' of the universe, with its periodic cycles of expansion and contraction.

10. Max Wilkinson, in his article, *'If God is the answer, what is the question?',* The Financial Times (Weekend FT), *18 April 1992.*

11. Cited by John Bunting in a letter to *The Daily Telegraph*, 7 July 1992.

12. From, 'Fitting the cosmic jigsaw', *The Times*, 25 April 1992.

13. From, 'One small step ... an infinity of actions', in *The Times Higher Education Supplement*, 5 January 2001.

14. See 'The mystical world of quantum mechanics', by Victor Stenger, in *The Times Higher Education Supplement*, 5 January 2001.

15. His article cited; see Note 4, above.

16. See David Blair and Geoff McNamara, *Ripples on a Cosmic Sea: The Search for Gravitational Waves*, St Leonards, NSW, Australia: Allen & Unwin, 1997, whose description (pp. 17-22) of Einstein's ideas on gravity have informed me. The authors use the phrase 'playing with words' (p. 20) in relation to difficulties inherent in the understanding of such concepts.

17. Max Wilkinson, from his article cited in Note 10, above.

18. In *The Times Higher Education Supplement*, 8 December 2000; reviewing the book by Ian Barbour, *When Science Meets Religion: Enemies, Strangers or Partners?* London: SPCK, 2000.

19. Kahl, A. J., *op. cit.*, London: Penguin, 1971 (Hamburg: 1968).

20. *Op. cit.*, London: Hodder and Stoughton (Sceptre), 1999.

Chapter 7: Information, Information, Information

1. In his book, *Crossing the Threshold of Hope*, London: Jonathan Cape, 1994.

2. Conducted by Professor Harold Thimbleby, who published his results at the Newcastle conference of the British Association for the Advancemant of Science, September 1995.

3. Speaking on the BBC World Service programme *Agenda*, 5 March 2000.

4. *Ibid.*

5. *Things Fall Apart*, New York: Anchor Books, Doubleday, 1994; first publ. 1959.

6. *The Dynamic Society*, London: Routledge and Kegan Paul, 1996.

7. 30 August 1998.

8. September 1998 (tr. Ed Emery).

9. 14 February 1999

10. 'Was May tremor a sign of much worse to come?', by David Kaunders, *Sunday Telegraph*, 15 July 2006; 'Wave hello to the bears ...', by Tom Stevenson, *Daily Telegraph*, 18 July 2006; 'The Return of the Bear', by Martin J. Pring, Pring Research, Inc., 2006 (www.pring.com).

11. London: Brealey, 1996.

12. London: Brassey's, 1991.

13. Job 28:12.

14. *The Shield of Achilles*, London: Allen Lane, 2002; cited by Larry Elliot, in 'Labour's market-state error', Guardian Weekly, 16-22 June, 2006.
15. T.S. Eliot, from Choruses of *The Rock*.

Chapter 8: Foundations

1. Frankfort, H., et al., *op. cit.*, p. 152.
2. *Ibid.*, p. 65.
3. Proverbs 8:1, 27-30a, 35.
4. See Kahn, C.H., *The Art and Thought of Heraclitus*, Cambridge: Cambridge University Press, 1979, p. 250; cited by Freke, T., and Gandy, P., in *The Jesus Mysteries: Was the Original Jesus a Pagan God?* London: Thorsons, 1999; paperback ed., p. 101.
5. As quoted by Clement of Alexandria, *Clement of Alexandria*, p. 167; cited by Freke and Gandy, *op. cit.*, p. 102.
6. *The Hermetica*, Book 1, 5 and 6; see the edition by Copenhaver, B.P., Cambridge: Cambridge University Press, 1992; cited by Freke and Gandy, *op. cit.*, p. 102.
7. John 1:1-5, 14.
8. *Tractate Sanhedrin*, 43b.
9. Mt 12:24.
10. e.g., Timothy Freke and Peter Gandy, *op. cit.*, p. 169. I am indebted to these authors for the Talmudic citations concerning 'Yeshu' that follow.
11. Klausner, J., *Jesus of Nazareth*, London, 1929 (English transl.), pp. 23f; cited by Bruce, F.F., *Are the New Testament Documents Reliable?* London: IVF, 4th ed., 1953, p. 102. Bruce points out that the 'virgin' reference does not mean that the original speaker, or later scribe, actually believed Jesus to have been born of a virgin.
12. Daniel 7:9.
13. Dan. 7:13.
14. Mk 14:61-2.
15. See Chapter 3, Note 8.
16. Mk 14:63-4. For the account of the discussion in the Sanhedrin involving Rabbi Akiba, I am indebted to F.F. Bruce, *The Spreading Flame*, Exeter: Paternoster Press, 1958, pp. 265-6.
17. Babylonian Talmud, *Tractate Sanhedrin*, 41a; Jerusalem Talmud, *Sanhedrin* I, 1, and VII, 2; Jn 18:31.
18. Babylonian Talmud, *Shabbath*, 30b.
19. Acts 22:3.

20. *From Jesus to Paul*, 1944, pp. 310, f.; cited by F.F. Bruce (1958), p. 81. Klausner refers to other literature, besides the Babylonian Talmud, in support of his thesis.

21. For John the Baptist: *Ant.* xviii. 5. 2; for James, *Ant.* xx. 9. 1; for *Testimonium Flavianum*, Ant. xviii. 3. 3. The translation here is that given by F.F. Bruce (1953), pp. 109-10.

22. *Hist. Eccl.* I, 11; *Dem. Evang.* iii. 5.

23. *Contra Celsum*, i. 47; *Comm. in Matt.*, x, 17.

24. *Jesus of Nazareth*, 1929, pp. 55 ff; cited by Bruce (1953), p. 110.

25. Professor J.R. Porter refers to this version in a letter to *The Times*, 4 April 1991, in which he writes of 'an increasing tendency among scholars to see here an original reference to Jesus, which has been expanded by one or more Christian copyists'.

26. Bruce (1953), p. 112. The argument as a whole is developed on pp. 110-12.

27. *Annals*, xv. 44; cited by Bruce (1953), p. 119.

28. *Chronicle II*, 30: 6; cited by F.F. Bruce (1958), p. 156.

29. Eusebius, *Hist. Eccl.*, iii, 5.

30. *Letters*, x. 96.

31. xvi. 2.

32. xxv. 4.

33. Acts 18:2.

34. *Ant.* xviii. 6. 4.

35. Mt 27:45; Mk 15:33; Lk 23:44. Tertullian claimed to have found in Roman records a note about an inexplicable worldwide darkness at the time of Jesus' death. Further, Phlegon wrote that in the fourth year of the two hundred and second Olympiad there was a darkness over Europe, at which time also an earthquake caused extensive damage in Nicaea. (The Greeks adopted the system of dating by successive Olympiads, beginning in 776 BC, in the third century BC.) This Greek dating of a strange darkness equates to 32 AD, which is on other grounds a possible date (besides 30 AD, favoured in this work) for the death of Jesus. See Bishop, J., *The Day Christ Died*, London: Weidenfeld and Nicolson, 1957, p. 308, Note.

36. Quoted by Bruce (1953), p. 115; for all the extant fragments of Thallus' work, he refers the interested reader to Müller, C., *Fragmenta Historicorum Graecorum*, iii, pp. 517ff.

37. See Origen, *Contra Celsum*, i. 38; ii, 48. Celsus wrote *The True Doctrine* in about 170 AD, some 70 per cent of it surviving in the form of quotation in Origen's foregoing work.

38. See Eusebius, *Hist. Eccl.*, iv. 3.

39. London: S.C.M. Press.
40. London: S.C.M. Press.
41. *Op. cit.* (1976), pp. 2-3.
42. London: S.C.M. Press.
43. Carsten Peter Thiede and Matthew d'Ancona, *The Jesus Papyrus*, London: Wiedenfield and Nicolson, 1996, paperback ed., p. 46.
44. *Op. cit.* (1976), pp. 9-10.
45. *Ibid.*, p. 9.
46. Robinson mentions (*ibid.*, pp. 19-20) that Mt 22:7 has been cited as a retrospective reference to the fall of Jerusalem. The verse, part of the parable of the wedding feast, reads: 'The king was angry, and he sent his troops and destroyed those murderers and burnt their city.' However, Robinson points out that the wording of this verse represents a fixed description of ancient expeditions of punishment in Near Eastern, Old Testament and rabbinical literature, so that it cannot be held to reflect any one such event. He further argues that if it were a description after the event it would have included more detail, such as the fact that only the Temple perished by fire, as in the truly *post eventum* 'vision' of the city's destruction given in the Jewish apocalypse II Baruch (7:1; 80:3).
47. *The Birth of the New Testament*, 1962, p. 123; cited by Robinson (1976), p. 14.
48. Mt 24:15. He speaks of the 'desolating sacrilege spoken of by the prophet Daniel'.
49. The Dead Sea Scrolls were sealed into the caves at Qumran in Palestine in 68 AD, two years before the fall of Jerusalem.
50. From Dan. 9:24-26 (all the foregoing quotations).
51. Lk 1:1-4; Acts 1:1-2.
52. *Op. cit.* (1976), p. 86.
53. Papias of Hierapolis (*c.* 60-130), *Frag.* 2. 15, and as quoted by Eusebius (*c.* 260-340), *Hist. Eccles.* iii. 39.14ff; Irenaeus (*c.* 130-200), *Adv. Haer.* iii. 1.2; Clement of Alexandria (150-215), as quoted by Eusebius, *Hist. Eccl.* vi. 14.6f, and as quoted also in *Adumbrationes ad I Peter 5:13* (*see* Aland K., *Synopsis Quattuor Evangeliorum* [539], Stuttgart: Württembergische Bibelanstalt, 1964); Origen (*c.* 185-254), as quoted by Eusebius, *Hist. Eccl.* vi. 25.5.
54. Eusebius, *Hist. Eccl.* ii. 16, 24; *Theoph.* iv. 7; Epiphanius (*c.* 315-403), *Adv. Haer.* li. 6; Jerome (342-420), *De Vir. Ill.* 8; from fourth-century Syria, *The Apostolic Constitutions*, vii. 46.
55. Acts 28:30-1.

56. *The Date of Acts and the Synoptic Gospels* (English translation), London: Williams and Norgate, and New York: Putnam, 1911, p. 96f; cited by Robinson (1976), p. 90.

57. *Op. cit.* (1976), p. 89-90.

58. Tacitus, *Annals*, xv. 44.

59. Acts 11:28.

60. On these two points, Robinson cites (*op. cit.* [1976], p. 257), for John's great age, Irenaeus, *Adv. Haer.* ii. 22.5 and iii. 3.4, quoted by Eusebius, *Hist. Eccl.* iii. 23.3f; Jerome, *De Vir. Ill.* 9, who places his death in 'the 68th year after our Lord's passion', i.e. c. 98 CE; for John the last to write, Irenaeus, *Adv. Haer.* iii. 1.1; Clement, quoted by Eusebius, *Hist. Eccl.* vi. 14.7; Eusebius (here speaking for himself), *Hist. Eccl.* iii. 24.7.

61. *Op. cit.* (1976), p. 258.

62. *Ibid.*, pp. 302-3.

63. *Ibid.*, p. 310.

64. *Ibid.*, p. 276. *Cf.* Jn 1:17; 2:19,21; 4:21; 5:10-18; 6:31-35; 9:39-41; *etc.* Robinson also refers (pp. 276-7) in this context to Jn 11:47-48, where the Jewish religious leaders express the fear that, if they do not take action against Jesus, 'the Romans will come and take away both our temple and our nation.' It is surely remarkable, if the gospel were written after 70 AD, that it contains no hint of the fulfilment of this unwitting prophecy – though of course these leaders *did* take action against Jesus.

65. *Ibid.*, pp. 277-8. See Jn 2:20; 5:2.

66. *Ibid.*, pp. 284, 307, 352-3. Robinson (p. 308) points to an article by F.L. Cribbs as 'much the weightiest statement so far of the case for an early dating' ('A Reassessment of the Date of Origin and the Destination of the Gospel of John', *Journal of Biblical Literature 89*, 1970, pp. 38-55). Cribbs believes it was written by 'a cultured Christian Jew of Judaea during the late 50s or early 60s'.

67. See Edwards, H.E., *The disciple who wrote these things*, 1953; cited by Guthrie, D, *New Testament Introduction*, London: Tyndale, 1965, p. 261.

68. *Op. cit.* (1976), p. 306.

69. e.g., C.F. Burney, *Aramaic Origin of the Fourth Gospel*, 1922, and C.C. Torrey, *Our Translated Gospels*, 1937, pp. x,xi; cited by Bruce (1953), p. 58. Torrey argues that the gospel was composed in Palestine, probably before 50 AD, and was later translated into Greek at Ephesus, the translator adding chapter 21.

70. *The Structure and Message of St. John's Gospel*, 1928, pp. 225ff; cited by Bruce, F.F. (1953), pp. 58-9.

71. London: Hodder and Stoughton, 1991.

72. *Op. cit.*, pp. xxii-xxiii.

73. Both Wenham and Robinson lean heavily upon 'the long-forgotten Bampton lectures of G. Edmundson' (Wenham, p. xxiii), entitled *The Church in Rome in the First Century* (London: Longmans, 1913). The argument of this 'scrupulously documented' work (Robinson, p. 114) is summarised by Wenham (p. 149): (1) There was a large and world-famous church in Rome in 57 AD with which Paul had had contact for some years. (2) A well-grounded tradition says that its foundation was laid by Peter in the second year of Claudius. (3) This fits without difficulty into the account of Peter in Acts. (4) Rome's claim to Petrine foundation was unchallenged throughout the church.

C. P. Thiede (*Jesus: Life or Legend*, 2ⁿᵈ ed., Oxford: Lion, 1997, pp. 44-6) argues that Peter's visit to Rome in 41 or 42 AD is referred to in an intentionally cryptic form in Acts 12: 17, where we read that Peter 'departed and went to another place'. Comparison with Ezekiel 12:3, in the Greek version of the Old Testament, reveals the phrase 'other place' as referring to Babylon, and 'Babylon' is used in the New Testament to stand figuratively for Rome (*cf.* I Peter 5:13; Rev. 17:5,18). Thiede also believes that Irenaeus refers to Peter's presence in Rome at this time, where he speaks of the 'exodus' (*exodon*) of Peter (and Paul) in the context of the writing of Mark's gospel. Many have taken 'exodus' to refer to the death of those apostles (in the 60s), but the natural sense of the word is 'departure' from a place.

74. *Op. cit.*, p. 223.

75. On this point, Wenham cites J. Chapman, *Matthew, Mark and Luke*, London: Longmans, 1937, pp. 16f.

76. *The Origin of the Synoptic Gospels*, Oxford: Blackwells, 1922, pp. 91f; cited by Wenham, *op. cit.*, p. 94.

77. e.g., Papias, as quoted by Eusebius, *Hist. Eccl.* iii. 39.16; Irenaeus, *Adv. Haer.* iii. 1.1; Pantaenus (died *c.* 190), as quoted by Eusebius, *Hist. Eccl.* v. 10.3; and as quoted by Jerome, *De Vir. Ill.* 36; Origen, as quoted by Eusebius, *Hist. Eccles.* vi. 25.4; Eusebius, *Hist. Eccl.* iii. 24.6; *Ad Marinum*, Question 2; Epiphanius, Adv. Haer. xxix. 9.4; xxx. 3.7; Cyril of Jerusalem (*c.* 315-86), *Catecheses* xiv. 15; Jerome, *De Vir. Ill.* 3; *also* Gregory of Nazianzus (329-389), Chrysostom (*c.* 347-407) and Augustine (354-430).

An interesting tradition current in Cyprus has it that St Barnabas always carried with him a copy of Matthew's gospel. A native of Cyprus, he found martyrdom at his home city of Salamis (near Famagusta), where he was buried under a carob tree, together with his copy of the gospel. When his grave was opened by order of Bishop Anticituis in 477 AD, the gospel was still lying on his chest.

78. *Op. cit.*, p. 117.

79. 'Firstly', *Chronicon*; 'secondly', *Hist. Eccl.* iii. 24.6.

80. *Op. cit.*, p. 239, referring to Acts 12:2,17.

81. *Ibid.*, pp. 239-242. Irenaeus, *Adv. Haer.* iii. 1:1, as quoted by Eusebius, *Hist. Eccl.* v. 8:2-4.

82. *Ibid.*, p. 110; the sentence quoted from Matthew is in Mt 1:21.

83. *Ibid.*, pp. 112-3. Wenham cites M. Lowe and D. Flusser ('A Modified Proto-Matthean Synoptic Theory', *New Testament Studies 29* [1983] p. 47, n88), who write, 'It was common practice for the disciples of rabbis to make notes of their sayings. It is also notable that Justin Martyr repeatedly refers to the gospels as *apomnemoneumata* ... a technical term for memoirs.'

84. See Thiede, C.P. (1997), pp. 23-36. *Cf.* Lk 4:16-20.

85. For learning by rote in the Greek world, Wenham refers the reader to R.O.P. Taylor, *The Groundwork of the Gospels*, Oxford: Blackwell, 1946, pp. 23ff; among the Jews, H. Riesenfeld, 'The Gospel Tradition and its Beginnings', in *Studia Evangelica* (1959) 43-65, and B. Gerhardsson, *Memory and Manuscript*, Lund: Gleerup, 1961.

86. *Op. cit.*, p. 96. Wenham refers to the judgement of B.H. Streeter: 'Mark reads like a shorthand account of a story by an impromptu speaker.'

87. Lk 1:1-2.

88. Acts 13:5. Carsten Thiede (1997, pp. 49-50) points out that in Acts the word applied to Mark signifies 'an attribute given to Mark himself, in his own right, not in relation to Paul and Barnabas'. He is thus to be seen as ministering or serving the word, or gospel, not some person senior to him.

89. Luke 1:3. This verse actually reads *parekolouthekoti anothen*, 'having followed all things closely *from the first*', as the New International Version translates; the Revised Standard Version, for no obvious reason, renders the second Greek word 'for some time past'.

90. The idea that Paul was the creator of a Gentile form of Christianity, contrasting starkly with a Jewish form of the faith delivered to his first followers by Jesus, has entered deeply into people's consciousness, at both a popular and scholarly level (*cf.* Casey, M., *From Jewish Prophet to Gentile God*, Cambridge: James Clarke, 1991). Emanating long ago from the Tübingen School of biblical criticism, the viewpoint has proved extremely resilient, despite the lack of evidence for it, whether within or without the New Testament.

91. Exeter: Paternoster, 1992.

92. C.P. Thiede and M. D'Ancona, *The Jesus Papyrus*, Wiedenfield and Nicolson, 1996, pp. 55-6.
93. Thiede (1997), pp. 130-2.
94. *Ibid.*, pp. 77-8.
95. *Ibid.*, p. 135.
96. *Ibid.*, pp. 127-9.
97. *Ibid.*, p. 133.
98. See further Chapter 9, below, in the section 'Death of a king'; also Note 140 to Chap. 9, which offers an alternative (though, I believe, less satisfactory) explanation.
99. *Ibid.*, 117-22. Regarding Jesus himself having had a relationship with the Essenes, Thiede refers to Mark 14:12-15, where we read that Jesus, planning the last supper with his disciples, told two of them to follow 'a man carrying a jar of water'. Thiede points out that jars of water were normally carried by women, unless by a male slave, who would however have used a skin, not a jar. So, concerning this 'man' the two disciples had to follow, he writes: 'Everything points to a member of the one community which did not include any women, nor slaves – the celibate Jerusalem Essenes.' For 'the large number of priests', see Acts 6:7. For Christian collective living, see Acts 2:44-5.
100. London: Wiedenfeld and Nicolson, 1996.
101. See Matthew D'Ancona's article in *The Times*, 24 December 1994, 'Eyewitness to Christ'.
102. Mt 26:22, where the text in the 'Jesus papyrus' does not have the disciples speaking one after the other; see Thiede (1997), pp. 99-101.
103. Thiede (1997), pp. 94-5, 103.
104. *Ibid.*, pp. 95-6.
105. *St Paul the Traveller and the Roman Citizen*, London: Hodder and Stoughton, 1920, p.8; cited by E. Yamauchi, *op. cit.*, pp. 94-5.
106. *Roman Society and Roman Law in the New Testament*, Oxford: Clarendon Press, 1963, p. 189; cited by E. Yamauchi, *op. cit.*, p. 97.
107. Acts 13:7; 18:12; 19:38; 17:6,9; 19:35; 28:7; *see* Bruce (1953), pp. 85-89; he cites Tacitus, *Annals*, xiii. 1, and Dio Cassius, *Hist.* lxi. 6, for Asian 'proconsuls'.
108. *The World of Josephus*, London: Secker and Warburg, 1964, p. 290; cited by E. Yamauchi, *op. cit.*, p. 96.
109. *Op. cit.*, p. 187-8.
110. *Ibid.*, p. 189.
111. e.g., the uncovering in 1929 of a first-century pavement in Corinth inscribed, 'Erastus, curator of public buildings, laid this pavement at his

own expense', confirming Paul's reference in Romans 16:23 to a fellow-Christian in Corinth, 'Erastus, the city's director of public works' (NIV); see Ramsay, W.M., *The Bearing of Recent Discovery on the Trustworthiness of the New Testament*, London: Hodder and Stoughton, 1915.

112. Bruce (1953), pp. 92-3.
113. Ramsay (1915), pp. 80f, 222.

Chapter 9: The Real Jesus

1. Mk 1:9,24; 10:47; 14:67. A.N. Wilson, in his book *Jesus*, is another who misleads on the issue of Jesus' birth, as also on his genealogy. He writes (p. 75): 'The fourth gospel very specifically states that Jesus was not born in Bethlehem, and that he was not born of David's line.' The fourth gospel does nothing of the kind. The verses to which Wilson refers (Jn 7:41-2) imply that certain Jews *thought* Jesus was born in Galilee and was (therefore?) not a descendant of David – a very different matter.
    The above point witnesses to a perennial problem for Christian apologists: the feeding of misinformation to the public by authors who should know better.
2. Mt 1:18-21; Lk 1:34-5.
3. Acts 2:25-35; 13:22-3; Rom. 1:3; II Tim. 2:8).
4. See Guthrie, *New Testament Introduction: The Gospels and Acts*, London: Tyndale, 1965, pp. 164-5. *Cf.* also Lk 2:51b. Jn 19:26-7 tells us that Jesus from the cross instructed the beloved disciple, his cousin John, to take Mary under his care – probably because John believed in him whereas his own brothers did not. In due course, according to tradition, Mary accompanied John to Ephesus. Luke could have consulted Mary directly, though he may have obtained her story from John.
5. *Our Mysterious God*, Basingstoke: Marshalls, 1983, p. 105.
6. e.g., Blair, H.A., *A Stranger in the House: the astonishing gospel*, London: Darton, Longman and Todd, 1963, p. 5-11. He adduces evidence to suggest Matthew preserved Mary's genealogy, an early copyist's error having crept into the text.
7. Lk 2:1-7.
8. See Taylor, L.R., 'Quirinius and the Census of Judaea', *American Journal of Philology*, LIV (1933), p. 133; cited by E. Yamauchi, *op. cit.*, p. 97.
9. See Deissmann, A., *Light from the Ancient East*, London: Hodder and Stoughton, 1927, pp. 270f.
10. See Gwynne, N, in a letter to *The Sunday Telegraph*, 4 February 1990.
11. *Ant.* xviii. 1.1; *Jewish War*, xi, 8.1; Acts 5:37.

12. Mt 2:1; Lk 1:5.

13. See Ramsay, W.M. (1915), pp. 275ff; cited by Bruce (1953), p. 89. *Cf.* E. Stauffer (*Jesus and his Story*, London, 1959 [English transl.], pp. 35-8), who shows that the census could have been taking place from 8 BC onwards.

14. Jack, J.W., in *Expository Times*, xl (1928-9), pp. 496ff; Tertullian, *Adv. Marc.*, iv. 19; cited by Bruce (1953), p. 89.

15. Josephus, *Ant.* xvii. 10.10.

16. Anti-Marcionite Prologue to Luke; *cf. also* Eusebius, *Hist. Eccl.*, iii. 4; cited by Bruce (1953), p. 83. Luke shows a special interest in the Herod family, and Bruce suggests (p. 46) that this may have been due to his acquaintance with Manaen, foster-brother of Herod Antipas ('the tetrarch') and brought up with him (Acts 13:1; NIV). Manaen was a teacher in the church at Antioch.

17. Lk 1:5.

18. Lk 3:1-3.

19. See Balmforth, H, *The Gospel according to St Luke*, Oxford: Clarendon, 1930, p. 132, who cites Tacitus, *Ann.* i. 3.3, for Tiberius as 'collega imperii'. *See also* Bruce (1953), pp. 89-90, who gives 27/28 AD as the 'fifteenth year of Tiberius'; Dodd, C.H., *op. cit.*, p. 121, favours 28/29 AD.

20. Two items are of particular interest in Luke's list. Firstly, Herod Antipas of Galilee, though given the courtesy title 'king' by his subjects, was not given this status by the Emperor; Luke is therefore careful to call him 'tetrarch' (*cf.* Mt 14:9; Mk 6:14; Lk 3:19). Secondly, Luke was for long thought to be mistaken about Lysanias of Abilene (a region west of Damascus) as the only person of that name known from other sources had died in 34 BC. Two Greek inscriptions then turned up in Abila, confirming that 'Lysanias the tetrarch' ruled in the region between 14-29 AD (see Yamauchi, E., *op. cit.*, p. 99; also Ramsay, W.M. (1915), pp. 297ff.).

21. Lk 3:21,23. There is slight ambiguity about Luke's wording in relation to Jesus' age, usually translated 'about thirty years of age'. The Greek text (Nestle/Kilpatrick; 2nd ed., Bible Society, 1958) reads literally, 'And himself was Jesus beginning about thirty years'. The word for 'beginning', *arxomenos*, is usually thought to refer to the beginning of Jesus' ministry, but the translation given in the AV is possible, 'And Jesus himself began to be about thirty years of age.' We cannot therefore be sure whether Jesus had completed thirty years or was beginning his thirtieth year. The former seems more likely, however, especially in view of the fact that the patriarch Joseph, seen as a type of the coming Messiah, was elevated to the position of viceroy of Egypt when 'thirty years old' (Gen. 41:46), which

indicates the completion of thirty years. It is possible that Jesus inferred from this that his own 'elevation', that is, his call to minister to the people, would come when he was of a similar age. John the Baptist, it appears, also commenced his ministry at the age of thirty.

22. *Ant.* xvii. 6.4.

23. See Seymour, P.A.H., *The Birth of Christ: Exploding the Myth*, London: Virgin, 1998, pp. 56-7.

24. *Cf.* Tasker, R.V.G., *The Gospel according to St Matthew*, London: Tyndale, 1961, p. 41. For the statements in Matthew implying Jesus was born some time before Herod's death, see Mt 2:7,11,16 (and p. 150, below).

25. e.g., Seymour, P.A.H., *op. cit.*; also David Whitehouse, BBC science correspondent, in *The Independent*, 24 December 1990. Both offer a specific date: 15 September 7 BC.

26. See Nigel Hawkes, 'Star of Bethlehem was a comet in springtime', *The Times*, 1 November 1991; *also* Seymour, *op. cit.*, p. 5. Mark Kidger, a British astrophysicist, supports the theory that the star was a nova in his book *The Star of Bethlehem: An Astronomer's View* (Princeton University Press, 1999); he points to a nova that occurred in the constellation of Aquila in 5 BC, though he suggests that planetary conjunctions taking place in 6 and 7 BC were also construed as signs. Hugh Montefiore, in *Josephus and the New Testament* (Mowbray, 1962; pp. 8-16), argues similarly, adding that the story of the star of Bethlehem could have given rise to Josephus' reference to a star and/or comet standing over Jerusalem to portend its destruction.

27. Lk 1 and 2:1-39; Mt 1 and 2, *passim.*

28. *Op. cit.* (1991), p. 295.

29. Mt 2:22.

30. Lk 2:39.

31. Lk 1:36,39.

32. Lk 1:39,56.

33. Mt 2:11. The Greek word *paidion* ('little/young child') is used, the diminutive of *pais* ('child'), rather than *brephos* ('child while yet in the womb/new-born babe') as in Lk 2:12. See Liddell, H.G. and Scott, R., *Greek-English Lexicon*, Oxford: Oxford University Press, 7th ed., 1883. For Herod's decision to kill male children of 'two years old or under', see Mt 2:16.

34. Lk 2:41.

35. Lk 2:42-52.

36. Mk 1:6; Mt 3:1.

37. *Ant.* xviii, 5.2.

38. Lk 3:7,16-17.

39. Mt 3:14-15.

40. Lk 3:21-22.

41. Jn 1:32-33.

42. Is. 42:1-7 (*esp.* 6b); 49:5-7.

43. Is. 50:4-9; 52:13 - 53:12.

44. Lk 4:1-2; Deut. 8:2,3a.

45. We do not have to take the figure 'forty' literally, either in the gospels or in the Old Testament. In ancient Semitic society it was often used to refer to an indefinite large amount or long period, as in the Turkish language and culture to this day; *cf.* Lewis, G, *Turkish*, London, Hodder and Stoughton, 1989 (2nd ed.), p. 45.

46. Mt 4:1-10.

47. Jn 3:24.

48. Jn 1:35-51 (Andrew, and Philip); 2:1-11 (wedding feast).

49. Jn 2:12 – 3:21; for people believing because of the signs, 2:23.

50. Jn 4:1.

51. Mt 4:12; Mk 1:14.

52. Lk 3:19-20; Mk 6:17-29.

53. Is. 9:1-2.

54. Mt 4:12-17.

55. Mk 1:14-15.

56. Lk 4:16-30.

57. Mt 4:18-22; Mk 1:16-20.

58. Mk 3:14-15.

59. *The Founder of Christianity*, London: Collins, 1971, pp. 126-7.

60. Lk 4:18-19; Is. 61:1,2a.

61. I follow the RSV margin here, and the NIV text, in translating the Greek word *entos* 'within', this being the normal meaning of the word (see Liddell and Scott, *A Greek-English Lexicon*). The translation 'in the midst' or 'among' is possible; if adopted, it would presumably signify that Jesus was referring to the kingdom's embodiment, at the moment of speaking, in himself. This would still preserve the idea of the kingdom being 'inward' or 'personal'.

62. Mt 5-7; *cf.* Lk 6:20-49.

63. Mt 13; *cf.* Mk 4:2-34; Lk 8:4-15.

64. Lk 6:20-1; Mt 5:3-6; Mt 10:28, 39; Jn 12:24-5; Mt 18:1-4; *inter alia*.

65. *Op. cit.* (1953), pp. 70-1. See also Notes 41 and 42 to Chapter 8.

66. For miraculous works being signs of some deeper truth, *see*, for example: on the feeding of the multitudes, Mt 16:5-12; Mk 8:14-21; Jn 6:25-51; on his healings, etc, pointing to his true identity and role for those who had eyes to see, Lk 7:19-23; 11:20; Jn 10:25, 37-8; on bodily healing being the outward sign of sins forgiven, Mt 9:1-8; Mk 2:1-12; on the significance of healing a blind man, Jn 9:1-7, 35-41; on the significance of raising Lazarus from the dead, Jn 11:4, 23-7, 40-2. For the fact that signs were not given to those with no prior faith, *see* Mt 16:1-4; Mk 6:1-6; *cf. also*, Mt 17:14-20; Mk 9:20-7.

67. Jn 6:1-14.
68. Jn 6:14-15.
69. *Op. cit.*, p. 134.
70. Mk 6:45.
71. Jn 6:66.
72. Jn 6:63.
73. Mk 7:1.
74. Mt 16:15-16.
75. Mt 16:20-1.
76. Examples of Jesus' claims (*inter alia*): lord of the Sabbath, Mt 12:1-13; control over nature, Mt 8:23-7; Jn 2:1-11; right to forgive sins, Mt 9:1-8; *cf.* Jn 5:5-9,14; authority over powers of evil, Lk 4:33-6; 9:1; 10:17-20; Jn 12:31; right to judge, Mt 11:20-4; 16:27; 23:13-39; Jn 5:22-7; 8:16; 9:39; God as his Father, Mt 11:24-7; 26:63-5; Jn 5:17-18; 10:22-39; one with the Father, Jn 10:30; to be Messiah, and therefore Son of God, Mt 16:13-20; 26:63-5; Jn 4:25-6; 10:22-39; 11:25-7.
77. *Cf.* Chapter 3, Note 8. I follow Dodd, C.H., *op. cit.*, pp. 110ff, on this point.
78. Dan. 7:13.
79. Chapter 8, in the section 'Early Jewish sources'.
80. Dan. 7:27a.
81. Mk 14:61-2. Cf. Mt 26:63-4; Lk 22:67-70. The titles 'the Blessed' and 'Power' are pious references to God, the Jews considering it improper to refer to him directly as 'Jehovah' ('YHVH/YHWH', the holiest divine name, the Tetragrammaton).
82. In Psalm 110:1, David foresees 'my lord', who is Messiah, receiving an invitation from God to sit at his right hand.
83. Mk 14:63-4. *Cf.* Mt 26:65, 'He has uttered blasphemy'.
84. e.g., Winter, P., *On the Trial of Jesus*, Berlin: de Gruyter, 1961, pp. 148f.
85. *Op. cit.*, p. 102.
86. According to John, Peter had already made a confession of faith in Jesus as 'the Holy One of God'. This was when many were deserting him, following the feeding of the five thousand and the discourse on the bread of life; *see* Jn 6:67-9.

87. Jn 7:1-10.
88. From Jn 7:25-46.
89. Jn 10:22.
90. Jn 10:22-39.
91. Jn 10:40.
92. Jn 11:47-50.
93. Jn 18:15.
94. Lk 23:50; Jn 3:1; *cf.* Jn 19:38-40.
95. Jn 11:53-55.
96. From Mk 8:31-9:32.
97. Mk 9:33-10:23.
98. Mk 10:32.
99. Lk 18:34. *Cf.* Lk 19:11 for the disciples expecting an immediate worldly kingdom.
100. Mk 10:45; for the paragraph as a whole, Mk10:32b-45.
101. Mk 10:1a.
102. Jn 10:40.
103. Mk 11:1.
104. Mt 21:5; Zech. 9:9; *cf.* Mk 11:1-7.
105. *Op. cit.*, p. 144.
106. *Wars of the Jews*, ii. 14.3.
107. Mt 21:9a; Jn 12:13b; Mk 10:9-10.
108. The Zealot movement arose in the wake of the popular rising in 6 AD led by Judas 'the Galilean' against the census mounted then by the Romans. One of the 'apostles' appointed by Jesus, Simon (not Simon Peter), was or had been a Zealot; *see* Mk 6:15. *Cf.*, for expectation of a worldly kingdom, Lk 19:11; Lk 24:21; Acts 1: 6.
109. The idea that though Jesus was crucified he did not die, but only swooned on the cross and revived in the coolness of the tomb, has a long history. Implied by Celsus in the second century, it was taken up by German writers in the eighteenth and nineteenth centuries as also by the Englishman Samuel Butler in 1865. Modern writers arguing similarly include H.J. Schonfield, in *The Passover Plot*, London: Hutchinson, 1965, and Barbara Thiering, in *Jesus the Man*, London: Doubleday, 1992. Muslims argue, on the basis of a passage in the Koran ('Women', verse 156), that the Jews did not succeed in killing Jesus, but that he was caught up to heaven by God. They explain that someone else (like Simon of Cyrene, who was made to carry Jesus' cross to Calvary) was crucified in place of Jesus.

110. e.g., Kahl, J., *The Misery of Christianity*, London: Penguin, 1971; *cf.* pp. 103, 121, where he writes, 'The name of Jesus is empty ... we may as well freely admit that we just do not know.'
111. Jn 19:32-5.
112. See Bishop, J., *op. cit.*, p. 318; *also* Tasker, R.V.G., *The Gospel according to St John*, London: Tyndale, 1960, pp. 212-13.
113. Lk 13:33b, 34.
114. Ps. 48:2.
115. Mt 21:13; Mk 11:17; Lk 19:45; cf. Is. 56:7; Jer. 7:11. *Cf.* also Zech. 14:20-1, especially 21b, 'And there shall be no longer be a trader in the house of the Lord in that day.'
116. Mt 21:12-17; Mk 11:15-19; Lk 19:45-8.
117. See Note 119, below.
118. Mk 12:17; cf. Mt 22:21; Lk 20:19-25.
119. e.g., the Jewish writers Eisler, R., *The Messiah Jesus and John the Baptist*, London: Methuen, 1931, and Carmichael, J., *The Death of Jesus*, London: Gollancz, 1963; also Brandon, S.G.F., *Jesus and the Zealots*, Manchester: Manchester University Press, 1967.
120. For not bringing peace but a sword, Mt 10:34-9; *cf.* Lk 12: 51-2a; for 'men of violence', etc, Mt 11:12; *cf.* Lk 16:16; for the two swords, Lk 22:38; for Peter striking off someone's ear, Jn 18:10; Lk 22:50.
121. *The Political Christ*, London: S.C.M., 1973, p. 46. Richardson points out that the saying about not bringing peace but a sword in its context clearly refers to the division that may be created in a family when one of its members believes in Jesus, and that 'men of violence' (Greek, *biastai*) in the passage about the kingdom of heaven suffering violence probably refers not to men but to the 'supernatural powers of evil' with which the spiritual kingdom inaugurated by Jesus was in deadly combat.
122. Jn 18:36.
123. *The Trial of Jesus: A Study in the Gospels and Jewish Historiography from 1770 to the Present Day*, Leiden: E.J. Brill, 1971.
124. *What on Earth? The Church in the World and the Call of Christ*, Cambridge: Lutterworth, 1993, pp. 60-3.
125. *Op. cit.*, pp. 126, 271. The conclusions of the Jewish writer Hugh Schonfield (*op. cit.*, pp. 149-50) are worth recording: 'Jesus never said he would fall into the hands of the Jewish people, but into the hands of the chief priests, elders and scribes. The Gospels testify that the commons of the Jewish nation heard him gladly, and that the Council acted secretly without the knowledge of the people, because they feared a popular demonstration by the Jews in Jesus' favour. We have the evidence that

they decided on the removal of Jesus in private conclave, and, taking advantage of his betrayal by one of his own disciples, arrested and interrogated him by night so that the Jewish people assembled in their multitudes at Jerusalem for the Passover should be totally ignorant of what was taking place ... The motives of the Council ... in the main were those of self-preservation and self-interest, though not wholly divorced from considerations of national and spiritual survival.'

126. Mk 11:27-33; *cf.* Mt 21:23-7; Lk 20:1-8.
127. Mt 21:33-46; *cf.* Mk 12:1-12; Lk 20:9-19.
128. Mk 12:38-40a; also from Mt 23:13-33.
129. Mk 13:1-2; *cf.* Mt 24:1-2; Lk 21:5-6.
130. Mt 24:3; *cf.* Mk 13:3-4; Lk 21:7.
131. Mt 24:30b. For the whole passage, or 'apocalypse', together with related parables: Mt 24 and 25; *cf.* Mk 13. Lk 21 is similar, but has a slightly less Jewish emphasis.
132. Dan. 7:13; see also Chap. 8, under *Early Jewish sources.*
133. Jn 11:16.
134. Mt 25.
135. Mt 26:2.
136. Mt 26:3-5; *cf.* Mk 14:1-2; Lk 22:1-2.
137. Lk 22:3-6; *cf.* Mt 26:14-16; Mk 14:10-11.
138. Jn 12:6.
139. See Note 99 to Chap. 8 for the possible Essene connection.
140. Mt 26:17-19; Mk 14:12-16; Lk 22:7-16; Jn 13:1-2a; Babylonian Talmud, *Tractate Sanhedrin,* 43b.

R.V.G. Tasker and others have approached the chronological discrepancy differently, and their argument is worth summarising. Of the verse in John (13:1) that has the time-reference 'before the feast of the Passover', Tasker writes (*The Gospel according to St John,* London: Tyndale, 1960, pp. 153-4): 'I would suggest that verse 1 should be separated from the incident which immediately follows it, and be regarded as an introduction to the whole of the remaining chapters ... It is not necessary to suppose that the events in the upper room took place before the feast of the Passover, or to conclude in consequence that the last supper could not have been the Passover meal.' *Cf.* also Lightfoot, R.H., *St John's Gospel,* Oxford: OUP (paperback ed.), 1960, p. 260-2. John's comment that certain disciples thought Jesus wanted Judas to 'buy what we need for the feast', (13:29a) when he said, 'What you are going to do, do quickly', (13:27b) does seem to suggest that the Feast was yet future; yet if it was, the disciples' inference is surprising since there would have been no need for haste as provisions could easily have been bought the following morning. Their mistaken inference makes as good sense if we assume they thought something was lacking for a celebration in hand or about to take place, making it necessary for Judas to go out quickly, buy something, and return immediately.

We must also, of course, explain John's use of the terms 'Preparation of the Passover' (19:14) and 'Preparation' (19:31) with reference to the day of Jesus' death, a Friday. Again, at first sight this seems to mean the day of preparation for the Passover, that is, before the Feast had begun. On the other hand, Mark (15:42) and Luke (23:54) refer to this Friday as the day of Preparation for the Sabbath. The term 'Preparation' may have the same meaning in John, in which case 'Preparation of the Passover' means 'preparation day [Friday] during the Passover festival'– as we might say, 'Friday in Easter week'. The festival lasted for seven days. The reference to the Passover in Jn 18:28b could refer to the whole festival, not just the Passover meal. See Tasker, *op. cit.* (1960), pp. 205, 209, 217. While the above explanation is possible, there remains the witness of the Babylonian Talmud that Jesus was put to death 'on the Eve of Passover'. Though it is conceivable that the Talmud is mistaken, it seems unlikely; for this reason I consider the explanation based on the use of differing calendars the more satisfactory.

141. *Op. cit.* (1997), p. 118.
142. Lk 22:17-20.
143. Jn 14-17.
144. Mark (14:51-2) records that 'a certain young man' was present in the garden at this time. He is probably referring to himself, especially as his family may have owned the house of the upper room. John Mark, therefore, could have secretly followed the party of master and disciples from the house to the garden following the Passover meal. See Cole, R.A., *The Gospel according to St Mark*, London: Tyndale, 1961, pp. 223-4. See also Thiede (1997), pp. 119-21.
145. Mk 14:32-6. *Cf.* Mt 26:36-44; Lk 22:39-42 (43-4).
146. Lk 22:45.
147. Shakespeare, *Macbeth*, ii. 2.36.
148. Jn 18:2-12. *Also* Mt 26:47-56; Mk 14:43-50; Lk 22:47-54a.
149. Jn 18:13; Lk 22:54,63-5. *Cf.* Lk 3:2.
150. Jn 18:19-24; Mt 26:57-68; Mk 14:53-65; Lk 22:63-71. There is slight ambiguity about whether or not the questioning recorded (solely) by John about Jesus' disciples and teaching was before Annas or Caiaphas; according to some manuscripts, verse 18:24, recording that Annas sent Jesus bound to Caiaphas, has become displaced. See R.V.G. Tasker, *op. cit.* (1960), pp. 196-8.

151. Mk 14:55.

152. Mt 26:61; Mk 14:57-9. *Cf.* Jn 2:19-21 (what Jesus actually said).

153. Mt 26:69-75; Mk 14:66-72; Lk 22:54b-62; Jn 18:25-7.

154. Lk 23:1-2.

155. Lk 23:3-4; Jn 18:33-38a.

156. Lk 23:6-12.

157. Lk 23:13-25; Mt 27:15-26; Jn 18:38b-19:16. Mk 15:25 records that it was 'the third hour', that is, 9 a.m., when Jesus was crucified; Jn 19:14 says it was 'the sixth hour' a little while before Pilate passed sentence. Tasker (*op. cit.* [1960], p. 209) gives good reason for us to believe that John was using the modern method of signifying time, counting the hours from midnight and midday.

158. Mk 15:16-21; Lk 23:26-32.

159. Mt 27:33-54; Lk 23:33-47; Jn 19:17-37.

Chapter 10: 'He is always there'

1. Jn 16:31-33.

2. Dodd, C.H., *op. cit.*, p. 163.

3. I Cor. 15:26,54-7.

4. Mt 28:20.

5. Jn 20:8; *cf.* Lk 24:24. For the full accounts of the finding of the empty tomb, *see* Jn 20:1-18; Lk 24:1-12; Mt 28:1-10; Mk 16:1-8.

6. Matthew records (28:2) that as dawn broke that Sunday 'there was a great earthquake'; he has already mentioned (27:51; *cf.* Mk 15:38; Lk 23:45) that at the moment of Jesus' death, following a three-hour period of unnatural darkness, 'the earth shook, and the rocks were split', when also 'the curtain of the Temple was torn in two, from top to bottom'. Interestingly, the Talmud (j. Yoma vi, 43c; cited by H. Montefiore, *op. cit.*, p. 18) records that 'forty years before the fall of the Temple [70 AD], the doors of the Temple opened of their own accord', suggesting seismic activity in 30 AD, the probable year of Jesus' death. See also Chapter 8, Note 35.

7. Acts 2:29-32.

8. The following passages refer to the various appearances in the order given: Jn 20:14-18; Mt 28:8-9; Lk 24:34 and I Cor. 15-5; Lk 24:13-31; Lk 24:33-49 and Jn 20:19-23; Jn 20:26-29; Jn 21:1-14; Mt 28:16-20; I Cor. 15:6-8.

For further study of the accounts of Jesus' resurrection, I would recommend: Morison F., *Who Moved the Stone?* London: Faber, 1930; Wenham, J., *Easter Enigma*, Paternoster Press, 2nd ed., 1992; and the novel by Stuart Jackman, *The Davidson Affair*, London: Faber, 1966.

Bibliography

ET = English Translation

Achebe, Chinua, *Things Fall Apart*, New York: Doubleday, 1994 (1st ed., 1959).

Allis, O.T., *The Unity of Isaiah*, London: Tyndale, 1951.

Armstrong, Karen, *A History of God*, London: Heinemann, 1993; Mandarin, 1994.

'Azzâm, 'Abdul Rahmân, *The Eternal Message of Mu'•ammad*, New York; Mentor, 1965 (Devin- Adair, 1964).

Baker, Derek, ed., *Sanctity and Secularity: the Church and the World*, Oxford: Blackwell, 1973.

Balmforth, H, *The Gospel according to St Luke*, Oxford: Clarendon Press, 1930.

Barrow, J.D., and F.J. Tipler, *The Anthropic Cosmological Principle*, Oxford: Oxford University Press, 1988.

Bishop, J., *The Day Christ Died*, London: Wiedenfield and Nicolson, 1957.

Blair, David, and Geoff Mcnamara, *Ripples on a Cosmic Sea: The Search for Gravitational Waves*, St Leonards, Australia: Allen and Unwin, 1997.

Blair, H.A., *A Creed Before the Creeds*, London: Longmans, Green and Co., 1955. – *A Stranger in the House: the astonishing gospel*, London: Darton, Longman and Todd, 1963.

Blair, Philip, *What on Earth? The Church in the World and the Call of Christ*, Cambridge: Lutterworth, 1993.

Bobbitt, Philip, *The Shield of Achilles*, London: Allen Lane, 2002.

Bruce, F.F., *Are the New Testament Documents Reliable?* 4th ed., London: I.V.F., 1953 (1st ed., 1945). – *The Spreading Flame*, Exeter: Paternoster Press, 1958.

Butterfield, Herbert, *Christianity in European History*, London: Collins, 1952.

Catchpole, David R., *The Trial of Jesus: A Study in the Gospels and Jewish Historiography from 1770 to the Present Day*, Leiden: E.J. Brill, 1971.

Chapman, J., *Matthew, Mark and Luke*, London: Longmans, 1937.

Cole, R.A., *The Gospel according to St Mark*, London: Tyndale, 1961.

219

Corey, M.A., *God and the New Cosmology*, Lanham, Maryland: Rowman and Littlefield, 1993.

Couperie, T. De La., *The Language of China Before the Chinese*, Taipei: Ch'eng-wen Publishing   Co., 1966.

Cragg, G.R., *The Church and the Age of Reason (1648-1789)*, London: Penguin, 1960.

Crefeld, Martin van, *On Future War*, London: Brassey's, 1991.

Crick, Francis, *Life Itself*, London: MacDonald, 1981.

Cupitt, Don, *The Sea of Faith*, London: BBC, 1984.

Darwin, Charles, *On the Origin of Species by Means of Natural Selection*, London: John Murray,   1859.

Davies, Paul, *Superforce*, London: Simon and Schuster, 1984.

Dawkins, Richard, *The Selfish Gene*, Oxford: Oxford University Press, 1976 (paperback 1989). – *The Blind Watchmaker*, London: Penguin, 1988 (Longman, 1986).

Dawood, N.J., ET from the Arabic of *The Koran*, London: Penguin, 1956.

Dodd, C.H., *The Founder of Christianity*, London: Collins, 1971 (New York, 1970).

Eldredge, Niles, *The Triumph of Evolution and the Failure of Creationism*, Basingstoke: Freeman, 2001.

Fox, R.L., *Christians and Pagans in the Mediterranean world from the second century AD to the   conversion of Constantine*, London: Penguin, 1988 (1986).

Frankfort, H. and H.A., J.A. Wilson and T. Jacobsen, *Before Philosophy*, London: Penguin, 1949;   originally *The Intellectual Adventure of Ancient Man*, Chicago: University of Chicago, 1946.

Frazer, J.G., *The Golden Bough*, London: Macmillan, 1890.

Freke, Timothy, and Peter Gandy, *The Jesus Mysteries: Was the Original Jesus a Pagan God?*   London: Thorsons, 1999 (paperback, 2000).

Furneaux, Rupert, *The Empty Tomb*, London: Panther, 1963.

Gould, S.J., *Ontogeny and Phylogeny*, Harvard University Press, 1977 (London: John Wiley).

Guthrie, Donald, *New Testament Introduction: The Gospels and Acts*, London: Tyndale, 1965.

Hamilton, K., *Earthly Good: The Churches and the Betterment of Human Existence*, Grand   Rapids: Eerdmans, 1990.

Handcock, P.S.P., *Mesopotamian Archaeology: An Introduction to the Archaeology of Babylonia and Assyria*, London: Macmillan, 1912.

Harnack, A. von, *The Date of Acts and the Synoptic Gospels*, ET, London: Williams and Norgate, 1911.

Harrison, R.K., *Introduction to the Old Testament*, London: Tyndale, 1970 (Grand Rapids: Eerdmans, 1969).

Highfield, Roger, and Peter Covency, *The Arrow of Time*, London: W.H. Allen, 1990.

Hume, David, *Dialogues Concerning Natural Religion*, ed. Norman Kemp Smith, Edinburgh: Nelson, 1935.

Jackman, Stuart, *The Davidson Affair*, London: Faber, 1966.

Jameson, H.G., *The Origin of the Synoptic Gospels*, Oxford: Blackwells, 1922.

John Paul II (Pope), *Crossing the Threshold of Hope*, London: Jonathan Cape, 1994.

Jones, Steve, *Almost Like a Whale: The Origin of Species Updated*, London: Doubleday, 1999.

Kang, C.H., and Ethel R. Nelson, *The Discovery of Genesis: How the truths of Genesis were Found Hidden in the Chinese Language*, St Louis: Concordia Publishing House, 1979.

Kennedy, Ludovic, *All in the Mind: A Farewell to God*, London: Hodder and Stoughton (Sceptre), 1999.

Khal, J., *The Misery of Christianity*, ET, London: Penguin, 1971 (Hamburg, 1968).

Klausner, J, *Jesus of Nazareth*, ET, London, 1929. – *From Jesus to Paul*, ET, London, 1944 (New York, 1943).

Lester, Robert, *Buddhism: The Path to Nirvana*, New York: Harper and Row, 1987.

Lewontin, Richard, *Human Diversity*, Scientific American Library, 1982.

Lightfoot, R.H., *St John's Gospel*, Oxford: Oxford University Press, 1960.

Lyons, J., *Language and Linguistics*, Cambridge: Cambridge University Press, 1981.

Manley, G.T., *The Book of the Law: Studies in the Date of Deuteronomy*, London: Tyndale, 1957.

Meek, C.K., *Tribal Studies in Northern Nigeria*, London: Kegan Paul, Trench, Trubner & Co, 1931.

Milton, Richard, *The Facts of Life: Shattering the Myth of Evolution*, London: Fourth Estate, 1992.

Montefiore, Hugh, *Josephus and the New Testament*, London: Mowbray, 1962.

Morison, F., *Who Moved the Stone?* London: Faber, 1930.

Moule, C.F.D., *The Birth of the New Testament*, London, 1962.

Nelson, Byron C., *After Its Kind: The First and Last Word on Evolution*, 2nd ed., Minneapolis: Augsburg Publishing House, 1952 (1st ed., 1927).   – *The Deluge Story in Stone: A History of the Flood Theory of Geology*, Minneapolis: Augsburg Publishing House, 1931.

Neusner, J., *The Way of the Torah*, Belmont, California: Wadsworth, 1988.

Oesterly, W.O.E., and T.H. Robinson, *Hebrew Religion: Its Origin and Development*, 2nd ed.,   London: S.P.C.K., 1937 (New York: Macmillan, 1930).

Peacock, *A Brief History of Eternity*, Wheaton: Crossway Books, 1990.

Ramsay, William M, *The Bearing of Recent Discovery on the Trustworthiness of the New   Testament*, London: Hodder and Stoughton, 1915.   – *St Paul the Traveller and the Roman Citizen*, London: Hodder and Stoughton, 1920.

Rattray, R.S., *The Tribes of the Ashanti Hinterland*, Oxford: Clarendon Press, 1932.

Richardson, Alan, *The Political Christ*, London: S.C.M., 1973.

Robinson, J.A.T., *Redating the New Testament*, London, S.C.M., 1976.   – *Honest to God*, London: S.C.M., 1962.   – *The Priority of John*, London: S.C.M. Press, 1985.

Ross, J., *The Original Religion of China*, London: Oliphant, Anderson and Ferrier, 1909.

Rudolf, Otto, *The Idea of the Holy*, ET, London: Penguin, 1959 (German original, 1917).

Schonfield, H.J., *The Passover Plot*, London: Hutchinson, 1965 (Corgi, 1967).

Schwartz, J.H., *Sudden Origins: Fossils, Genes and the Emergence of Species*, London: John   Wiley, 2000.

Seymour, P.A.H., *The Birth of Christ: Exploding the Myth*, London: Virgin, 1998.

Sherrard, Philip, 'The Desanctification of Nature', in *Sanctity and Secularity: the Church and the   World*, Oxford: Blackwell, 1973.

Sherwin-White, A.N., *Roman Society and Roman Law in the New Testament*, Oxford: Clarendon   Press, 1963.

Snooks, Graeme, *The Dynamic Society*, London: Routledge and Kegan Paul, 1996.

Stone, R., *Mammoth: The Resurrection of an Ice Age Mammoth*, London: Fourth Estate, 2002.

Strauss, D.F., *The Life of Jesus, Critically Examined*, ET, London: John Chapman, 1846.

Tasker, R.J.V., *The Gospel according to St John*, London: Tyndale, 1960. – *The Gospel according to St Matthew*, London, Tyndale, 1961.

Thiede, Carsten Peter, and Matthew d'Ancona, *The Jesus Papyrus*, London: Wiedenfield and Nicolson, 1996.

Thiede, Carsten Peter, *The Earliest Gospel Manuscript? 7Q5 and its Significance for New Testament Studies*, Exeter: Paternoster, 1992. – *Jesus: Life or Legend?* 2nd ed., Oxford: Lion, 1997 (1st ed., 1990).

Thurow, Lester, *The Future of Capitalism: How Today's Economic Forces Shape Tomorrow's World*, London: Brealey, 1996.

Toynbee, A.J., *A Study of History* (abridgement of Volumes 1-6 by D.C. Somervell), London: Oxford University Press, 1946.

Vidler, A.R., *The Church in an Age of Revolution: 1789 to the present day*, London: Penguin, 1961.

Wenham, John, *Redating Matthew, Mark and Luke: A Fresh Assault on the Synoptic Problem*, London: Hodder and Stoughton, 1991. – *Easter Enigma*, 2nd ed., Exeter: Paternoster Press, 1992 (1st ed., 1984).

Wheen, F., *Karl Marx*, London: Fourth Estate, 1999.

Williamson, G.A., *The World of Josephus*, London: Secker and Warburg, 1964.

Wilson, A.N., *Jesus*, London: Flamingo, 1993 (Sinclair-Stevenson, 1992). – *God's Funeral*, London: Abacus, 2000 (John Murray, 1999).

Wiseman, D.J., *Illustrations from Biblical Archaeology*, London: Tyndale, 1958.

Wiseman, P.J., *New Discoveries in Babylonia about Genesis*, 6th ed., London: Marshall, Morgan and Scott, 1953 (1st ed., 1936).

Wright, J.S., *Our Mysterious God*, Basingstoke: Marshalls, 1983.

Yamauchi, Edwin, *The Stones and the Scriptures*, London: Inter-Varsity Press, 1973 (New York: J.B. Lippincott, 1972).

Zaehner, R.C., *Hinduism*, London: Oxford University Press, 1962.

Index